AF556099

Development of Library Management

Development of Library Management

K. P. Singh

RANDOM PUBLICATIONS
NEW DELHI (INDIA)

Development of Library Management

ISBN 978-93-5111-243-3

Published in 2014 in India by

RANDOM PUBLICATIONS

4376-A/4B, Gali Murari Lal, Ansari Road
New Delhi-110 002
Phone : +91-11-43580356, +91-11-23289044
e-mail: randomexports@gmail.com, sales@randompublications.com,
info@randompublications.com

Reprinted 2026

Type Setting by : Keystoneprintads, Delhi-110051

Preface

Library management involves functions such as planning, organizing, leading, and controlling. Planning is about systematically making decisions about the library goals. Organizing is about assembling and coordinating human, financial, physical, informational, and other resources needed to achieve library goals. Leading is about functions that involve efforts on the part of the librarian to stimulate high performance by employees, and controlling about monitoring various library operations and services.

These four management functions are highly integrated, but libraries that excel in organizing material resources and in leading their human capital are known to give better performance. Keeping in view the fact that libraries in adult education set ups are, by design, small budget libraries, confined to one room space, and adult education staff manages them manually on part time basis, these four management functions would occur in varying degree. In such a typical set up, the functions of organizing and controlling would receive greater attention compared to other two functions.

For managing a library you may take the following step-by-step approach. Library Management System is essentially meant of collections. It is a multi-user version and can take care of all the fundamental functions of a Library like Cataloguing, Circulation, Accessioning and Housekeeping. Modern libraries are not made up of just Books but CD ROM's, Articles, Project Reports, Bound volumes are substantial part of the holding, Managing the holdings manually is a not a simple job.

In modern library system scientific management requires complete mental revolution on the part of workers and management. In the age of IT revolution, library system has also undergone drastic changes. Modern libraries often publish lists of accessions and may maintain a readers' advisory service. Interlibrary loan services, lecture series, public book reviews, and the maintenance of special juvenile collections are other important recent developments. The concept of modern library system is categorically narrated in this book. Academics and professionals in the field will find this work an authentic reference tool

I thank all members of my team who have helped in the preparation of the book. My special thanks go to "Random Publications" who have published the book.

– K. P. Singh

Contents

1

Library and in Our Society

THE ROLE OF LIBRARIES IN MODERN SOCIETY

First, the general development of the information society is pushing to re-evaluation of all the institutions which work with information, data, and knowledge-indirectly also with culture. In this connection the roles of education and media have been discussed already quite largely also in the European Union. But libraries-as well as other memory institutions like archives and museums-have not been considered.

Still, there is a clear need in the information society to maintain an institution which is concentrating in collecting and organizing information and offering general access to it. Until now, this work has been underestimated, but I argue the situation will change! Libraries are especially important now when the whole idea of education is stressing more and more independent learning and acting. All citizens must be able to find and use information. It is the key raw material-but it is a zero resource, if there are no access points to it and if documents are in chaotic order.

Here we can see libraries enter the stage:

- The unique function of libraries is to acquire, organize, offer for use and preserve publicly available material irrespective of the form in which it is packaged in such a way that, when it is needed, it can be found and put to use. No other institution carries out this long-term, systematic work. Culture must be nominated especially: it has an important and unique role in mobilizing resources of human beings. It has been described: To some extent, culture makes its influence felt more indirectly than knowledge, but it is impossible to imagine how people's creative powers could be fully activated without the impact of culture, which extends into the depths of the mind.

The challenge to modern societies is that the basic resource, knowledge, is developing from information in very individual, capricious and unpredictable process. It cannot be commanded. Still, societies can support this development, *e.g.* by offering access to cultural and knowledge treasures. This can even be translated into economic language: to get out the best from the human resources in Europe, this resource must be feeded up with rich and various cultural and infor-mation contents! I would like to stress especially the idea of organizing information by libraries.

It is often shadowed by the second important side of library work: offering access. But in the life-long learning and new technology context just all forms of organizing documents are getting more to the focus. This is clear to anybody who has tried to find something from not-so-often-used Internet websites.

NEW LINES IN THE EU-AND IN THE UNITED STATES

In accordance with these phenomenons, there are new political lines in the European Union: The Maastricht Treaty in 1992 launched the cultural aspects. This was only after a long discussion, which made it clear that we have to remember to separate the national view and the European view. The Amsterdam Treaty in 1997 declared citizenship as an important theme. A significant part of this are a.o. granting information skills and access to information to every European.

In addition to this, the European future strategies need to meet the democratic aspects of the information society development. One of the crucial points is again general access to information. Libraries, especially public libraries, are a good tool in all of these new areas. But the European union does not support whichever cultural or citizen concentrated projects in Europe.In the interests of the European Union there is always to find the European element. So, what can be done in library policy on the European level, taking in account that libraries are primarily a part of national education and cultural policies?

The own-initiative report "The role of libraries in modern societies," adopted by the European Parliament in October 1998, is the first effort to answer these questions. The same topics have been discussed in the United States. They have reached the point where especially the problems of those lacking access to digital resources have been studied. The report Falling Through the Net: Defining the Digital Divide by the U.S. Department of Commerce was released earlier in July 1999. The report finds that minorities, low-income persons, the less educated, and children of single parent households, particularly when they reside in rural areas or central cities, are risk groups.

The report calls for public policies and private initiatives to expand affordable access to critical information resources. But it also shows,, for the first time as far as I know, that libraries and community centres really can diminish the information gap between haves and not-haves. The 1998 data from the U.S. demonstrates very clearly that community access centers, primarily public libraries, are particularly well used by those groups who lack access at home or at work: *e.g.* unemployed groups used Internet in libraries three times as often as an average citizen.

EARLIER ACTIONS IN EU

In the European Union, there have been some efforts to mobilize "the treasures of the European libraries" since the mid-80'ies. These discussions and resolutions led to two special library programmes under the 3rd and 4th Framework programmes of research and development. The later programme has been known as "Telematics for Libraries". They have been strongly concentrated in IT, because it has been seen as a good tool to produce better access to the existing, underused library resources.

These programmes have had a clear impact in the European library co-operation and development. Benefits of this work come to public libraries indirectly: common standards and working methods help in the end all kind of libraries. But a fact is, that nearly all the libraries active in these EU projects are national libraries or big research and university libraries. Two main exceptions are Publican, a network of European public libraries, and ECUP, which was a copyright awareness raising project, and reached public libraries as well.

A new beginning was the so called Morgan report in 1997. In this report libraries were for the first time put clearly onto the place where they belong in the information society. As one result of the Morgan report, the European Commission informed that it will produce a Green Paper about the role of libraries in the information society.

For one or another reason, this was made quite ready but was never published. In this situation the Committee on Culture, Youth, Education and the Media in the European Parliament decided to produce an own-initiative report about libraries.

The main reason was that they wanted to influence the big issues under work in the EU, first of all the copyright directive and the 5th framework programme, which will have a direct impact to libraries. I was nominated the rapporteur of the own-initiative report. The report was adopted almost unanimously and with a very encouraging discussion in the Plenary session of the Parliament in October 1998.

DECISIONS OF THE EP CONCERNING LIBRARY POLICY

In short, when adopting the own-initiative report, the EP was calling the Commission and/or the member states to following actions:

- Libraries must be taken in account in national and EU information society strategies and in the respective budgets.
- Libraries need more resources for acquiring expensive books.
- The Green Paper on libraries by the Commission must be completed.

- The users position must be taken in account in the copyright directive process, the balance must be maintained-this was politically the most important decision in short run.
- Support to libraries was demanded from the 5th Framework programme of research and development, *e.g.* for networking, drafting standards, preserving, and transferring information; there is no more named library programme under the 5th framework programme
- A clearing-house to solve problems of long-term conservation should be founded.
- Studies concerning permanent paper should be done on European level.
- The member states should take care of digitizing their cultural heritage for future.
- There should be studies and concrete support to libraries in licensing matters, which are–will be the next big issue in library work.
- The EU cultural and information budget should be opened to libraries as well, libraries and their co-operation should be taken in account in planning new programmes.
- Problems of legal deposit in international and multinational materials, especially in electronic materials should be solved.
- The member states should provide all types of libraries with modern equipment, particularly with Internet connections.
- Free of charge use of public libraries, in the spirit of the UNESCO Public Library Manifest, was demanded.
- Free and easy access via libraries to material produced with the aid of tax revenues was demanded.
- The members states should organize for their library professionals up-dating education and training.
- A European Union focal point for libraries should be set up
- The member states should found European information points at libraries in countries where they do not yet exist.
- Library statistics should be better and more comparable both on national and European level.
- The national Parliament libraries should be opened to the MEP's in countries where this is not yet the practice.

In addition to these, the report strongly stresses that the library financing must be re-thought in the information society. Without new resources libraries are unable to do everything they are expected to do!

After the EP adoption of this report, the European Commission informed that it will next prepare a communication about actions to do. It was stated that the report had already served as a discussion paper, and so the need for the Green Paper had disappeared. The communication is in summer 1999 still under work in the Commission DGXIII/2.

TRADITIONS AND NEW FORMS OF WORK IN THE SAME HOUSE

The European Commission R&D framework programmes have concentrated in IT matters. The three cultural programmes, Caledoskope, Ariane and Raphael, have not been very useful for libraries, because their scope has been quite narrow. *E.g.* the books and reading programme Ariane has concentrated in translations. In the coming framework programme Culture 2000 libraries will have more possibilities to get support also for their cultural actions. What then will be the fate of the traditional tasks of libraries in general? Will the information society wipe out book loaning and poems?

THE PUBLIC LIBRARIES IN THE KNOWLEDGE SOCIETY

THE LIBRARIES IN A STATE OF FLUX

The municipal reform in 2007 had major consequences for the library service. The number of libraries decreased and the remaining libraries grew in size. The reform thus underlined and intensified various tendencies in library development over the past many years. The public library is in a state of flux. *Library service to children* from 2008 that chose as its point of reference the changes in children's use of the library. Thus this report had a strong focus on one target group and on how the library can develop new services to that group.

The present report also focuses on the target group, but slightly more on the institution–the public library. Based on a number of societal needs and new opportunities the report also considers how the library can be developed as an institution. The library offer is changing rapidly, but it continues to be much sought after. Two out of three Danes use the public library, and 29% of the adult population visit the library at least once a month. In 2008 the public libraries registered more than 34 mil. visits. This makes the library one of our most popular, public cultural offers, and this has been the case for many years. But the way we use the library is undergoing a change. On the one hand the loan of physical materials–books, CDs etc.–is falling. In the period 2000-2008 the public libraries' loan of physical materials has thus fallen by 22%, from ca. 62 mil. to app. 48 mil. materials. On the other hand the use of digital offers is growing, an offer that spans from downloads of music and e-books to renewals of loans via the library's homepage.

Bibliotekernes Netmusik, where as a library user you can via your municipality download music for free, experienced over 2,5 mil. downloads in 2008–an increase of 48% compared with 2007. One explanation of the change in borrowing patterns could be that the technology and media development has resulted in new media habits on behalf of the library users. At the same time the libraries' consistently high visiting show that they have succeeded in reorganizing and revitalizing themselves and continue to be attractive. This happens by developing new library services, particularly digital services, but also by turning the library into something more than just a collection of materials, so that the physical library maintains its desirability. Today the library is also a place for being and meeting, where one for example gets instruction, uses the Internet or gets help in the local citizen service centre. However, borrowing books remains the main reason why Danes visit the library. The latest cultural habits survey from 2004 shows that 85% of adult library users visit the library to borrow books and journals. The same tendency becomes apparent in more recent studies. In a Gallup poll conducted on behalf of the Danish Library Association, the Union of Danish Librarians and HK Kommunal (white collar workers' union (municipal) in 2009, "borrowing books" is the most frequent reason for visiting the library, followed by "borrowing electronic media", "taking the children to the library" and "watching events".

There is in fact also a growing interest in the library's non-users, as can be seen from the large number of new initiatives, which the libraries participate in at municipal level. In many cases these have a social aspect, and the library is here used as a partner in a targeted initiative towards certain target groups. This effort is particularly relevant in the light of the challenges that globalization presents to less resourceful citizens. The focusing on non-users also has another angle, which is i.a. clearly expressed in former minister for culture, Carina Christensen's strategy Culture for everybody from 2009. Here the emphasis is on the value of participating in a cultural community and the individual citizen's benefit from cultural offers. The strategy suggests that all citizens should be able to take advantage of the cultural offers and consequently–that the cultural institutions focus more purposefully on non-users.

THE POLITICAL BASIS FOR THE COMMITTEE'S WORK

The appointment of the Committee on the Public Libraries in the Knowledge Society was decided by the minister for culture in connection with several consultations in Folketingets Kulturudvalg (parliamentary cultural committee), which took place in the wake of a large number of public library branches being closed down during the first year of the municipal reform. The discussion fuelled by this naturally included the media and technology development.

A suggestion for a more extensive, interdepartmental committee work was rejected by the minister, who referred to the work that had already been done by the Globalisation Council. The committee's work builds on the report *Future library service to children* from 2008. The report contains a number of recommendations as to how to make sure that a strong library offer continues to be available to all Danish children. In 2008 the Danish Agency for Libraries and Media also published the report *The public libraries after the municipal reform,* which analysed the development within the public library area with particular focus on any consequences due to the municipal reform. The report concluded that the closure of the branches in 2006-2007 was a natural adaptation of the library service, and that at the same time it demonstrated a prioritisation in order to deliver a more up-to-date and value-enhancing library offer.

With the report from the Committee on the Public Libraries in the Knowledge Society we now have a number of recommendations as to how this prioritisation can be made so that the public libraries also in future will be able to meet the public's need for enlightenment, education and cultural activity. The committee presents its recommendations within an expenditure-neutral framework with the perspective that it may be both necessary and correct with local changes of priorities within the library field in order to support and strengthen the public library in the knowledge society.

THE COMMISSION'S ASSIGNMENT: MANDATE FOR THE COMMITTEE ON THE PUBLIC LIBRARIES IN THE KNOWLEDGE SOCIETY

The committee must focus on continuous development of the public libraries in Denmark. This includes the public libraries' interaction with other libraries and relevant institutions. Focus must be on the libraries as an easily accessible offer to everybody. The committee must build on the report *Future library service to children* and pay particular attention to service to youngsters and adults. The committee must assess the public libraries' role in relation to the challenges facing the knowledge society, the globalisation strategy's focus on education, lifelong learning and societal cohesive force. The committee must assess to which extent there is basis for establishing new concepts for a library service that meets the public's needs in terms of enlightenment, education and cultural activity, and close to the citizens.

Likewise the committee must asses the possibilities for continuous development of traditional core services such as literature dissemination. In particular, the committee must asses the need for further development of the libraries' digital infrastructure and the interaction between digital and traditional services. The committee must furthermore describe models for the mediation of digital cultural heritage and licensed digital media and models for various forms of learning and inspiration activities (*e.g.* in relation to citizens with poor reading and IT skills). The committee must likewise give examples of new partnerships, including inter-institutional cooperations and binding networking commitments. Finally the committee must assess the need for competence development of library staff. On the basis of its analyses the committee must put forward recommendations and suggestions as to how the strategy's objectives can be realised within the present legislation and existing division of labour between state and municipalities. The committee's suggestions must be expenditure-neutral. The committee is composed upon appointment, so that the minister for culture appoints three members, while Local Government (KL), Danish Library Association, Association of Library Directors, Danish Research Library Association, the Regional Libraries, Union of Danish Librarians and Børne-og Kulturchefforeningen each appoints a member. The Danish Agency for Library and Media's director general is chairman of the committee, and the Agency is the committee's secretariat. The committee must have completed its work primo 2010.

DIGITAL LIBRARIES AND SOCIETY

Digital libraries are large, organized collections of information objects. Whereas standard library automation systems provide a computerized version of the catalog—a gateway into the treasure-house of information stored in the library—digital libraries incorporate the treasure itself, namely the information objects that constitute the library's collection. Whereas standard libraries are, of necessity, ponderous and substantial institutions, with large buildings and significant funding requirements, even large digital libraries can be lightweight. Whereas standard libraries, whose mandate includes preservation as well as access, are "conservative" by definition, with institutional infrastructure to match, digital libraries are nimble: they emphasize access and evolve rapidly.

The five stages in this part provide an excellent illustration of the huge variety of interesting issues in digital library research that impacts the Asia Pacific region. Unlike the New World, where most of the research on technological aspects of digital libraries originates, Asia has an exceptionally rich cultural heritage. This manifests itself in a huge legacy of documents, in various forms—from paper to palm leaves—and in various different conditions. The need to preserve this legacy is particularly pressing in today's world, where political instability is rife and climate change is beginning to have an effect.

As recent events have shown, disasters, both manmade and natural, can have a devastating effect on fragile cultural artifacts. S.M. Shafi from the University of Kashmir, India, surveys the many issues involved with digital archiving of medieval manuscripts in Asia. Libraries are pillars of education, and it is natural to expect that digital libraries will provide new opportunities for innovative educational practices. These will be particularly relevant to the Asia Pacific region because of the huge disparities in access to education between the different communities there. Peer-to-peer learning has always been a crucial factor in personal development, although it is frequently ignored in educational studies.

Natalie Lee-San from Nanyang Technological University, Singapore, describes her studies of how digital libraries can provide an innovative, perhaps revolutionary, environment for peer-to-peer learning amongst youths. She touches on many practical issues: gender differences, different learning styles, different levels of media and computer literacy, and age-related differences. Many economies in the Asia Pacific region are agricul-turally-based. Modern agriculture is a knowledge-based activity that can benefit greatly from digital libraries. Mila Ramos from the International Rice Research Institute in the Philippines describes a large-scale digital library system designed to support the growth, nurturing, harvesting, and distribution of that most Asian of staples, rice. This digital library supports an institute whose goal is to improve the well-being of present and future generations of rice farmers and consumers, particularly those with low incomes.

The institute's library houses the world's most comprehensive collection of technical literature on rice, and provides a widely-used international reference service. As in many specialized libraries, digital library technology is seen to have special advantages in a world of shrinking library budgets. Intellectual property issues are a central driving force behind the market in information of which libraries are a part. And the questions become more complex as the nature of today's information shifts from a primarily book-based culture to one that embraces all types of multimedia objects, and large, carefully-curated, collections of such objects. The stage on *"Multimedia digital library as intellectual property"* by Hideyasu Sasaki and Yasujshi Kiyoki at Keio University in Japan clarify the copyright situation as it affects multimedia collections and compilations.

They go on to discuss the patentability of particular retrieval mechanisms, an essential component of digital libraries. The fifth stage in this part on how digital library research impacts the Asia Pacific region is the present one, on digital libraries in society. Most existing digital library projects, being research-oriented, are predicated on state-of-the-art equipment and interfaces, academic and research institutions, special collections. In contrast: digital library technology can and should be available to everyone, on all platforms, in all countries; and it can and should enable ordinary people to exercise their creative powers to conceive, assemble, build, and disseminate new information collections that are designed not just for western academics but for a wide diversity of different audiences throughout the world.

Though less glamorous, this may, in the end, be a more important goal for society. Digital libraries pose an inherent tension between the technologist's desire for advanced solutions that use the latest and greatest hardware and software, and the librarian's desire for wide, crossplatform availability and long-term preser-vation—as epitomized by the sustained success of paper as a delivery medium. To achieve universal access for both information consumers and collection-builders is really a problem for HCI. We examine the social need for digital libraries, particularly in developing countries, by briefly sketching some trends in commercial publishing and contrasting them with a growing international perspective of information as a public good. We draw out the implications for the user interface, which is the principal bottleneck in allowing non-specialist people to make public information available in focused collections that are universally usable. Then we introduce digital library technology and illustrate it with a particular example, the Greenstone digital library software, which is designed for a broad user base and is in widespread use in many corners of the world—from Uganda to the US, Kazakhstan to Canada, Nepal to New Zealand. Following that, we review a project that is applying digital library technology to the distribution of humanitarian information in the developing world, a context that is both innovative and socially motivated. Next we discuss issues of universal access and illustrate them with reference to the Greenstone software.

We include a brief demonstration of a prototype system that is intended to allow anyone to build and disseminate information collections, and illustrates some human interface challenges that arise when providing necessarily complex functionality to a non-computer-oriented user base. We close with the hope that future digital libraries will find a new role to play in helping to reduce the social inequity that haunts today's world, both within our own countries and between nations.

BOOKS, LIBRARIES, AND THE SOCIALLY DISADVANTAGED

Today, the long-standing three-way tension between the commercial interests of publishers, the needs of society and information users, and the social mandate of public libraries, is being pulled and stretched as never before. First, the very notion of a "book" is evolving in many different directions: books become more interactive; publishers rent content; books are distributed under restrictive conditions that mechanically prohibit sharing. While it would be premature to make specific predictions, it seems likely that these trends will further disadvantage the disadvantaged—particularly those in poorer countries who have yet to benefit from ready access to ordinary books. Second, a huge body of information is becoming freely available on the Internet.

Much is of questionable quality, but some is very good indeed. In many cases the information is provided for the "public good" rather than for commercial profit, and the redistribution of such information is likely to be encouraged, rather than prohibited, by those who make it available. Initiatives like UNESCO's "Information for all" programme and the upcoming World Summit on the Information Society highlight the importance of public information; they are founded on the belief that information literacy will help alleviate many of the problems confronting human societies. Third, the implications for libraries are mixed. Whereas new controls by publishers over how the content they own may be used presents libraries with significant problems, the ready availability of "public good" information meshes well with library philosophy. A new role is emerging for information professionals who can select material, index it, add appropriate metadata, and redistribute it in added-value form for the good of society. Suitable technological infrastructure is being provided by the open source movement, which is making available high-quality software for repackaging and distribution of information (and not just on computer networks). What future has the book in the digital world? The question is a complex one that is being widely aired. Authors and publishers ask how many copies of a work will be sold if networked digital libraries enable worldwide access to an electronic copy of it.

Their nightmare is that the answer is *one*: how many books will be published online if the entire market can be extinguished by the sale of one electronic copy to a public library? To counter this threat, the entertainment industry is promoting new *"digital rights management"* (DRM) schemes that permit a degree of control over what users can do that goes far beyond the traditional legal bounds of copyright. ndeed, the acronym is more aptly expanded as "digital restrictions management" because it is concerned solely with content owners rights and not at all with user's rights. It is, in effect, a "private governance system in which computer systems regulate which acts users are and are not authorized to perform".

nticircumvention rules are sanctioned by the *Digital Millennium Copyright Act* (DMCA) in the US. The DMCA has been used, for example, to prosecute a Norwegian teenager for writing software to play a DVD that he had purchased on a computer for which no commercial playback systems exist. an DRM be applied to books? The motion picture industry can compel manufacturers to incorporate encryption into their products because it holds key patents on DVD players. Commercial book publishers are promoting e-book readers that, if adopted on a wide scale, would allow the same kind of control to be exerted over reading material. asic rights that we take for granted—such as the ability to lend a book to a friend, resell it on the second-hand market, keep it indefinitely, continue to use it when your e-book reader breaks down, donate it to charity, preserve it for your grandchildren, copy excerpts without resorting to a handwritten transcription—are in jeopardy.

DRM allows such rights to be controlled, monitored, and withdrawn instantly, and DMCA legislation makes it illegal for users to seek redress by taking matters into their own hands. Fortunately, perhaps, lack of standardization and compatibility issues are delaying consumer adoption of e-books. n the realm of scholarly publishing, digital rights management is more advanced. Academic libraries license access to content in electronic form, often in tandem with purchase of print versions too. They have been able to negotiate reasonable conditions with publishers—probably because they represent the lion's share of the scholarly market. owever, the extent of libraries' power in the consumer book market is moot. One can envisage a scenario where publishers establish a system of commercial, pay-per-view, libraries for e-books and refuse public libraries access to books in a form that can be circulated. These new directions present our society with puzzling challenges, and it would be rash to predict what society's response will be. But one thing is certain: they will surely increase the degree of disenfranchisement of those who do not have access to the technology. In parallel with publishers' moves to reposition books as technological artifacts with refined and flexible control over how they can be used, an opposing trend has emerged: the ready availability of free information on the Internet. Of course, the world-wide web is an unreliable source of enlightenment, and undiscriminating use is dangerous—and widespread. As early as 1996 complaints arose that the Web's contents are largely unattributed, undated, unannotated, unreliable; information about author and publisher is unavailable or incomplete; far too many resource catalogues are chasing far too few original or non-trivial documents—complaints that are very familiar today.

But one thing has changed: search engines and other portals have enormously increased our ability to locate information that is at least ostensibly relevant to any given question. Teachers complain bitterly that students view the Web as a replacement for the library, harvesting information indiscriminately to provide answers to assignments that are at best shallow and at worst incoherent and incorrect. One consolation is that the very same search facilities can be used to detect plagiarism. •Nevertheless, the Web abounds with accessible, high-quality information. Many social groups, non-profit societies and charities make it their business to create sites and collect and organize information there.

To take a single example at random, a Google search for *diabetes* returns three national diabetes associations in the top ten hits, and of course many more exist. ach of these sites offers a cornucopia of valuable information on the disease, which is not commercial and provided for the public good. Widespread use is strongly encouraged, and it seems likely that arrangements could be made for re-distribution of the material presented there, particularly it was intended as a not-for-profit service and appropriate acknowledgement was made. ne of the key problems with information distribution via the Web is that it disenfranchises developing countries. Although the Web does not extend into the homes of the socially disadvantaged in developed countries either, various national programmes are working to provide access. ut network access varies enormously across the world.

Whereas in 1998 more than a quarter of the US population were surfing the Internet, the figures for Latin America and the Caribbean was 0.8%, for Sub-Saharan Africa 0.1%, and for South Asia 0.04%. Schools and hospitals in developing countries are poorly connected. ven in South Africa, the bestconnected African country, many hospitals and 75% of schools have no telephone line. Universities are better equipped, but even there up to 1,000 people can depend on just one terminal. The Internet "is failing the developing world". Prompted by this inequity, the importance of information, and particularly public information, is today being highlighted by prominent international bodies. For example, UNESCO's "Information for all" programme was established in 2001 to foster debate on the political, ethical and societal challenges of the emerging global knowledge society and to carry out projects promoting equitable access to information. It reflects a growing awareness that information is playing an increasing role in generating wealth and human capital, and that participation in the "global knowledge society" is essential for social and individual development. Information literacy is described as "a new frontier" by the Director of UNESCO's Information Society Division.

The Inter-national Telecommunications Union has established a World Summit on the Information Society, held in Geneva in December 2003 and Tunis in 2005, to promote a global discussion of the fundamental changes that are being brought about in our lives by the transformation from an industrial to an information society, and to confront the extreme disparities of access to information between the industrialized countries and the developing world. What is the librarian to make of all this? The mandate of today's public libraries, in sharp contrast to that of publishers, is to facilitate the open distribution of knowledge. Librarians strive to enable the free flow of information. Their traditions are liberal, founded on the belief that libraries should serve democracy.

To help fulfill their mission as resource centers for citizens, public libraries maintain collections of records, policy statements, government documents, and so on. A recent promotional video from the American Librarian's Association exults that "the library is democracy's place of worship". learly, the impending redefinition of the book as a digital artifact that is licensed rather than sold, tied to a particular replay device, with restrictions that are clearly laid out and mechanically enforced, is an innovation that goes right to the heart of libraries. he changing nature of the book may make it hard, or even impossible, for libraries to fulfill their mandate by providing quality information to readers.

And on the other hand, the emergence of a vast storehouse of information on the Internet poses a different kind of conundrum. Librarians, the traditional gatekeepers of knowledge, are in danger of being bypassed, their skills ignored, their advice unsought. Earch engines send users straight to the information they require—or so users think—without any need for an inter-mediary to classify, catalogue, cross-reference, advise on sources. The ready availability of information on the Internet, and its widespread use, really presents librarians with an opportunity, not a threat. Avvy users realise they need help, which librarians can provide. A good example is Infomine, a cooperative project of the University of California and California State University. Infomine contains descriptions and links to a wealth of scholarly and educational Internet resources, each of which has been selected and described by a professional academic librarian who is a specialist in the subject and in resource description generally. Participating librarians see this as an important expenditure of effort for their users, a natural evolution of their traditional task of collecting and organizing information in print. What kind of technical infrastructure is needed to support and promote this kind of work? Open source software is a powerful ally for librarians who wish to extend liberal traditions of information access. These systems make the source code freely available for others to view, modify, and adapt; and the very nature of the licensing agreement prevents the software from being appropriated by proprietary vendors.

But the open-source movement is more than just a vehicle for librarians to use: its link with library traditions goes much deeper. Public libraries and open source software both enshrine the same philosophy: to promote learning and understanding through the dissemination of knowledge. Both are pervaded by a sense of community, on the one hand the kind of inter-institutional cooperation exemplified by interlibrary loan and on the other teams of designers and programmers that frequently cross national boundaries.

Ew trends in information access present librarians in developed countries with difficult and conflicting challenges. Meanwhile, however, the situation in the developing world is dire. Here, traditional publishing and distribution mechanisms have failed tragically. or example, whereas a US medical library subscribes to about 5,000 journals, the Nairobi University Medical School Library, long regarded as a flagship center in East Africa, last year received just 20 journals. In Brazzaville, Congo, the university has only 40 medical books and a dozen journals, all from before 1993, and the library in a large district hospital consisted of a single bookshelf filled mostly with novels. Traditional libraries are substantial institutions that occupy physical space, present a physical appearance, and exhibit tangible physical organization. When standing on the threshold of a large bricks-and-mortar library you gain a sense of presence and permanence that reflects the care taken in building and maintaining the collection inside.

Digital libraries, in contrast, are lightweight. But they provide potentially far greater accessibility, which means that they will have even greater social effects. Once created, they can, without significant institutional support, continue to serve users. They can be distributed throughout most of the developed world over the Internet. In developing countries and remote corners of the developed world they can be circulated on removable media—CD-ROM, DVD, or 100 Gb disk units the size of videocassettes—and updated over radio.

Issues of copyright pose difficult problems, but they are manageable. or example, there is plenty of non-copyright material, or material whose owners are prepared to donate copyright for socially useful purposes, and trends towards more open access to academic and humanitarian information are visible. Not everyone sees digital rights management and the DMCA as the way forward, and in the longer term publishers, to remain viable, will have to investigate alternative revenue models for the information they own. No wonder international organizations such as the United Nations, along with many smaller *non-government organizations* (NGOs), are keenly interested in digital library technology.

Advances in digital library technology are radically lowering the bar for the design and production of richly-organized, coherent, focused collections of information. Now, anyone with access to sufficient source material can use public-domain software to build large, fullysearchable, collections the size of traditional personal or institutional libraries—in minutes. Let the minutes stretch to hours and the collection can be polished, organized, branded, distributed. It can include fully-illustrated text, images, video, music. t can present attractively-designed pages with consistent use of icons.

Keywords, key phrases, even acronyms and their definitions, can be extracted—automatically—and used to underpin novel means of access. Let the hours stretch to days and metadata can be manually added that permits further levels of organization. Given access to programming skills, creative new facilities that stretch the imagination can be rapidly integrated into the system. All this, one might say, can be done with ordinary Web sites: there is no need for digital library technology. owever, bitter experience has shown that all but the most rudimentary sites do require significant institutional support—for organization and maintenance.

The Web is littered with incomplete, unfinished, unmaintained, out-dated, inconsistently-organized, useless information collections. ust as traditional library cataloging procedures integrate new works into existing collections with minimal overhead so that they immediately become first-class members of the collection, so digital libraries allow new documents to be added completely automatically. In the case of traditional libraries this is done through the small but nonnegligible overhead of generating a new catalog entry. With ordinary Web sites it requires inserting links manually into index pages and the like, and may involve adding links not only into the new document but also into existing ones that ought to reference it—it's like rewriting the book, and maybe revising all other books in the library too!

In contrast, digital libraries bring access structures instantly and effortlessly up to date whenever new documents are added. The challenge for HCI is to design and build digital library systems that fulfill the potential of digital libraries as a "killer app" for computers in developing countries, which will bring concomitant benefits in almost every other sphere of application. or the information consumer we need access to information that is guaranteed across space, time, and culture. We need flexible distribution mechanisms for documents, and for information objects of all types, that can be accessed on all computer platforms—including the lowliest. We need a choice of distribution over the Web or on removable media such as CD-ROM or DVD. igital libraries can incorporate flexible presentation that caters to individual differences, such as large-font displays or spoken output for the visually impaired. Libraries are places where information is preserved, not rendered obsolete, and digital libraries must instill confidence that information prepared today can be accessed next week, next decade, next century—regardless of technological changes.

An important aspect of digital libraries is their ability to work in local languages, promoting pluralism and reducing the risks of homogeneity. Because language is the vehicle of thought, communication, and cultural identity, this will encourage diversity and strengthen individual cultures. But there is a long way to go: even Unicode is woefully incomplete in certain areas, such as African languages. Naturally, today's digital library systems focus principally on the reader: the consumer of the material stored in the library's treasure-house.

But digital libraries make a more radical, and perhaps ultimately more important, contribution by empowering ordinary users to conceive, assemble, build, and disseminate new information collections themselves. n principle, modest computing resources are quite sufficient to enable users to build new collections by gathering together material in local files or on the Web; augmenting it with appropriate metadata that supports convenient search and browsing operations; incorporating advanced features like key-phrase extraction, document summarization, and metadata extraction; designing an attractive and functional interface; and publishing the collection on a variety of different media that are suitable for the intended readership. •The HCI challenge is to realise this potential for users—such as most librarians—who have a strong understanding of information and its organization, but no more interest in computers than they have in papermaking technology, last millennium's vehicle for information dissemination.

UNIVERSAL ACCESS

Universal access to digital libraries presents huge challenges to software engineers and HCI practitioners. The Greenstone digital library software allows us to glimpse some of the issues, although it certainly does not yet effectively address them all. Most digital libraries are accessed over the web, using any web browser. However, in many environments, particularly in developing countries, web access is insufficient and the system must run locally. And if people are to build and control their own libraries, a centralized solution is inadequate: the software must run on their own computers. Thus digital library systems intended for broad access should run on a wide variety of computer systems, particularly low-end ones. Developed under Linux, the Greenstone server runs on any Windows, Unix, or MacOS/X system. All versions of Windows are supported, from 3.1 up. Supporting primitive platforms poses substantial challenges of a rather mundane nature: for example, Microsoft compilers no longer support Windows 3.1 and it is necessary to acquire obsolete versions. Under Windows, pre-built collections can be viewed on any system with at least 8 Mb RAM, but collections cannot be built under Windows 3.1/3.11—for this at least a Pentium processor is generally required, except for very small collections. The fact that Greenstone does not run on early Macintosh systems is a serious drawback in certain environments.

In an international cooperative effort established in August 2000 with UNESCO and the Belgium-based Human Info NGO, Greenstone is being distributed widely in developing countries with the aim of empowering users, particularly in universities, libraries, and other public service institutions, to build their own digital libraries. UNESCO recognizes that digital libraries are radically reforming how information is acquired and disseminated in its partner communities and institutions in the fields of education, science and culture around the world, and particularly in developing countries. Their hope is that this software will encourage the effective deployment of digital libraries to share information and place it in the public domain. he UNESCO distribution of Greenstone is a CD-ROM that contains the full source code and executable binaries for Windows and Linux, along with all necessary associated software.

Full documentation and five demonstration collections are included. he current CD-ROM is trilingual, with complete interfaces, instructions, and documentation in English, French and Spanish. For those with Web access, the same package is also available for download from the Greenstone Web site, often in a form that is slightly ahead of the CD-ROM version—for example, many other language interfaces are included and full documentation is available in Russian and Kazakh too. Providing accessibility in different languages is more difficult than one might at first realise. As well as the manuals, installation instructions and installation prompts, the licensing agreement, and the readme files have to be translated too.

Greenstone collections like the Humanity Development Library can be published as standalone collections on removable media such as CD-ROM, or presented on the Web. CD-ROM is a very practical format in developing countries. Any Greenstone collection can be converted into a self-contained Windows CD-ROM that includes the Greenstone server software itself and an integrated installation package. The installation procedure has been thoroughly honed to ensure that only the most basic of computer skills are needed to install and run a collection under Windows. Even standalone Greenstone users interact through a Web browser: Netscape is supplied on each CD-ROM for those who do not already have a browser. In standalone mode the software runs locally but incorporates a Web server so that if the system happens to be connected to a network—say a hospital or school intranet—information is available to other machines that may not possess CD drives. This happens automatically: no special configuration is necessary. Another difficult engineering challenge is checking for the existence of a network. While installed network software is easily detected, it is hard to determine non-intrusively whether it is operational. Incorrectly installed or configured software is endemic in developing countries, because computers there are often cast-offs whose software is inappropriate to their present environment, yet system support to rectify the problems is unavailable.

It is essential for universal access that such problems are addressed properly and solved satisfactorily without involving the user, even though they are mundane and timeconsuming. Greenstone provides some support for the visually impaired by incorporating a "textual" mode of access that replaces all images by textual prompts. This output is suitable for users with speech synthesizers or other specialized access devices. However, the facility is not well advanced: in particular, we have not yet refined it through usability testing and interface improvement.

2

Historical Development of Library

GROWTH OF LIBRARIES IN INDIA

GROWTH AND DEVELOPMENT OF ORIENTAL LIBRARIES IN INDIA

Libraries have always had a pivotal role in the storage, processing, and dissemination of information. Some may serve general needs, but special libraries serve the needs of a particular community of users. Among special libraries, Oriental libraries hold an important place because they preserve the cultural heritage of a nation or a civilization.

Oriental Libraries

"Oriental Libraries" are those libraries that have literature pertaining to Oriental studies and languages. "Oriental" in this context refers to the ancient Near East, including India, Persia, and ancient Arabia, among other places, and the languages and literatures of those places and peoples.

Growth and Development

India is a vast repository of different cultures, both because it was invaded by a number of foreign countries and peoples, and because of its contacts with people from the East. The languages from those Eastern countries are part of Indian literature. The literature in those Eastern languages created India's Oriental libraries.

Their history can be traced back to the Vedic period, when the written literature was kept in Ashrams or Gurukuls. Gurukuls were mostly located peaceful forest environments. With the passage of time, Gurukuls were also established in cities.

Jain and Buddhist Era

Taxila was one of the famous educational centres where students came from different parts of the country. Varanasi also distinguished itself by having a large number of Gurukulas. During this period, the literature was preserved in the Sutra style of composition. Buddhist and Jain Monastries acted as repositories of knowledge, for religious literature as well as other types. Monastic Oriental Libraries were also called Viharas. Over time, these Viharas developed into institutions of higher learning. A federation of Viharas constituted a Mahavihara, which was a larger educational institutional institution.

Nalanda Mahavihara is the best example. Fa-Hien, a Chinese traveller, also found a number of monastaries in India. Kanyakubja, Sravasti, Kusunagara, Vaisali, and Patliputra were centres of Oriental literature according to Fa-Hien. Hiuen-Tsang, another Chinese traveller, visited India during 629-645 A.D.

He left a detailed account of his visit, which gives us significant information about Buddhist educational institutions possessing a rich variety of Eastern literature. Taxila was a center of learning in Ancient India and a large number of people from all over the world and the subcontinent itself visited this place to gain knowledge.

Literature related to medicine and archery enriched the library at Taxila. Rahula Sankrityayana, Angiris set up a seminary with a Granthakuti attached to it at Taxila, which later flourished in to an academy or university. Nalanda University is the best known of ancient India 's universities. It has been called the treasure house of information by European archeologists.

The information there helped locate Buddhist shrines in India. It is believed that King Kumara Gupta built the first monastery at Nalanda to train Buddhist monks. Nalanda University was an expansion of this seminary. King Buddha Gupta, Jagatha Gupta, Baladitya, and Vijra made additions and expansions to the building. There were three large libraries with vast amount of literature in Oriental languages on subjects such as science, medicine, astrology, fine arts, literature.

The University of Valabhi was built by the Maitraka Kings during the years 475-775 A.D. Its library had a variety of Eastern literature. This great university and its library lasted until the 12th century, when they were completely destroyed by Arab invaders. Odantapuri University was founded by King Gopala and was a well-known center of learning. It had a library that was rich in Brahmanical and Buddhist works. Mohammad Bakhtiyar Khilji destroyed this monastic university along with its library. Somapuri also possessed a wealth of Oriental literature, but it was destroyed by fire in the middle of the 11th century.

Vikramasila monastery, built by King Dharmapala, had a variety of literature on metaphysics, tantras, grammar, ritualism, and logic. The library fulfilled the demands of outsiders, especially those from Tibet, by providing them copies of manuscripts in a most liberal way. Another University with a significant Oriental collection, especially in Tantric Buddhism, was Jagaddala, founded by King Ramapala. Another monastery with a rich wealth on different aspects of Oriental literature was Kanheri University, built during the reign of Amoghavarsha. By the 10th century, the corpus of Jain literature had increased many times, and Jain monks had contributed substantially to nearly all branches of knowledge known at that time. The Jayendra monastery of Kashmir had a good library where the Chinese traveller Hiuen–Tsang spent two years copying manuscripts.

Similarly, he spent fourteen months at the Chinapati monastery. Several Hindu kings and their ministers, who flourished between 10th and 12th centuries AD, are credited with establishing libraries and supporting the library movement. Among them was King Bhoja of Dhara, who flourished in the 11th century, and was a distinguished scholar with a rich library. King Kumarapaladeva of the Chaulakyas is said to have established 21 Jain Libraries. He kept a copy of Kalpasutra written in golden ink in each one of them.

Mughal Empire

When the Muslims established their rule in India at the beginning of the 13th century, Muslim emperors paid special attention to libraries, taking care to establish libraries in educational institutions. They constructed no separate library buildings; rather, books were deposited and preserved in educational institutions, mosques, and Khangahs.

Many Muslim rulers were from the East, and they helped enrich libraries with Oriental literature. Paper began be used as a writing material in the 12th century, and this helped book production in this periods. Mughal sovereigns and their courtiers were educated and accomplished, and some maintained personal libraries.

The Muslim sovereigns collected and preserve the Vedas, the Ramayana, and other Hindu religious books. They also translated a variety of books in Hindi in to Persian and Arabic, and helped disseminate Hindu art and culture. After the establishment of Sultans of Delhi in 1202, a new period in the history of Oriental libraries came in to existence. These minor Muslim rulers and nobles encouraged Islamic learning and established *maktabs* (primary schools), *madrasas* (schools of higher learning), libraries, and mosques.

They encouraged Arabic and Persian literatures in all branches of learning, and enriched Oriental literature in the libraries. They gave shelter and protection to scholars, who brought literature from other parts of the world to India. The Library of Khwajah Nizam-ud-din Auliya was an important Oriental library.

It was the property of the *Waqf* (religious board) and was open to every man of letters. During the reign of the Khilji dynasty the number of Oriental libraries increased. Jala-ud-din Khiljee established the Imperial Library at Delhi and appointed Amir Khusru as its librarian.

The Tughluq Dynasty opened a new chapter in the history of Oriental libraries in India. Mohammad Tughluq built one thousand madrasas, each with a library with collections in Arabic and Persian. Humayun ascended the throne in 1530 and a library known as Khan-i-Tilism. Humayun's library played a significant role in Mughal history. Akbar, the greatest of Mughal emperors maintained a very rich library. He added a sizable number of books, obtained from his conquest, from libraries in Gujrat, Jaunpur, Kashmir, Bihar, Bengal, and the Deccan.

His library was unique in its collection of rare books, among which was the Persian *Divan of Human Shah.* By the time of Akbar's grandson, Shah Jahan, the library was a complex organization with a large staff, and headed by Nazim, a noble of the court. In Kashmir, a picture of the first library is found in the Shrine of Hazrat Bulbul Shah, which was established by Muslims. A magnificient monastery and mosque were constructed by the emperor of Kashmir, Sultan Sadruddin, for Hazrat Bulbul Shah. A library was attached to this mosque.

Amir Kabir Syed Hamdani, a theologian and scholar had a well established personal library that contained Oriental literature. He established a number of libraries in Kashmir which added to the wealth of the Indian Oriental libraries. The Sultans of Kashmir had given funds to establish madrasas and libraries. Each madrasa had a library. Sultan Zain-ul-Abedin-ul constructed a library which historians tell was one of the best in the world. Among the other libraries built by Budshah, Darul-ul-Uloom Nausherah was the best.

Another library, by the name of Madrasa-i-Sher, was built by Budshah near modern Islamabad. During the Chak Sultanate many libraries thrived and brought Oriental literature to the limelight. Akbar conquered Kashmir in 1587 and established many madrasas and libraries there. In Gujrat and Malwa, a number of libraries were introduced by Ahmad Shah I and Dilawar Khan.

Shah Jahan, like his predecessors, patronized learning and education and built a library with a rich collection of Arabic and Persian manuscripts. Dara Shikkoh, Aurangzeb, and Bahadur Shah Zafar also contributed to the development of Oriental libraries. Mughal rule was a period of literary excellence. Most of the emperors were themselves scholars, and also extended their patronage to scholarship and learning.

Other Kingdoms

There were kingdoms in other parts of India that also had libraries enriched by Oriental literature. The kingdoms of Bahmani and Deccan had independent kings who reigned for 340 years, and who were patrons of learning, as were the Bahmani kings, who continued their rule up to 1526 AD and had an empire that stretched from coast to coast. They founded many colleges and libraries. Ahmad Shah built a magnificient college near Gulbarga. Muhammad Shah Bahmani II built another imposing college at Bidar that is one of the many beautiful remains of the grandeur of the Bahmanis. All these colleges had libraries that possessed an enormous amount of Oriental literature.

Arabian and Iranian literature brought by visitors and travellers were added to the libraries of Bahmanis. The Urdu language was at its zenith during the reign of Firoz Shah Bahmani, and a vast amount of Urdu literature enriched the Bahmani Libraries. The library of Gesudaraj was distinguished among the libraries of Deccan. Books on Sufism and religion were available in this library.

The emperors of Qutub Shahi also established a good number of libraries during their reign, and a vast amount of literature in Persian was included. Tipu Sultan, son of Haider Ali and emperor of Mysore established a number of libraries. "Zaimul-Umoor" was the great university of Seringa Patnam in his reign. He collected books from many countries including Europe. The library had a copy of the Holy Quran which was written by the hand of Aurangzeb Alamgir. It is estimated that the library had nearly 2,000 volumes of Persian, Arabic, and Hindi manuscripts from all branches of Islamic literature.

After the downfall of the Mughals, and with the invasion of Ahmad Shah Abdali, the literary wealth of the Indian libraries was looted away. In 1857, after the Sepoy mutiny, thousands of books were destroyed and thousands of important, valuable, and rare books were siphoned to England.

British and other Europeans

The growth and development of Oriental libraries was regenerated again during European and British rule. The interest shown by the British and European scholars in Oriental Learning and Indology, along with the social, cultural and religious movements spearheaded by eminent Indians, resulted in new Oriental libraries.

These institutions established libraries for Oriental scholarship. The result of this renaissance is a number of special libraries devoted to Oriental and Indological collections in various parts of the country. Rampur Raza Library, very rich in Indo-Islamic studies and arts, was created by Nawab Faizullah Khan in 1794, and has tremendous manuscript wealth. One can find manuscripts in Arabic, Persian, Urdu, Sanskrit, Sinhali, Tamil, Kannada, and other Oriental languages.

The Asiatic Society Library, Kolkatta, a premier and leading oriental institutions of the country was established in 1784 by Sir William Jones. Colonel Mackenzie, an Englishman and an engineer by profession established an Oriental Library by the name of " *Government Oriental Manuscript Library* (GOML) " in Chennai.

Contemporary Libraries

Khuda Baksh Oriental Library was founded in 1842 by Maulvi Khuda Baksh Khan, who donated his entire personal collection. Since 1977 it has been issuing regularly a multi-lingual research quarterly *Khuda Baksh Library Journal.* The library has been recognized as a research center by seven Indian universities. The collection has a rich repository of Persian and Arabic manuscripts. Maulana Azad Library, Aligarh Muslim University was initially founded as "Anglo Oriental College (MAOC) at Aligarh in 1875 and raised to the status of a university in 1920.

The personal collection of Maulana Azad also enriches the library. The library has a total collection of over 1 million volumes and 14,571 manuscripts. The Maulana Azad Library has the largest collection of Urdu books in the Indian subcontinent, which is perhaps largest in the world as well.

The collection includes:

- Urdu
- Arabic
- Persian
- Sanskrit
- Hindi
- Sir Syed Collection
- Gandhian Collection
- Aligarh Collection
- Thesis Collection
- Archives
- Microfiche
- Manuscripts

Hakim Mohammad Syed Library, Jamia Hamdard, New Delhi is a leading university founded in 1906.

It has a well known Oriental library, which has a number of special collections:

- Nazaria Collection
- Abdul Sattar Siddiqui Collection
- Maulana Abdul Salam Niazi Collection
- Jaffri Collection
- Shafi Ahmad Collection
- Dr Tanveer Alvi Collection

The library has 4,500 rare manuscripts. Osmania University Library was established in 1918 and is considered seventh oldest in India, the third oldest in South India, and the first to be established in state of Hyderabad. The library has a collection of rare books and manuscripts including Palm Leaf manuscripts. The National Library of India, which came in to existence in 1948, is the largest library in India. Previously it was known as the Imperial

Library which was formed in 1891 by combining a number of Secretariat libraries. It has a wide range of collections in a variety of national and international languages. A good number of Arabic and Persian documents are also available here.

The Oriental library initiative that took place in ancient India reached its zenith in the period when the British and other Europeans came to India. The Mughals also contributed a great deal to the development of Oriental libraries. Eventually, their extravagant ways caused the libraries to deteriorate, but social and political conditions eventually led to better libraries with larger collections.

ACADEMIC LIBRARIES IN INDIA: A HISTORICAL STUDY

Research in library history in India has remained largely neglected area which has resulted into availability of very limited and scanty literature. Commenting on the status of library history in India, Donald G. Davis, Jr. of the University of Texas at Austin, writes that "although a core literature on Indian library history exists, it has many imbalances and gaps. The scholars are very dispersed in their interests and their geographical location. With one person rarely contributing more than one work. There is little pattern to existing research efforts."

In this context, the role of historian happens to be much more crucial and significant to make an assessment of the growth and development of libraries in India, the factors responsible for their development and the impact of those factors on the library progress. Rajgopalan, in his 1987 presidential address to the Indian Library Association rightly said, "it is generally acknowledged that our libraries are underutilized in relation to investments being made in them.

Non-use and low-use of libraries amount to wastage of facilities being made available. Maybe the literacy rate, lack of reading habits, etc., are the causes for low use from the side of patrons... User education programmes must be organized by libraries in a way that libraries are fully utilized." He further remarked that, "if library historians would address the roots and trends of library issues, they would provide a valuable service to the profession and society."

The Father of Library and Information Science in India,Padmashri Dr. S.R. Ranganathan while giving a radio talk in April 1956 said, "an account of the libraries in the first four periods must necessarily depend upon the historical research. This has not yet been done. The library profession is too small in India to spare a person to fill up this antiquarian gap. Those trained in the scientific method of tracing history are too preoccupied with dynastic and political history to spare sufficient time for cultural history in general and library history in particular."

Thus, an historical study of the growth and development of academic libraries in India, is a desideratum, the fulfillment of which should go a long way in removing the imbalances and gaps. Such a study becomes significant not only in view of the tremendous activity concerning the growth and development of libraries in India, but also because their growth has been shaped in the first phase by the phenomena that have shaped the historical course of this period and, secondly, the rise of library as an important instrument in the advancement of knowledge and socio-economic transformation.

Source Material for Writing History of Libraries

For the purpose of scientific writing of history of libraries, an understanding of the nature of existing source material and knowing the art of using it is essential. The sources for writing the history are available in Pali, Sanskrit, Chinese, Arabic, Persian and European Languages and most of them have been translated into English. These exist in various formats, such as Manuscripts, inscriptions, copper plates etc. They are either indigenous or foreign.

The contribution of foreign travelogues such as Tibetan, Chinese, Muslim, Portuguese, English and other Europeans is highly useful. Some noteworthy foreign travelogues are Itsing, Fahien, Hieun Tsang, Alberuni, Ibn Batuta, Minhaj, Firishta, Badauni, Afif, bernier, mandelso, Manrique de Lara, Martin, Count Noer.

In addition to the contribution of the travelogues, the contribution of historians like Henry M. Eliot, John Dawson, Stanley Lane-Pool, Ishwari Prasad, R.C. Majumdar, Jadunath Sarkar, V.D. Mahajan, Mohammed Muhammed Zubair, J.S. Sarma and N.N. Law etc. is also significant. Though scanty, yet there are articles written by the library professionals on history of libraries. A few efforts have also been made for conduct of research in the area of history of libraries and such like works have been consulted for the purpose of writing this paper.

University Libraries in Ancient India

In the Vedic age instructions were imparted "orally, without the medium of books." Taxila from 700 B.C. to 300 A.D. was considered to be the most respected seat of higher learning and education in India but still there is no evidence found so far in the archaeological excavations at Taxila that there had been a good library system in the Taxila University.

Fa-Hien noticed such libraries at Jetavana monastery at Sravasti. In 400 A.D., there came into being one of the biggest known universities, the Nalanda University, which by 450 A.D. became a renowned seat of learning, its fame spreading beyond the boundaries of India. Nalanda near Patna grew to be the foremost Buddhist monastery and an educational centre. Most of what we know of the Nalanda University during the 6th and the 7th centuries A.D. is due to the accounts left by Hiuen-tsang, who lived in the institution for three years in the first half of the 7th century, and I-tsing who also stayed there for ten years towards the latter part of the same century.

Information on the Nalanda University Library is also found in the Tibetan accounts, from which we understand that the library was situated in a special area known by the poetical name the Dharmaganja, which comprised three huge buildings, called the Ratnasagara, the Ratnodadhi and the Ratnaranjaka of which the Ratnasagara was a ninestoried building and housed the collection of manuscripts and rare sacred works like Prajnaparamita Sutra etc.

The library at Nalanda had a rich stock of manuscripts on philosophy and religion and contained texts relating to grammar, logic, literature, the Vedas, the Vedanta, and the Samkhya philosophy, the Dharmasastras, the Puranas, Astronomy, Astrology and Medicine. The University of Nalanda and its library flourished down to the 12th century A.D. until Bakhtiyar Khalji sacked it in 1197-1203 A.D.7 and set fire to the establish-ment of Nalanda. The world famous universities, such as, the Vikramasila, the Vallabhi and the Kanchi were coming up in other parts of the country during the period from the 5th century A.D. to the 8th century A.D. All these universities possessed rich libraries and in the hall containing such books there used to be an image of the goddess Saraswati with a book in her hand.

The Nalanda and the Vikramshila universities were under the control of the king Dharmapala. He founded the Vikramshila monastery in the 8th century A.D. It had a rich collection of texts in the Sanskrit, the Prakrit and the Tibetan languages. Regarding the library of the university, the *Tabaqat-i-Nasiri* informs us that there were great number of books on the religion of Hindus there; and when all these books came under the observation of the Mussalamans, they summoned, a number of Hindus that they might give them information regarding the import of these books; but the whole of the Hindu community was killed in the war.

Muslim vandalism caused the disappearance of the excellent collection at Vikramashila. The Jaggadal Vihara in Varendra-bhumi was also an important centre of learning with considerable collection of the reading material. It was established by the king Kampala, who ruled from 1084 to 1130 A.D. The provision of facilities for reading, writing, editing and translating manuscripts shows that this library was in no way less than its contemporary libraries in importance. Though not as large as the library of Nalanda, it abounded in private collection of texts.

Likewise Mithila had been famous for its scholars since the days of Rajrishi Janaka and had a rich collection of various commentaries on the different branches of the Hindu *Shastras.* The library of its university played an important role in teaching and learning. A needle *(Shalaka)* was pierced through the manuscript on the subject of the student's specialization and he was expected to explain the last page pierced. In this way the student's all-round mastery of the subject was tested. Mithila continued to enjoy its all India importance in the field of learning till the end of the 15th century AD. The university at Sompuri, like that of Vikramshila, occupied a significant position since the days of Dharampala.

Like Nalanda, this university also had its own library. Atisa Dipankar, a noted scholar, lived there. He with the help of other scholars, translated into the Tibetan the *Madhyamkaratnapradipa* of Bhavaviveka. This university was destroyed by fire in the middle of the 11th century A.D. Efforts were made by the monk Vipulsrimitra to renovate the university but it could not regain its past glory.

At a time when Nalanda was famous for its *Mahayana* courses of study, the Maitrakakings provided their patronage to the Mahavihara of Vallabhi. This university was famous for its *Hinayana* studies. The fact that this university had a good library is supported by a reference in a grant of Guhasena, dated 559 A.D., wherein a provision was made out of the royal grant for the purchase of books for the library. This important seat of learning at Kanheri, on the West Coast, flourished during the reign of Amoghavarsha in the 9th century A.D. The library occupied a significant position within the establishment, and the donors provided money to buy books for the library. The last of the famous seats of learning in Eastern India was Navadwipa in Bengal.

It reached its height of glory from 1083 to 1106 A.D. as a centre of intellectual excellence as well as its rich library facilities, when Lakshman Sen, a king of Gauda, made it his capital. However, this library was also destroyed along with the centre by Bakhtiyar Khalji. Situated in South India at Amaravati, on the banks of the Krishna, the Nagarjuna Vidyapeeth flourished in about 7th century A.D. Its library housed in the top floor of the five storyed building of the university had an enormous collection on the Buddhist philosophy, particularly of the *Mahayana* school that Nagarjuna had founded, science and medicine.

There is enough archaeological evidence that supports the existence of this 7th century university and its library. The enormity of the collection in this library is borne out by the fact that it not only had works on the Buddhist literature and the *Tripitakas,* but also works on several branches of scientific knowledge, such as, Botany, Geography, Mineralogy and Medicine. It was a great attraction for scholars from the different parts of India and from countries, like, China, Burma and Ceylon.

University Libraries in Medieval India

The existence of academic libraries during the medieval period of Indian history is not known, though the Muslim rulers did patronize libraries in their own palaces. A lone exception, however, was a library attached to a college at Bidar, having a collection of 3000 books on different subjects. Aurangzeb got this Library transferred to Delhi to merge it with his palace library. During the medieval period, due to Muslim invasions and political troubles, the powerful empires and kingdoms of Indian rulers fell one by one. This affected higher education and the development of academic libraries as well.

Libraries in Modern India

During the British rule in India, number of academic institutions were established by the East India Company, and by the Christan missionaries. Some of the worth mentioning events which led to the growth and development of higher education in India during this period were the establishment of the Calcutta College in 1781, Jonathan Duncan, then a British agent, founded the Benaras Sanskrit College in 1792. The Calcutta Fort William College was founded in 1800.

All these colleges were having their own libraries. The Charter Act of 1813, the foundation of Fort William and Serampore Colleges, Calcutta, Madras and Bombay universities and their libraries, Hunter, Raleigh and Calcutta University Commissions, library training programmes, the establishment of Inter University Board, Sargent Report and appointment of the University Grants Committee, the establishment of Madras University, University of Bombay, University of Calcutta and their libraries, the constitution of Inter-University Board, the appointment of Hartog Committee, the Montague-Chelmsford reforms of 1919, the Government of India Act of 1935, and the Sargent Committee Report etc.

laid foundation for establishment of libraries in various parts of the country. The Fort William College was founded in Calcutta on 18th August 1800 by the Marquis of Welleselay, the Governor-General of India during 1798-1805. Reverend David Brown, Provost of the college was instrumental in setting up the library which had a well rounded collection of Eastern manuscripts. In the absence of adequate financial support, the library could not survive for long and in 1835 it was decided to close the library and its valuable collection was transferred to the Asiatic Society Library in Calcutta between 1835-39. The Charter Act of 1813 passed by the British Parliament gave the East India Company complete responsibility for educating Indians. The establishment of C.M.S. College in Kottayam, Hindu college in Calcutta in 1816 and Raven Shaw College in Cuttack in 1816 was the immediate result of the Charter Act 1813.

These and other colleges came into existence thereafter had their own libraries the day they were established. Serampore College during this period was founded by the Danes in 1818 and the King of Denmark in 1927 agreed to give this college an academic status by providing equivalence to the Danish Universities with power to confer degrees. The library of this college too was established along with its foundation and at a later stage the college was given affiliation to the University of Burdwan for the purpose of conferring degrees. The 7th March 1835 decision of the British Indian Government to promote English literature and sciences in India was resulted into the spread of number of colleges in India and by 1839 there were over forty colleges with attached libraries in the British territory in India.

For their establishment, lots of money was made available by the Indians in the form of donations. In 1840 Presidency College was founded in Madras, followed by a medical college in Bombay in 1845. This progress in education was instrumental in establishing universities in India. The Charles Wood dispatch of 1854 popularly known as the 'Magna Carta of English Education' in India also paved the way for the establishment of the universities in the presidency towns. Sir John Colville introduced the Bill to establish universities in India and it was passed by the Governor General of India Lord Dalhousie on 24th January 1857, paved the way for the foundation of three universities based on the London Universities Model in the Presidency towns of Calcutta, Madras and Bombay.

Indian Education Commission, popularly known as Hunter Commission was appointed by the British Indian Government in 1882 to study the progress of education under the new policy adopted in 1854 by the East India Company and transferred to the Crown and accepted by the Secretary of State in 1859. Sir William W. Hunter in his report had clearly stated that the conditions of the libraries was in a very poor state and declared them "hardly creditable." The Commission paid special attention to the colleges and their libraries and other facilities.

The direct result of the Commission was the establishment of Panjab University, Lahore and Allahabad University in 1882 and 1887 respectively but still the condition of the education and libraries remained in a poor state. The Raleigh Commission 1902 appointed by Lord Curzon to investigate the conditions and prospects of the Indian universities and to recommend measures to improve their constitution and working and standards of teaching also paid special attention to the academic libraries and found that, "the library is little used by graduates and hardly at all by other students." Further, the Commission commented, "In a college where library is inadequate or ill arranged, the students have no opportunity of forming the habit of independent and intelligent reading."

Thus, the Commission specifically recommended that reference services must be made an integral part of all libraries in colleges and universities, and that one of the prerequisite conditions for the grant of university affiliation to a college be the accessibility of students to the library of the institution. The recommendations of the Raleigh Commission were included in the Universities Act of 1904 and provided the power to all universities to require that all colleges applying for affiliation maintain proper libraries, equipment, library building, and lend books to all students but the situation and the status of libraries could not be improved much simply because the recommendations made by the Commission and the provisions made in the act could not be implemented properly. The Calcutta University Commission popularly known as Sadler Commission was appointed by the government in 1917 to study the situation and the status of education in the country and to make recommendations to solve the existing problems.

The Commission noticed that "one of the greatest weak-nesses of the existing system is the extraordinarily unimportant part which is played by the library" and found that "in some colleges the library is regarded not as an essential part of teaching equipment but merely as a more or less useless conventional accessory." The Commission made the recommendations regarding the libraries that college libraries be strengthened and that training should be given to the students and occasionally to the teachers about use of the library.

One of the immediate result of the Calcutta University Commission was the establishment of a few new teaching-cum-residential universities at Patna in 1917, Osmania in Hyderabad in 1918, Dacca, Aligarh, and Lucknow in 1921, Delhi in 1922 and Nagpur in 1923 and all of them were established along with the establishment of libraries as an integral part of the university system. As stated earlier, the impact of the Commission could very well be seen in the establishment of several universities along with their libraries. This was the period when in the libraries scenario, a person appeared who at a later stage turned the entire scene and become the father of library science in India.

The man was none other than Dr. S.R. Ranganathan. The University of Madras appointed Dr. S.R. Ranganathan as its Librarian in 1924. He was trained at the University of London Library School before joining his duties at Madras. Things did change rapidly after his joining. For example, he introduced the lending and reference services at the Madras University Library and extended the library hours for the benefit of the readers. Whereas the hours had previously been 7 a.m. to 4 p.m., they were changed to 7 a.m. to 6 p.m. He delivered a series of lectures to about two thousand teachers at the conference of the South Indian Teachers' Union in 1929 regarding the use and importance of the library services.

The Madras Library Association started a summer course in librarianship and the lectures for this course were mainly delivered by Dr. Ranganathan. The main objective of the course in its beginning was to spread the ideas of the value of good library services and modern library methods among potential users of the library. The budget of the university library of Madras had been very poor from the beginning and it was really a difficult task to manage, run and administer the library effectively within it. Ranganathan brought this poor financial position to the notice of the then Chief Minister, Dr. P. Subbaroyan, when he delivered a speech during an educational conference held at Madras in 1926. In his speech, Ranganathan "gave a graphic account of the library network in Europe and the United States of America and compared it with the poor, appalling facilities existing in India.... added that paucity of funds prevented him developing his library."

The Chief Minister was highly impressed by Ranganathan's speech and promised to give more State help to the University Library. Its immediate result was a grant of rupees 6,000 which was added to the annual grant from the State, and, in addition, rupees 100,000 in lump sum were sanctioned by the Madras State Government in the same year to buy books and periodicals in pure sciences, humanities, and social sciences. Provision was also made for additional grants to the library, as and when new departments of study and research were established.

In the words of Ranganathan, "This was the first time when such a forward financial step in the history of the university libraries in India was taken in the second quarter of the 20th century." The University of Madras library made a good start under Ranganathan's effective leadership and administration. In 1930, the library had five well-trained reference librarians to help the readers, and they "carried the work to a high pitch of efficiency."

This was the first time in the history of Indian libraries that a special reference service was introduced in a university library. The library collection increased to 93,000 volumes in 1935 and on September 3, 1936, the library was shifted to its first new and permanent functional building. By 1944, when Ranganathan resigned from the position of the Librarian, to become the University Librarian at the *Banaras Hindu University* (BHU), the collection of the Madras University Library had augmented to 1,20,000 volumes. The contribution of Dr. Ranganathan to the growth and development of libraries in general and the Madras University Library in particular is undoubtedly tremendous and unforgettable. It will not be wrong to say that the Library School of Madras and the Madras University Library were the laboratories of Ranganathan to propound his ideas in library science and to test them practically.

Some of the important and major ideas of Ranganathan were the Five Laws of Library Science which were enunciated by him in 1924, and their formulation and publication in 1929 and 1931 respectively. These laws are still considered a unifying theory for all library practices and services, and set of guidelines for the dynamic development and study of library science as a whole.

The University of Bombay Library received a special grant of rupees 50,000 from the Central Government in 1939 to strengthen its collection for graduate studies. During the period from 1931 to 1939, a few more special grants were given to the library for its collection development. A very special grant of rupees 10,000 was given by Kikabhai and Maniklal, sons of the late

Premchand Roychand, in 1931 to replace the electric clock of the library tower. The collection, which stood at 4,504 volumes in 1900, rose to 70,000 in 1939 and 73,582 in 1947. Though higher education and academic libraries made some progress during the first quarter of the present century, yet their growth and development was not very well organized.

Academic institutions and their growth after 1916 created a few problems also and the general feeling was that the "quality of Education was being sacrificed for quantity." While such a situation prevailed, the Indian Statutory Commission, popularly known as the Simon Commission, was appointed by the Government in 1927 to study the conditions prevailing in India. The Simon Commission appointed an Auxiliary Committee to look into the growth of education in India. Sir Philip Hartog, a former member of the Calcutta University Commission, and a former Vice-Chancellor of the University of Dacca, was appointed its Chairman.

In its report, submitted in 1929, the Committee stated that "the dispersal of resources for university teaching among a number of colleges had made it difficult to build up university libraries of the type required for advanced work both at the Honours and the research stage majority of the university libraries were inadequate and all needed great additions." In addition to want of books, libraries also lacked good current periodicals in their collections. The Committee also made a special note of the low academic standards in many colleges and universities and the "unhealthy competition for candidates between neighbouring universities".

This report, however, did not offer any comprehensive, detailed, and realistic solutions to the problems. In 1935, Ministry of Education was formed in each province, as per the provisions of the dyarchy in the Montague-Chelmsford Reforms of 1919, supplemented by those of the new Government of India Act of 1935. The Ministry of Education in India requested the Central Advisory Board of Education in 1944 to survey the educational conditions in the country.

The Board's report, known as the Sargeant Report, after its Chairman, Sir Sargeant, the Educational Advisor to the Government of India, came up with a master-plan for the development of education in the post-World War II India. Its terms of reference covered education at all levels-primary, secondary, and higher. The Indian universities, as they existed then, despite many admirable features, did not fully satisfy the requirements of a national system of education. During the British rule, several committees and commissions set up periodically, paved way for the foundation of several colleges and the establishment of many universities and in many cases the libraries were also established along with them.

It is also true that as compared to the first two decades the development of university libraries after 1924 did make better progress but the college libraries were still neglected and were struggling to get their recognition.

There were only 12 universities in India in 1924 and their number swelled to 18 by the time India got freedom in 1947. In fact, the academic libraries during the British rule had no significance in the academic life of the institutions of higher education and the pivotal role that can be played by the academic libraries in the life of the institutions could very well be seen in the policy statement of higher education of the free India and the fact was also proven when at the time of national reconstruction, the importance of libraries in teaching and research was recognized, and libraries received the early attention of the Government of India.

Academic Libraries in India after Independence

The actual process for the development of university libraries in India can be said to have been set in motion with the appointment of the University Education Commission presided over by Dr. S. Radhakrishnan and its recommendations, such as, annual grants, open access system, working hours, organization of the library, staff, steps to make students book conscious and the need to give grants to teachers to buy books. The section on libraries of the report opens with a powerful statement on the importance of libraries in university education and states, "teaching is a cooperative enterprise. Teachers must have the necessary tools for teaching purposes in the shape of libraries and laboratories as also the right type of students."

The Commission in the course of its study of the academic libraries, found that "libraries were hopelessly inadequate to serve the curricular needs of a modern university. They were ill-housed, illstocked, and ill-staffed and were totally lacking in standard literary and scientific journals. Service was in the hands of personnel that had hardly any notion of the objectives of university education. The annual appropriation for book purchase seldom exceeded the ten thousand mark."

In addition, the annual grant for these libraries were not sufficient. Therefore, the Commission recommended that at least six per cent of the total budget of each academic institution should be set aside for the library. Only then will the condition of these libraries improve. It added that if institutions were not willing to allocate six per cent of their budget to libraries, they should spend ₹40 per student enrolled. The Commission also suggested that greater attention should be paid to improve the reference services in the university libraries. Therefore, "documentation and biblio-graphical services must be developed in order to promote research among the faculty and students, make libraries proper centres for research activities, and to raise the standards of services."

As far as the library staff is concerned, the Commission was of the view that it is very important to have well-qualified staff, including the Director, in order to provide excellent service in any library. The Director's qualifications must include Ph.D. in Library Science and he must have the rank and salary of a professor, capabilities of organization and management, and should have full powers of an administrator to run the library effectively. University Education Commission. There is no doubt that the recommendations of the Commission "were based on the needs of the modern library services in universities for the promotion of research and creative learning." It was for the first time that such detailed attention was paid to the library matters by a commission on university education in India.

Ranganathan Committee (1957)

The most comprehensive and significant document on the university and college libraries is the Report of the UGC library committee, chaired by Ranganathan. The Report was published by the University Grants Commission in 1959 entitled 'University and College Libraries.' It was perhaps the first attempt by any Library Committee in India to systematically survey the academic libraries on a national basis, and it was also the first time that the government of India had decided to seek advice from a professional librarian regarding academic libraries. The committee was to advice the UGC on the standards of libraries, building, pay scales, and library training.

After the survey the library committee invited all academic librarians to a seminar on "Work flow in university and college libraries," at Delhi from March 4 to 7, 1959 to keep them informed about the progress the committee had made surveying the academic libraries. It wanted to discuss its recommendations with them. Some of the recommendations of the Committee included the provision that the UGC and the State Government should help the college and the university libraries in the collection development of both books and periodicals. The formula suggested by the committee was that funds be given "at the rate of ₹15 per enrolled student and ₹200 per teacher and research fellow. There should also be special initial library grants in the case of a new university and of a new department in an existing university, a similar scale should be followed for the college libraries. In order to promote co-operation among libraries, a Union Catalogue of books and a Union List of periodicals to be prepared.

The Committee strongly recommended that an open access system be introduced in every academic library. Committee also stressed "that reference service is the essential human process of establishing contact between the right reader and the right book by personal service. Reference service is vital in promotion of reading habit in student each library should provide an adequate number of reference librarians to function as library hosts and human converters."

Other recommendations included building up a microfilm collection, copying facilities for microfilms and book material, appointment of a committee to look into the standards of teaching, examination and research in the library schools, and appointment of full-time teaching faculty members rather than asking librarians to teach part time in the library schools. The Committee added that "the status and the salary of the library staff should be the same as that of the teaching and research staff', *i.e.*, Professor, Reader, and Lecturer etc." The recommendations of the committee had a farreaching effect on the development of the university libraries later. They had not only provided a framework to the UGC to implement its grants-in-aid programmes but also given to the university authorities important guidelines. Particular mention, in this connection, may be made of the recommendations concerning the library finances which had helped libraries to secure enough finances by way of annual grants from the universities themselves and of development grants from the UGC. The recommendations on the library personnel and staff strength have given to the library staff status and salaries equivalent to the academic staff and ensure provision for adequate staff for various library operations. The Committee submitted its report to the UGC with the hope that it will provide a blueprint for the systematic development of university libraries in the country. Hence, in-spite of many hurdles like education being a state subject in the Indian Constitution, considerable development in the university libraries has taken place and as such the condition of these libraries in 1953 was much better than in the 1940's and even the early 1950's.

Kothari Commission

The Education Commission under the chairmanship of Dr. D. S. Kothari marked another important stage in the history of university libraries in India.

The Commission devoted considerable attention to the develop-ment of the university libraries and made suitable recommendations on the following points:

- Norms for financial support;
- Long range planning for library development;
- The need for the establishment of a well equipped library before the starting of a university, college, or department;
- Suitable phasing over of the library grants;
- Encouraging the students in the use of books;
- Interdisciplinary communication; and
- Documentation service in libraries etc.

The Education Commission had also addressed itself to the role of libraries in adult education and recommended establish-ment of a network of public libraries. It wanted the school libraries to be integrated with public libraries for purposes of the adult education programmes. The Report, submitted by Dr. D. S. Kothari, on June 29, 1966, emphatically pointed out that "nothing can be more damaging than to ignore its library and to give it a low priority. No new college, university or department should be opened unless adequate number of books in the library are provided." The Commission was shocked to note that the recommen-dations of the

Radhakrishnan Commission had not been fully implemented, for only four universities in India has spent five per cent or more of their budget on books and periodicals acquisitions, though the 1948's Commission has suggested that six per cent of the total budget be spent on libraries. Other universities had spent less than five per cent of their budget on libraries, "Surprisingly enough there are five universities which spent even less than one per cent of the total budget on the libraries."

It was clear proof that the university libraries in India were not functioning properly to fulfill the needs of higher education. The Kothari Commission recommended that a long range plan for library development should be drawn up for each academic institution taking into consideration anticipated increase in enrollment, introduction of new subjects and research needs etc., and documentation service be encouraged in libraries, and documentation experts be appointed to help researchers and do indexing and abstracting.

It was further recommended that "the book selection should be oriented towards supporting instruction and research." The library should "provide resources necessary for research in fields of special interest to the university; provide library facilities and services necessary for the success of all formal programmes of instruction." Monetary guidelines were also suggested by the Commission. "As a norm, a university should spend each year about Rs.25 per student registered and ₹300 per teacher depending on the stage of development of each university library." It was also suggested that "the foreign exchange needed for university and college libraries should be allowed separately to the UGC."

The Wheat Loan Programme

During the 1950's and early 1960's the Indian academic libraries received huge grants from the UGC amounting up to ₹100,000 for books, buildings, equipment and even for additional staff. At the same time many libraries got additional grants from a special US fund called the 'Wheat Loan Programme.' The American Congress passed a special Act, in 1951 known as the 'Public Law 480' to loan India $ 19,000,000 to buy much needed wheat from the US. Under the agreement of the loan, India had to buy American books, periodicals and scientific equipment worth $ 50,000 to be used for research purposes in the Indian libraries. This, money India had to pay as interest on the loan. Part of the money was to be spent on the exchange of scholars, including librarians, between the two countries. The United States authorities bought some educational material and equipment from India for research purposes and higher education in the American Universities. During 1951-1961 Indian libraries spent US $ 1,400,000 of the purchase of American books, US dollar 160,000 on libraries, US $ 40,000 on the travel and study grants for thirty three Indian librarians to visit the United States and US $ 75,000 on the travel and study grants of the five Americans.

College Libraries

The College libraries in India have a significant role to play in higher education. Majority of the undergraduate students, *i.e.*, 88.5 per cent and graduate students, *i.e.*, 53 per cent, attend these colleges. When India attained Independence many among the 533 affiliated colleges did not have their own libraries, but at present, every college in the country has a library. Majority of the college libraries do not have proper facilities to meet the needs of their users. Their collections are not up-to-date, budgets are their very inadequate and limited, and a large number of them are single libraries. In many colleges, there is neither a library hall nor a sufficient big room, not to think of a separate building for the library.

Any unused room, quite often somewhere out of sight, would be considered adequate to house a few shelves of books. And in most college libraries there is complete darkness even during the day time, as the windows are closed out of a fear that the books may be stolen.. Different studies, conducted by scholars and Srivastva have explicitly established that the condition of the college libraries in India are far from satisfactory.

The college libraries are open only six to eight hours a day. Many do not have any qualified librarian on their staff and have closed stacks only. The several commissions and committees, like the Radhakrishnan Commission of 1948, did not stress the importance of the college libraries in their reports. However, the University Grants Commission gives more importance to the college libraries. As the quality of higher education and research, especially at the graduate level, depends upon, among other things, the standard of the college libraries and their services. Therefore, the UGC has played a significant role in the growth and development of college libraries since 1953 by giving grants for books, equipment, staff and library buildings and has done a remarkable job in salary improvement of the college librarians.

The UGC's contribution to the college libraries is at the rate of ₹15 per student with a maximum of ₹10,000 with some additional and special grants for text books, when a new subject is introduced in the Curriculum. On the other hand, the colleges and the state governments have failed to provide their equal share. The total Expenditure on the college libraries according to the recommendation of the Education Commission should be 6.25 per cent of the total budgets of the colleges, but in most cases it has remained between 1.5 per cent and 2.3 per cent.

Sardana Collection development of the college libraries are done without taking into consideration the actual needs of the faculty and the students of the colleges as sixty per cent of them consist of text books and 20 per cent cover fiction. Even this small inadequate collection, in depth and content, is not used effectively due to the closed stacks system and lack of staff and facilities for instruction concerning their use. The net result is that the utility factor of the college libraries comes practically to nothing. In most college libraries, books are neither properly classified nor catalogued. In several libraries no systematic classification is followed for collection arrangements. The only service the college library renders to its clientele is book-lending. There are colleges where students are not even allowed inside the library.

The UGC is aware of the slow progress of the college libraries. In addition to providing financial help for development, it has also from time to time organized seminars to keep the college librarians aware of the new developments in the field. But these seminars have made only a limited effect on the progress of the college libraries. The condition of the college libraries in the country should be a cause for alarm among the academic community. In the interests of the development of higher education in the country along proper lines, it is important to make a detailed study of the style of functioning of the college libraries and of the utilization of the library resources and facilities by the students and teachers.

This will help in the preparation of more realistic and operational policies and programmes for ensuring the proper functioning, utilization and development of the college libraries. The college library has to be made the intellectual hub of the institution, serving equally, both the students and teachers. This is all the more necessary because about 90 per cent of the students in higher education in India pursue their studies in colleges and they have only very small and substandard college library resources to fall back upon. Although, owing to various efforts of the UGC as well as other forces, the traditional concept that the college library is a custodian of books has changed, yet there is evidence enough to show that the condition of the college libraries is generally poor, their development is rather slow and that the position of the college libraries and their librarians in India, with a few exceptions, is pitiable.

University Libraries

University libraries all over the world have their own place of importance in the scheme of higher learning. Libraries are not only repositories of knowledge but also dispensers of such knowledge. There is no doubt that where libraries of universities and institutions of higher learning are ignored or not given due recognition, the country as a whole suffers because the standards of study, teaching and research very heavily depend upon the qualitative and quantitative service rendered by the university libraries.

The Radhakrishnan Commission expressed that "the library is the heart of all the university's work, directly so, as regards its research work and indirectly as regards its educational work, which derives its life from research. Scientific research needs the library as well as its laboratories while for humanistic research the library is both library and the laboratory in one. Both for humanistic and scientific studies, a first class library is essential in a university." The growth of university libraries since Independence can be seen in respect of the initiatives taken by the Central Government considering the vital importance of higher education and role of libraries in the educational development, commitment to fulfill the demand of higher education, and the foundation of the UGC in 1953 by an Act of Parliament. The Radhakrishnan Commission recognized the value and importance of a well equipped and organized library system and its role in higher education. It had found many drawbacks and pitfalls in the university libraries and had made many recommendations for the improvement of library facilities. The Ranganathan Committee, appointed by the UGC in 1957, made some outstanding recommendations, which included standards for library building, collection development, staff and services and furniture etc. These recommendations were accepted by the UGC and forwarded for implementation.

The Kothari Commission also made valuable recommen-dations for this purpose, but the role of the University Grants Commission deserves special mention, because it has played a vital role by "regularly providing appropriate grants and funds to all universities for development of libraries, to purchase books and journals...., construction of new library buildings and for library equipment and furniture."

Dr. D. S. Kothari, the Chairman of University Grants Commission, said, "Libraries play a vital role in the development of institutions of higher learning. The University Grants Commission attaches great importance to the strengthening of library facilities in the universities and colleges and their efficient administration. The commission has also been giving grants to institutions for books and journals construction of library building and appointment of library staff."

One of the most remarkable and identifiable development in the history of higher education and libraries was the foundation of the INFLIBNET in 1991. Information and Library Network Centre is an autonomous Inter-University Centre of the UGC of India. It is a major National Programme initiated by the UGC in 1991 with its Head Quarters at Gujarat University Campus, Ahmedabad. Initially started as a project under the IUCAA, it became an independent Inter-University Centre in 1966.

Its objectives are:

- To promote and establish communication facilities to improve capability in information transfer and access, that provides support to scholarship, learning, research and academic pursuit through cooperation and involvement of agencies concerned.
- *To establish Inflibnet*: Information and Library Network a computer communication network for linking libraries and information centres in universities, deemed to be universities, colleges, UGC information centres, institutions of national importance and R&D institutions, etc. avoiding duplication of efforts.

Inflibnet performs following major activities:

- Provides grants to universities to automate the libraries, establishing the network facilities and create an information technology environment.
- Developed and distributed Software for University Libraries (Soul) which is an integrated userfriendly library management software. The latest version of the software is 2.0 which is competent to operate with the latest technologies and international standards such as MARC21, Unicode based and NCIP 2.0 based protocols for electronic surveillance and control.
- Indian Catalogue of University Libraries in India (IndCat) is Online Library Catalogue of books, theses and journals available in major university libraries in India which provides bibliographic description, location of the material in all subjects available in more than 112 university libraries. Thus, IndCat has over 10 million bibliographical records of books from more than 113 universities. In addition, the database of theses, expert databases, project databases and Sewakoffline database access facilities are also extended to the libraries of higher learning institutions.
- To enhance the skills of university library staff for implementation of Inflibnet programme, it conducts training programme for library staff, onsite training for member library staff, training on SOUL software, holding Caliber convention every year and workshops for senior level staff of the university libraries are conducted.
- It has brought out a document entitled 'Inflibnet Standards and Guideline for Data Capturing' prepared by a task force of experts based on Common Communication Format (CCF).

Another very important and significant landmark in the history of higher education and development of libraries in India is the establishment of "Ugcinfonet Digial Library Consortium" by the UGC on the concluding day of its Golden jubilee celebrations by his Excellency the then President of India, Dr. A.P.J Abdul Kalam at Vigyan Bhawan on 28th December 2003. UGC-Infonet is an innovative project launched by UGC to facilitate scholarly e-resources to Indian academies through joint partnership of UGC, Inflibnet and Ernet.

This includes interlinking of universities and colleges in the country electronically with a view to achieve maximum efficiency through Internet enabled teaching, learning and governance. The UGC-Infonet is overlaid on Ernet infrastructure in a manner so as to provide assured quality of service and optimum utilization of bandwidth resources. The network will be run and managed by Ernet India. The project is funded by UGC with 100 per cent capital investment and up to 90 per cent of recurring costs. UGC and Ernet India have signed the necessary MoU for this purpose. A joint technical and tariff committee, has been setup to guide and monitor the design, implementation and operations of Ugcinfonet. Information for Library Network (Inflibnet) an autonomous Inter-University Centre of UGC, is the nodal agency for coordination and facilitation of the linkage between Ernet and the Universities.

Under this programme, information and communication technologies (ICT) and internet will be used to transform learning environment from a monodimensional one to a multidimensional one. This was created to help and benefit more than 310 universities and about 14,000 colleges affiliated with these universities and approximately 10 million students with the e-journals, thus, is a boon to higher education system in many ways.

The UGC-Infonet digital Library consortium has the following objectives: Bhatt,

- To subscribe electronic resources for the members of the consortium at highly discounted rates of subscription and with the best terms and conditions.
- Promote the rational use of funds.
- Guarantee local storage of the information acquired for continuous use by present and future users.
- To impart training to the users, librarians, research scholars and faculty members of the institutions on the electronic resources with an aim to optimize the usage of the electronic resources.
- To have more interaction amongst the member libraries.
- To increase the research productivity of the institutions in terms of quality and quantity of publications
- Strategic alliance with institutions that have common interests resulting reduced information cost and improved resource sharing.

National Knowledge Commission

The National Knowledge Commission was set up by the Government of India on 13th June 2005 with a time-frame of three years, from 2nd October 2005 to 2nd October 2008. As a high-level advisory body to the Prime Minister of India, the National Knowledge Commission was given a mandate to guide policy and direct reforms, focusing on certain key areas such as education, science and technology, agriculture, industry, e-governance etc. Easy access to knowledge, creation and preservation of knowledge systems, dissemination of knowledge and better knowledge services are core concerns of the Commission.

The Commission envisaged the future road map for the growth and development of academic libraries by imbibing core issues such as, set up a national commission on libraries, prepare a national census of all libraries, revamp LIS education, training and research facilities, re-assess staffing of libraries, set up a central library fund, modernize library management, encourage greater community participation in library management, promote information communication technology applications in all libraries, facilitate donation and maintenance of private collections, and encourage public private partnerships in LIS development, etc.

SARASWATHI MAHAL LIBRARY

Saraswathi Mahal Library is located in Thanjavur, Tamil Nadu, India. It is one of the oldest libraries in Asia, and has on display a rare collection of Palm leaf manuscripts and paper written in Tamil, Hindi, English, Telugu, Marathi, and a few other languages indigenous to India. The collection comprises well over 60,000 volumes, though only a tiny fraction of these are on display. The library has a complete catalogue of holdings, which is being made available online. Some rare holdings can be viewed on site by prior arrangement.

HISTORY

The Saraswathi Mahal library started as a Royal Library for the private pleasure of the Nayak Kings of Thanjavur who ruled 1535-1675 AD. The Maratha rulers who captured Thanjavur in 1675 patronised local culture and further developed the Royal Palace Library until 1855. Most notable among the Maratha Kings was Serfoji II, who was an eminent scholar in many branches of learning and the arts.

In his early age Serfoji studied under the influence of the Dutch Reverend Schwartz, and learned many languages including English, French, Italian and Latin. He enthusiastically took special interest in the enrichment of the Library, employing many Pandits to collect, buy and copy a vast number of works from all renowned Centres of Sanskrit learning in Northern India and other far-flung areas. Since 1918 the Saraswathi Mahal Library has been a possession of the state of Tamil Nadu. Its official name of the Library was changed to "The Thanjavur Maharaja Serfoji's Sarasvati Mahal Library" in honour of the great royal Marathan patron.

EFFORTS

The library is open to the public; it also supports efforts to publish rare manuscripts from the collection, as well as ensuring all volumes are preserved on microfilm. The Library has installed computers in 1998 for the Computerisation of Library activities. As a first phase, the Library catalogues are being stored in the Computer for easy information retrieval. It is also proposed to digitalise the manuscripts of this Library shortly.

THE COLLECTION

The bulk of the manuscripts (39,300) are in Sanskrit, written in scripts such as Grantha, Devanagari, Nandinagari, Telugu. Tamil manuscripts number over 3500, comprising titles in literature, music and medicine. The Library has a collection of 3076 Marathi manuscripts from the South Indian Maharastrian of the 17th, 18th, and 19th centuries; this includes the hierarchy of the Saints of Maharashtra belonging to Sri Ramadasi and Dattatreya Mutts. The Marathi manuscripts are mostly on paper but a few were written in Telugu script on palm-leaf. There are 846 Telugu manuscripts in the holdings, mostly on palm leaf. There are 22 Persian and Urdu manuscripts mostly of 19th century also within the collection. Apart from these manuscripts there are 1342 bundles of Maratha Raj records available at the Library. The Raj records were written in the Modi script of the Marathi language. These records encompass the information of the political, cultural and social administration of the Maratha kings of Thanjavur.

SOME OF THE RARE BOOKS AND MANUSCRIPTS

- Dr. Samuel Johnson's dictionary published in 1784
- The pictorial Bible printed in Amsterdam in the year 1791
- The Madras Alamnac printed in 1807
- Lavoisier's *Traité Élémentaire de Chimie* ("Elements of Chemistry")
- The notes of Bishop Heber on Raja Serfoji II
- The correspondence letters of William Torin of London who purchased a lot of books for Raja Serfoji II and the Saraswathi Mahal Library
- The Globe used by the raja.
- Ancient maps of the world
- Town planning documents of Thanjavur including the underground drainage system, the fresh water supply ducting system
- Pictorial charts of the theory of evolution of man as evinced by Charles Le Brun

LIBRARY MUSEUM

A Museum is located in the Library building to reveal the importance of the Library to the Public. This Museum is small but organised into sections highlighting ancient Manuscripts, Illustrated Manuscripts, Printed copies of the Original Drawings, Atlases, Thanjavur-style Paper Paintings, Canvass Paintings, Wooden Paintings, Glass paintings, Portraits of the Thanjavur Maratha kings, and the Physiognomy charts of Charles Le-Brun. These materials give an idea of the total variety in the vast collection within the Library.

The Saraswati Library is situated within the campus of the Thanjavur Palace. Visitors can have a glimpse of preserved books and can sit and read in the library premises. Better preservation of books and facilities like air-conditioning with dehumidifiers, redesigning of space for comfortable reading, online catalogue facility should be taken up to preserve this internationally renowned treasure trove of books and palm-leaf manuscripts! Efforts were made to microfilm and catalogue the contents way back in 1965 when Indira Gandhi was Information and Broadcasting Minister, Government of India who sanctioned the fund for the library's development. Since then no efforts were made to scan the documents and computerise the same using present day technology. It is also a designated 'Manuscript Conservation Centre' (MCC) under the National Mission for Manuscripts established in 2003.

KHUDA BAKHSH ORIENTAL LIBRARY

Khuda Bakhsh Oriental Library is one of the national libraries of India. It was opened to public in October, 1891 by Khan Bahadur Khuda Bakhsh with 4,000 manuscripts, of which he inherited 1,400 from his father Maulvi Mohammed Bakhsh.

It is an autonomous organization under Ministry of Culture, Government of India, and is governed by a Board with the Governor of Bihar as its ex-officio Chairman. known for its rare collection of Persian and Arabic manuscripts. It also hosts paintings made during the Rajput and Mughal eras of India. It is also a designated 'Manuscript Conservation Centre' (MCC) under the National Mission for Manuscripts.

HISTORY

The library finds its origin in private collection of a bibliophile Mohammad Bakhsh and expanded by his son Khuda Bakhsh, who inherited 1,400 manuscripts and continued to add to the collection and eventually converted it into a private library by 1880. The library was opened to public upon its inauguration by Sir Charles Elliot, Governor of Bengal on 5th October, 1891.

In 1969 through a Federal Legislation, an Act of Parliament, namely 'Khuda Bakhsh Oriental Public Library Act (1969), the Government of India declared Khuda Bakhsh Oriental Public Library a centre of national importance and government took over the funding, maintenance and development of the library. Today it continues to attract scholars from all over the world.

Past directors of the library have been Dr. Abid Reza Bedar, who after remaining with the Raza Library, came as Director to the institution in 1972, and did some important work towards reviving the library along with his successor Habibur Rehman Chighani, at present the Director of the library is the Dr. Imtiaz Ahmad, since February, 2004.

COLLECTION

Some of the notable manuscripts are *Timur Nama* (*Khandan—Timuria*), *Shah Nama, Padshah Nama, Diwan-e-Hafiz* and *Safinatul Auliya,* carrying the autograph of Mughal Emperors and princes and the book of Military

Accounts of Maharaja Ranjit Singh. Apart of it the library also has specimens of Mughal paintings, calligraphy and book decoration and Arabic and Urdu manu-scripts, including a page of Quran written on deer skin.

BHANDARKAR ORIENTAL RESEARCH INSTITUTE

The Bhandarkar Oriental Research Institute (BORI) is located in Pune, Maharashtra, India. It was founded on July 6, 1917 to honour the life and work of Dr. Ramakrishna Gopal Bhandarkar (1837–1925), long regarded as the founder of Indology (Orientalism) in India. The institute is well known for its collection of old Sanskrit and Prakrit manuscripts.

THE INSTITUTE

This institute is of a public trust registered under Act XXI of 1860. Initially, the institute received an annual grant of 3000 Rupees from the Government of Bombay. Presently, it is partially supported by annual grants from the Government of Maharashtra. The Institute also receives grants from the Government of India and the University Grants Commission for specific research projects.

The institute has one of the largest collections of rare books and manuscripts in South Asia, consisting of over 1,25,000 books and 29,510 manuscripts. The institute publishes a journal, *Annals of the Bhandarkar Oriental Research Institute* four times a year.

The Institute also hosts the Manuscripts Resource and Conservation Centre under the auspices of the National Mission for Manuscripts, a project of the Ministry of Culture, Government of India. In 2007, the Rigveda manuscripts preserved at the Institute were included in UNESCO's Memory of the World Register.

THE MANUSCRIPT COLLECTION

The Government of Bombay, in 1866, started a pan Indian Manuscript Collection project. Noted scholars like George Bühler, F. Kielhorn, Peter Peterson, Ramkrishna Gopal Bhandarkar, S. R. Bhandarkar, Kathavate and Ghate collected more than 17,000 important manuscripts under this project. This collection was first deposited at Elphinstone College in Bombay. Then it was transferred to Deccan College (Pune) for better preservation. After the Bhandarkar Oriental Research Institute was founded in 1917, the BORI founders proposed to offer even better preservation and research.

Hence Lord Willingdon, the then Governor of the Bombay Presidency and the first president of BORI, transferred the valuable Government collection of manuscripts to the BORI on April 1, 1918. The first curator, P.K. Gode took active initiatives to enhance this collection. Presently, the Institute has over 29,000 manuscripts. The largest part of the collection (17,877 Manuscripts) is part of the "Government Manuscript Library", while there is an additional collection of 11,633 manuscripts also. The most prized collections include a paper manuscript of the Cikitsâsâra-sangraha dated 1320 and a palmleaf manuscript of the Upamiti-bhavapra-pañcakathâ dated 906. Among the several scholars referring to the works at BORI, the most well-known person arguably is the Bharat Ratna awardee, Pt. Pandurang Vaman Kane.

THE CRITICAL EDITION OF THE MAHABHARATA

A long term project under the auspices of BORI, started on April 1, 1919, was the preparation of a Critical Edition of the Mahabharata. V.S. Sukhtankar was appointed general editor of the project on August 1, 1925 and he continued until his death on January 21, 1943. After his death, S.K. Belvalkar was appointed general editor on April 1, 1943. On April 1, 1961 P. L. Vaidya appointed as General Editor of the project on the retirement of S. K. Belvalkar. R. N. Dandekar appointed as the joint general editor on July 6, 1957. To widespread acclaim, the completion for publication was announced on September 22, 1966, by Dr. Sarvapalli Radhakrishnan, then President of India, at a special function held at the institute.

The Critical Edition was collated from 1,259 manuscripts. This edition in 19 volumes (more than 15000 demi-quarto size pages) comprised the critically constituted text of the 18 *Parvas* of the Mahabharata consisting of more than 89000 verses, an elaborate Critical Apparatus and a Prolegomena on the material and methodology.

Further work since the initial publication has produced a Critical Edition of the Harivamsa, a Pratika Index, a Bibliography of ancillary materials, and a Cultural Index. The project of preparing a critical edition of the Harivamsa was inaugurated by the President of India, Rajendra Prasad on November 19, 1954. The publication was completed in November, 1971. The critical edition in two volumes consists the 4 *Parvan*s of the Harivamsa. The Pratika Index in 6 volumes consists 360000 verse quarters with appendices. Two volumes of the Cultural Index have been published so far. The constituted text of the critical edition has also been made available on the CD-ROM.

VANDALISM IN 2003

The institute was vandalized in December 2003 by a mob made up of members of an extremist self styled Maratha youth squad, calling themselves the Sambhaji Brigade, named after Shivaji's elder son. They claimed to be angered by the help provided by the institute's staff (in translating manuscripts) to a Western writer, Dr. James Laine, who discussed the telling and retelling of stories about Shivaji's parentage and life in his book on narrations of the Shivaji story.

The mob also damaged thousands of manuscripts and attacked Shrikant Bahulkar, a Sanskrit scholar who had only explained some Sanskrit references to Laine. The incident provoked widespread reaction and historian Gajanan

Mehendale to destroy parts of his in-progress biography of Shivaji. The vandalism and a ban on the book were denounced by historians who put their signatures to the statement include R.S. Sharma, R.C. Thakran, Suraj Bhan, Irfan Habib, D.N. Jha, Shireen Moosvi and K. M. Shrimali. Oxford University Press-publisher of James Laine's, 'Shivaji: Hindu king in Islamic India', withdrew the book after protests from Ninad Bedekar and other right-wing politicians as it contained allegedly objectionable statements about Shivaji.

ASIATIC SOCIETY LIBRARY

At present, the library of the Asiatic Society has a collection of about 1,17,000 books and 79,000 journals printed in almost all the major languages of the world. It has also a collection of 293 maps, microfische of 48,000 works, microfilm of 387,003 pages, 182 paintings, 2500 pamphlets and 2150 photographs.

The earliest printed book preserved in this library is Juli Firmici's *Astronomicorum Libri* published in 1499. It has in its possession a large number of books printed in India in the late 18th and early 19th centuries. The library also possesses many rare and scarcely available books. The library has a rich collection of about 47,000 manuscripts in 26 scripts. The most notable amongst them are an illustrated manuscript of the *Qur'an,* a manuscript of the *Gulistan* text, and a manuscript of *Padshah Nama* bearing the signature of Emperor Shahjahan. The number of journals in thepossession of the library is about 80,000 at present.

The early collection of this library was enriched by the contributions it received from its members. On March 25, 1784 the library received seven Persian manuscripts from Henri Richardson. The next contribution came from William Marsden, who donated his book, *History of Island of Sumatra* (1783) on November 10, 1784.

Robert Home, the first Library-in-Charge (1804) donated his small but valuable collection of works on art. The first accession of importance was a gift from the Seringapatam Committee on February 3, 1808 consisting of a collection from the Palace Library of Tipu Sultan. The library received the Surveyor-General Colonel Mackenzie's collection of manuscripts and drawings in December 1822.

MANUSCRIPT COLLECTION

Manuscript Collection of the society is varied and rich, and covers most of the Indian languages and scripts and even several Asian ones, *e.g.,* Assamese, Bengali, Gujarati, Gurumukhi, Kanarese, Urdu, Marathi, Modi, Nagari, Newari, Oriya, Rajasthani, Sarada, Armenian, Sinhalese, Arabic, Persian, Pushto, Javanese, Turki, Burmese, Chinese, Siamese, Tibetan etc. The materials used for the manuscripts are also varied: palm and palmyra leaves, barks of different trees, papers of various grades.

Sanskritic Manuscripts

The manuscripts cover the period from 7th c. A.D. down to the 19th century. These are useful source materials to illustrate the development of the Indian scripts (especially Bengali, Nagari etc.). The colophons and post-colophons contain information relating to socio-economic conditions of the people.

Besides, they help us to fix the chronology of the Royal dynasties of India. Where the inscriptions fail to ascertain dates and chronology, the manuscripts may throw some light, provided a thorough critical study of these and their colophons and postcolophons were made.

Some of the rare Sanskrit manuscripts may be mentioned here:

- Brihati,
- Amrita Vindu,
- Kiranavali,
- Charucharya,
- Nartaka Nirnaya,
- Parasika-prakasa,
- Sanskrita-ratnakara,
- Lalitavistara,
- Horoscope of a Muslim of the Mughal Court (1640 A.D.) A Deed of Mortgage (1639),
- Ramayana (Bengali) of Ramananda Yati,
- Vajrayana text (11th c.),
- A text on Buddhist Nyaya,
- Rigveda Padapatha,
- Laghu-Kalachakra-tika,
- Kalachakravetara,
- Kuttanimatam,
- Vajravalinama mannadalopayika,
- Ramacharita of Sandhyakar Nandi,
- Bhattikavyatika of Srinivasa, and
- Paragali Mahabharata.

The manuscript of Kubjikamatam is of the 7th Century A.D. The manuscript of Rigveda Padapatha, copied in 1362 A.D., is perhaps "the oldest manuscript of the Rigveda."

Islamic Section

Of the many Islamic Manuscripts there are some which are extremely rare and unique.

Of these only a few may be mentioned:

- Tahdhib Sharh As-Sab' at Mullaqat (early 12th c. Arabic),

- Qalaid al-Iquian wa Mahasin al-Ayan (12th c.),
- Kharidat al-Qasr (12th c.),
- Al-Jam Baynas as-Sahihin abridged version with autograph, (13th c.),
- A-Madkhul(13th c.),
- Tafsir-i-Quran (Persian, 13th c., important also for calligraphy),
- Tuhfat al-Ahbar fi usul at Hadith wa'l Akhbar (15th c.),
- Kitab al-I'lan (18th c.),
- Saha' if-i-Shara' if or Duraral Mansur (Persian, 19th c., an autographed copy), and
- Adab-i-Alamgiri (18th c.).

There are large numbers of illuminated and illustrated manu-scripts of different schools, many of which are unique for their calligraphy, delicacy of their lines, and elegance of composition and charming colour schemes.

These miniatures still afford glimpses of India's past achievements, Of these unique manuscripts (earliest belonging to the 10th Century A.D.) mention may be made of a few:

- Astasahasrika Prajnaparamita,
- Aparimitayurnama Mahayana sutra,
- Pancharaksha,
- Paramarthanama Sangati,
- Devimahatmya,
- Viveka Panchamrita,
- Bhagavatgita,
- Shahnama,
- Kullayat-i-Saadi,
- Suwaru'l aqalim,
- Farang-i-Aurang Shahi,
- Ain-i-Akbari,
- Diwan-i-Makhfi,
- Qissa-i-Nush-Afarin,
- Jamiut-Twarikh,
- Amir nama Tutinama,
- Iyar-i-Danesh,
- Bihar-i-Danesh,
- Tarjuma Mahabharata,
- Tafribul-Imarah (by Silchand, dedicated to J. H. Lushington), and
- Imaratut-Akbar (by Chitarmal for James Duncan).

Many scholars are using the collection for editing their texts and for translation in modern languages.

English Manuscripts

In the Library there are preserved a large number of old letters some of which date back to1784, just after the Society was founded. These letters were received by the Society from persons belonging to different walks of life, requesting information on such subjects as old and rare manuscripts, ancient monuments, coins etc. Some among the writers of these letters were persons well known for their literary, scientific and other cultural accomp-lishments. These old files constitute important documents relating to the history of the Society, as also of many other scientific and humanistic organisations that were established in India either in the 19th or in the 20th century.

Urdu Manuscripts

The Society has a fine collection of about 234 Urdu manu-scripts many of which were received as a gift from the Fort William College.

Sino-Tibetan and Burmese Manuscripts

The Society has a complete set of Kanjur and Tanjur texts of the Buddhist scriptures and some extra-canonical works. These were collected by B. H. Hodgson and A. Csoma de koros. A section of the collection has been catalogued. There are over one hundred titles of Chinese books, some of which are rare and valuable for Chinese studies. These cover almost all the subjects relating to Chinese Culture, Civilization and Science and Buddhism. Subjects covered include Classical Literature, Language. History, Geography, Topography, Philosophy, Religion, manners and customs, biography of scholars, sciences (Botanical, Astronimical, Zoological). The Society has a valuable collection of about 162 Burmese manuscript written on parabaikes and palm leaf. The manuscripts deal with Buddhistic texts, Religion, History of the world and also of Burmja and Arakan, works on Gramour (including that of kaccayana) and Rhetoric, Buddhist cosmography, Astrology, Medicine etc.

Bengali Manuscripts

Other than Sanskrit, a few Bengali manuscripts have been found written by Bengali Brahmins residing in Varanasi. Parageli Mahabharat, Chuti Khan's Asvamedha Parva, and many other important manuscripts were purchased. Mss. donated by Justice Ramaprosad Mukherjee and Sri A Roy enriched the collection.

The society has 703 Bengali and 12 Assamese manuscripts in the collection. It comprises Asiatic Society's own collection, Government collection, Indian Museum collection and donors' collection. At present, the collection of Bengali manuscripts in the possession of Asiatic Society is rich in respect of number and rarity. The Society has manuscripts on Ramayana, Mahabharata, Srimadbhagavat, Mangala Kavyas, treatises on Vaisnava faith and its allied subjects. Folk literature, erotic verses and Vaisnaba Sahajiya Cult etc.

Rajasthani Manuscripts

The Society possesses very rare, valuable and important Rajasthani Manuscripts which date the pre-middle and middle years. The Society prepared and brought out a descriptive catalogue of Rajasthani manuscripts comprising 636 manuscripts.

RARE BOOK DIVISION

In 1978 the Council decided to open a Rare Book Division. The preliminarhy screening of the collection has since been started.

Among the earliest printed books mention may be made of the following:

- Julii Firmici Astronomicorum libri octo integri (Venice 1499),
- Kitabal-Qanum (Arabic/Romae 1595),
- Kripar Sstrer Arthabhed (Bengali in Roman Character, Kisbon 1743);
- S. Purchas's Purchas: His Pilgrimage (London, 1 61 4),
- N. Halhed's Grammar of the Bengal Language, (Hooghly, 1778),
- Malabar and English Dictionary, (Madras, 1779),
- Rasamanjari (Sanskrit, Banaras, 1791),
- Ram Ram Bose's Lipimala (Bengali, Serampore, 1802),
- The Ramayana 3 vols, (Bengali, Serampore, 1803),
- Hitopadesa (Sanskrit, Serampore, 1804),
- Colebrooke's Grammar of the Sanskrit language vol. 1 (Serampore, 1805).

3

Kinds of Libraries

PUBLIC LIBRARY

A public library is a library that is accessible by the public and is generally funded from public sources and operated by civil servants. There are five fundamental characteristics shared by public libraries. The first is that they are supported by taxes; they are governed by a board to serve the public interest; they are open to all and every community member can access the collection; they are entirely voluntary in that no one is ever forced to use the services provided; and public libraries provide basic services without charge. Public libraries exist in many countries across the world and are often considered an essential part of having an educated and literate population. Public libraries are distinct from research libraries, school libraries, and other special libraries in that their mandate is to serve the general public's information needs.

Public Libraries also provide free services such as preschool story times to encourage early literacy, quiet study and work areas for students and professionals, or book clubs to encourage appreciation of literature in adults. Public libraries typically allow users to take books and other materials off the premises temporarily; they also have non-circulating reference collections and provide computer and Internet access to patrons.

SERVICES OFFERED

In addition to print books and periodicals, most public libraries today have a wide array of other media including audiobooks, e-books, CDs, cassettes, videotapes, DVDs, and video games, as well as facilities to access the Internet and inter-library loans. Readers' advisory is a fundamental public library service that involves suggesting fiction and nonfiction titles.

Public libraries may also provide other services, such as community meeting rooms, storytelling sessions for infants, toddlers, preschool children, or after-school programmes, all with an intention of developing early literacy skills and a love of books. In person and on-line programmes for reader development, language learning, homework help, free lectures and cultural performances, and other community service programmes are common offerings. One of the most popular programmes offered in public libraries are summer reading programmes for children, families, and adults. In rural areas, the local public library may have, in addition to its main branch, a mobile library service, consisting of one or more buses furnished as a small public library, serving the countryside according to a regular schedule.

Public libraries also provide materials for children, often housed in a special section. Child oriented websites with on-line educational games and programmes specifically designed for younger library users are becoming increasingly popular. Services may be provided for other groups, such as large print or Braille materials, Books on tape, young adult literature and other materials for teenagers, or materials in other than the national language. California and Nevada now offer a new service called Link+. This new programme links county libraries across the two states, allowing patrons access to books their library may not have in their collection.

Librarians at most public libraries provide reference and research help to the general public, usually at a reference desk but can often be done by telephone interview. As online discussion and social networking allow for remote access, reference is becoming available virtually through the use of the Internet and e-mail.

Depending on the size of the library, there may be more than one desk; at some smaller libraries all transactions may occur at one desk, while large urban public libraries may employ subject-specialist librarians with the ability to staff multiple reference or information desks to answer queries about particular topics at any time during regular operating hours. Often the children's section in a public library has its own reference desk. Public libraries are also increasingly making use of web 2.0 services, including the use of online social networks by libraries. Public libraries in some countries pay authors when their books are borrowed from libraries. These are known as Public Lending Right programme.

DIGITAL DIVIDE

As more commercial and governmental services are being provided online, public libraries increasingly provide Internet access for users who otherwise would not be able to connect to these services. Part of the public library mission has become attempting to help bridge the digital divide. A study conducted in 2006 found that "72.5 per cent of library branches report that they are the only provider of free public computer and Internet access in their communities".

A 2008 study found that "100 per cent of rural, high poverty outlets provide public Internet access, a significant increase from 85.7 per cent last year". The *American Library Association* (ALA), addresses this role of libraries as part of "access to information" and "equity of access"; part of the profession's ethical commitment that "no one should be denied information because he or she cannot afford the cost of a book or periodical, have access to the internet or information in any of its various formats." In addition to access, many public libraries offer training and support to computer users. Once access has been achieved, there still remains a large gap in people's online abilities and skills. For many communities, the public library is the only agency offering free computer classes and information technology learning.

As of 2008, 73.4 per cent of public libraries offered information technology training of some form, including information literacy skills and homework assignment help. A significant service provided by public libraries is assisting people with e-government access and use of federal, state and local government information, forms and services. Internationally, public libraries offer *information and communication technology* (ICT) services, giving "access to information and knowledge" the "highest priority." While different countries and areas of the world have their own requirements, general services offered include free connection to the Internet, training in using the Internet, and relevant content in appropriate languages. In addition to typical public library financing, *non-governmental organizations* (NGOs) and business fund services that assist public libraries in combating the digital divide.

ORIGINS AS A SOCIAL INSTITUTION

The culmination of centuries of advances in the printing press, moveable type, paper, ink, publishing, and distribution, combined with an ever growing middle class, increased commercial activity and consumption, new radical ideas, massive population growth and higher literacy rates forged the public library into the form that it is today. Public libraries are not a new idea; Romans made scrolls in dry rooms available to patrons of the baths, and tried with some success to establish libraries within the empire.

Naturally, only those few that could afford an education would be able to use the library, where those less than rich or without control of money; women, children and slaves could not. In the middle of the 19th century, the push for truly public libraries, paid for by taxes and run by the state gained force after numerous depressions, droughts, wars and revolutions in Europe, felt mostly by the working class.

Matthew Battles states that:

- "It was in these years of class conflict and economic terror that the public library movement swept through Britain, as the nation's progressive elite recognized that the light of cultural and intellectual energy was lacking in the lives of commoners".

Libraries had often been started with a donation, an endowment or were bequeathed to various, parishes, churches, schools or towns, and these social and institutional libraries formed the base of many academic and public library collections of today. Andrew Carnegie had the biggest influence in financing libraries in the United States of America, from the east to west coast. From just 1900 to 1917, almost 1,700 libraries were constructed by Carnegie's foundation, insisting that local communities first guarantee tax support of each library built.

The establishment of circulating libraries by booksellers and publishers provided a means of gaining profit and creating social centers within the community. The circulating libraries not only provided a place to sell books, but also a place to lend books for a price. These circulating libraries provided a variety of materials including the increasingly popular novels. Although the circulating libraries filled an important role in society, members of the middle and upper classes often looked down upon these libraries that regularly sold material from their collections and provided materials that were less sophisticated. Circulating libraries also charged a subscription fee, however the fees were set to entice their patrons, providing subscriptions on a yearly, quarterly or monthly basis, without expecting the subscribers to purchase a share in the circulating library. Circulating libraries were not exclusively lending institutions and often provided a place for other forms of commercial activity, which may or may not be related to print. This was necessary because the circulating libraries did not generate enough funds through subscription fees collected from its borrowers. As a commerce venture, it was important to consider the contributing factors such as other goods or services available to the subscribers.

Many claims have been made for the title of "first public library" for various libraries in various countries, with at least some of the confusion arising from differing interpretations of what should be considered a true "public library". Diffi-culties in establishing what policies were in effect at different times in the history of particular libraries also add to the confusion. The first libraries open to the public were the collections of Greek and Latin scrolls which were available in the dry sections of the many buildings that made up the huge Roman baths of the Roman empire. However, they were not lending libraries. The "halls of science" run by different Islamic sects in many cities of North Africa and the Middle East in the 9th century were open to the public. Some of them had written lending policies, but they were very restrictive. Most patrons were expected to consult the books on site. The later European university libraries were not open to the general public, but accessible by scholars.

PUBLIC LIBRARIES IN INDIA

Public library is largely regarded as the People's University. It has tremendous developments in India from the early period to till date at various stages. Most of the Indian states now have free public library services to develop the people of India at different levels.

ANCIENT PERIOD

- "The history of the development of the public library may be said to be as old as that of education in India". During Vedic times, the pupils stayed in the *guru-gruha* for several years for education. Since ancient times, India is being very much pertinent in search of knowledge and wisdom. Oral communication was the best means amongst the people of India and writing was not available. "The earliest written and recorded materials found in India are the inscriptions on stone pillars of King Asoka; these inscriptions could be called the first outside open libraries". Later, *Ashrams* came into existence in India and students study under the supervision of well-known teachers. They kept many manuscripts for use of the teachers and students as well as for the visitors. Many students joined ashrams and such big ashrams were known as *vidyapeeth,* where numbers of teachers are engaged to teach the students. These educational institutions collected many different manuscripts and other materials which can help in their teaching and daily routine. They kept and preserved carefully. "The reading materials, of course, related to many subjects formed the source material for transmitting knowledge in different streams of education and culture. The collections might be likened to modern libraries since they were carefully maintained and extensively used by students and teachers alike". Such *ashrams* or *vidyapeeths,* where manuscripts and other reading materials were reserved, may be regarded as a kind of library as they serve information and knowledge to the students and community in different ways. Pandey S K Sharma stated that; "In India, since the ancient times libraries have been functioning as light houses for those who wanted to read and to extend the boundaries of various disciplines. References are available to prove that Nalanda University had its own multistoried library in 600 AD with massive collection of manuscripts. The collection of the library was housed in three buildings, each having nine floors and three hundred rooms. This library was opened by the then Emperor of India, King Davapal. The library was open for any body that was known scholar and took interest in reading, interpreting and even copying the documents kept in the library. Chinese traveller Whuen Sang is known to have consulted this library in the seventh century and to have taken from here hundreds of treatises to China and Japan. This library was completely destroyed by Bakhtiar Khilaji, who invaded India in 1205 AD. And burnt the library. The library kept on burning for about six months".

Libraries in ancient India also developed at other famous centers of learning, such as *Vikramshila* and *Odantapuri.* Universities of ancient India, like Taxila and Vikramshala also have valuable collection on *tantras* and manuscripts in their libraries.

MEDIEVAL PERIOD

Muslims mostly rule the Medieval Period of India. Historically, it is also known as Mughal Period. There were great changes not only in social and political, but also on education and library system during this period. The Muslim rulers made great contributions to Indian culture and libraries played a significant role in the sociocultural development of the nation. "The period of Mughal is considered as the golden period of Indian history for its educational, literary, and library activities".

Babur, king of Kabul invaded India and annexed Delhi to his kingdom. "He established the first Mughal Imperial Library in 1526". Babur inherited manuscripts from his father and kept in his library and also collected books from different sources of his kingdom. Babur died in 1530 and was succeeded by his son Humayun. Humayun much lived in Agra and established library in his palace. He set up a library at Agra Fort, which was managed by Lal Beg.

In his library, he kept books, gilded pen cases, portfolios, picture books and beautiful works of calligraphy. After the death of Humayun, his son, Akbar, succeeded him in 1356. Akbar is regarded as one of the greatest Mughal king. Akbar improved the management of library with some technical works. He appointed Sheik Faizi to manage and control library services.

Akbar was very interest in manuscripts and appointed calligraphers to copy good manuscripts. He established a separate library for women at Fatehpur Sikri and made great improvement to the library. At the time of his death in 1605, the Imperial Library has twenty-four thousand books. Jahangir, another rule of Mughal period, made a law that when a wealthy man died heirless, the property should be used for building and repairing schools, monasteries, libraries, and other institutions. Some wealthy and scholars, like Abdul Rahim Khan-i-Khanan, Shaik Faizi, Gulbadan Begum and ruler of Mysore and Jaipur also have their private libraries.

Some Hindu learning centers also have libraries. "The libraries of these centers contain huge collections of manuscripts on religion and philosophy as well as other subjects like medicine, science and history". Christian missionaries have also contributed for the libraries since the coming of Vasco da Gama in India.

During the Mughal period, library technical works, *viz.* Accessioning, Classification and Cataloguing were also carried out in some ways. The head librarian was known as *"Nizam"* and the assistant librarian *as "Muhatin"* or *"Darogha"*. Other staff of libraries during Mughal period is Scribes, Book Illustrators, Calligraphers, Copyists, Translators, Bookbinders and Gilders.

THE BRITISH PERIOD

The Britishers came to India primarily to establish trade and commerce. Some of them were very interested for the upliftment of rich cultural heritage of India. "A number of Academic institutions were established during the British period by the East India Company and by the Christian missionaries". The University of Calcutta was established in 1857 and its library was opened in 1873. Other Universities, University of Bombay and University of Madras were established in 1879 and 1907 respectively. There were only nineteen Universities in India before 1947. Universities were equipped with libraries in accordance with the Indian University Act of 1904.

The Bengal Royal Asiatic Society set up library in 1784, Bombay Royal Asiatic Society in 1804 and Calcutta Public Library in 1835. Establishment of these libraries enlightened the community and may be regarded as the foundation of the concept of public libraries to the Indian people. Some of the important libraries set up in 19th. Century in India are Andrews Library, Surat in 1850, Gaya Public Library, Gaya in 1855, Long Library, Rajkot in 1856, Connemara Public Library, Madras in 1860, Government Library, Janagarh in 1867, Adyar Library, Adyar in 1886 and Dahi Laxmi Library, Nadiad in 1892. Apart from these, other libraries, like Gujarat Vernacular Society along with a library, in Ahmedabad 1848 and Barton Library, Bhavnagar in 1882 were also established.

Some of the Indian states also established public libraries. Such as Baroda established Baroda State Library in Baroda in 1877, Cochin established Public Library and Reading Room in Trichur in 1873, Dhar established Victoria General Library in Dhar in 1856, Indore established General Library in Indore in 1852, Jaipur established Maharajah's Public Library in Jaipur in 1899. Others states also established such kind of libraries, *viz.* Jammu and Kashmir in 1879, Kahtiawar, in 1886, Kolhapur in 1850, Nizam's Dominion in 1891 and Travancore in 1829.

The first significant date in the development of public libraries in India is 1808 when the Bombay Government initiated a proposal to register libraries, which were to be given copies of books published from the 'Funds for the Encouragement of Literature'. The contributions of His Highness the Maharaja Sayajirao III, Gaekwar of Baroda towards library movement in India cannot be overlooked. He is remembered today as the Father of Library Movement in India. At the age of 18, in 1881, he was entrusted with full power of the government of Baroda in the Gujarat speaking region of the Bombay Presidency and the Peninsula of Kathiawar.

Baroda's population was predominantly rural, the main occupation was agriculture. The people in general were economically poor and socially backward. Education was the foundation to reconstruct a new social and economic life and education should be the right of the humblest villager. He introduced free and compulsory education in his princely states. Baroda became the first territory not only among the native states but also in British India to have compulsory free primary education. He opined that primary education was to be the very base and decided to preserve it by means of libraries, which were the only agencies for perpetual universal self-education. He decided to establish library as an experiment in one of the towns of a *taluka* and in order to implement his idea immediately; he issued orders to his ministers.

"In conformity to his ruler's instructions, the Minister of Education prepared a detailed plan to open Circulating Libraries in the State, which was approved in March, 1907. Every public library instituted through the State's financial assistance was to be named as Circulating Library". In 1906, he went to America as "an observer, a student desirous of acquiring all the knowledge and experience that could enable him to make his own State a model one in India". He was very much impressed by the library services of America for the development of the people in their social, economic and educational life. He then invited an American, William Alanson Borden, a pupil-assistant of Charles A Cutter, who is working as Librarian of the Young Men's Institute, New Haven, Connecticut to come and established library services in India.

In response to his invitation, Borden reached Baroda on November 6, 1910, and became the Director of State Libraries. It can be traced back that public library movement started since 1910 in India. Borden makes a survey of libraries in Baroda and concludes that there were over 241 libraries, holding a little over 100000 volumes. But he did not find any of those libraries adequately housed, nor did he find them shelved in such a manner as to make them most attractive to readers or convenient to those in charge.

He then make proposal for the best services of libraries in the State as:

- Should Your Highness feel disposed to grant me the necessary authority, I propose to organize a Department of Public Libraries, to rank with the other Departments of Your State, with the necessary equipments of officers and clerks, etc. and to bring all the libraries under its control and management;
- To unify all the collections of books in Baroda City into one Central library;
- To add to this Central library, general and technical books;
- To erect a suitable library building of fireproof construction, with reading grooms, study rooms, Women's Library, Children's library, Lecture hall, Library school, and executive offices;
- To make that library to be Free Public Library of Baroda City, and also the main storehouse for all the valuable historical documents and papers now in private hands in the State, but which the owners would probably be glad to have stored in a safe place;
- To make it also the center from which traveling libraries should start and from which the books, new and old, could be distributed

to the various branch libraries in the different towns, cities, and villages of the State.

The Maharaja apparently accepted Borden's proposals, and ordered that the whole scheme might be implemented in parts. The Library Department was created under Order No.9/19, January 30, 1911, for organizing libraries in Baroda. As the Director of state libraries, he planned a network of free public libraries consisting a state central library, four district or divisional libraries, forty-five town libraries, and more than a thousand village libraries-all integrated into one chain system.

Borden played a leading role for the establishment, management and organization of public libraries in India. As a result of system, within two decades 85% of the Baroda urban and rural population had access to libraries.. Borden developed library classification scheme to suit Indian libraries. Another great contribution of Borden was the establishment of the first library school in India, in which he trained his own assistants and successors. Borden conducted the first formal library-training programme in India at Baroda in 1911. He was instrumental in the foundation of the Baroda Library Club and its journal, "Library Miscellany", published quarterly in three languages between 1912 and 1919.

University of Madras created the post of University Librarian in 1923 and Dr. S R Ranganathan joined the post on 4 January 1924. Ranganathan published his Five Laws of Library Science in 1931, Colon Classification in 1933 and Classified Catalog Code in 1934. He also prepared Model Public Library Bill and drives to legislate library bill in Indian states. He made a tremendous contribution for the development of libraries in India. Scholars, educationists and people of library bent of mind founded Calcutta Public Library in 1835 and the same was opened on 21 March 1836 for the public.

In 1944, Calcutta Public Library was shifted to a new and spacious building, constructed in honour of the Governor-General of India, Lord Metcalf. Indian War of Independence broke out in 1857 resulted in to Europeans of Calcutta withdrew their support for the library management in 1899. Consequently, the management and establishment of the library were gradually waning and by the end of the century, the activities of the library came into standstill.

Lord Curzon, the then Viceroy and Governor-General of India visited Calcutta in 1899 and found a miserable condition of Calcutta Public Library. He bought the rights of the Library from the proprietors and later merged it with the Official imperial Library consisting of government departmental libraries of the East India Company. He then declared open of a new Imperial Library of India on 30 January 1903 in the Metcalf Hall. In 1948, one year after the independence of India, Imperial Library was transformed into National library of India and was housed to the Viceroy's Palace in Calcutta, namely, the Belvedere Palace.

POST-INDEPENDENCE PERIOD

Public libraries in India made a tremendous growth after the independence of India in 1947. The central and the state governments took a number of steps forward for the development of the nation from the point of education and considered library as essential part of it. The programmes executed by provincial and central governments since 1910 for the social and adult education of the populace paved the way for the enactment of library laws and rules for grants-in-aid in the country. Hence public library became part of the education budget.

To enhance the level of literacy of 16% in 1941, the government undertook some programmes such as extension services, continuing education, social education, non-formal education and adult education. The government further initiated steps for the development of community and organized some projects in this regard. Libraries were considered to be an essential part of the Community Development Project that was launched during the first plan period.

In order to accelerate the pace of socioeconomic development, the government considered public libraries to be an integral part of development projects.. The Connemara Public Library in Madras became the State Central Library in 1950 under the provision of Madras Public Libraries Act 1948, and became one of the three depository libraries in 1955. Delhi Public Library was established in 1951 as the first UNESCO Public Library Pilot Project under the joint auspices of UNESCO and Government of India to adopt "Modern Techniques to Indian Conditions" and to serve as a model public library for Asia.. In 1954, the Delivery of Book Act was passed to include newspaper. The act obligated every publisher in India to deposit one copy each of its publications to the National Library in Calcutta, the Asiatic Society Library in Bombay, Connemara Public Library in Madras, and Delhi Public Library in New Delhi The Advisory Committee for Libraries as constituted in 1957 by the Government of India, with K P Sinha as the Chairman.

The Committee submitted its report in 1959 with a drafted Model Library Bill. The Planning Commission constituted a Working Group on Public Libraries in 1964 and the Commission submitted its report in 1965 with a Model Public Libraries Act. The model bill was sent to all the states/UTs, which do not have Public Libraries Act. In 1972, the Government of India, Planning Commission constituted Working Group on Development of Public Libraries to make recommendations for library development. Raja Rammohun Roy Library Foundation, an autonomous body under the Department of Culture, Ministry of Education, was established in 1972.

The main objective of the Foundation was to assist state library services in developmental works. In 1979, a library section was established in the Department of Culture under the Ministry of Education, which section was under the charge of an Under Secretary. The objective was to promote the development of public libraries in India. A Working Group on Modernization of Library Services and Informatics was appointed by the Planning Commission in 1983 and submitted its report in 1984 with the formulation of National Policy on Library Services and Informatics. Delhi Public Library became a copyright library in 1982.

National Literacy Mission was adopted in 1986, which emphasized education for women and also establishment of rural libraries. Library networks and systems were strengthened at the national level institutions in the development of literature in neoliterates. Fourteen states namely, Tamil Nadu, Andhra Pradesh, Karnataka, Maharashtra, West Bengal, Manipur, Kerala, Haryana, Mizoram, Goa, Orissa, Gujarat, Uttaranchal and Rajasthan have enacted Public Libraries Bills during 1948 to 2006.

The Government of India, Department of Culture, appointed a Committee on National Policy on Library and Information System in 1985. The National Policy on Education, 1986 states that a nationwide movement for improvement of existing libraries and the establishment of new ones will be taken up, provision will be made in all educational institutions for library facilities, and the status of librarianship improved.

The National Book Policy, 1986 also had an impact on libraries, as:

- Provision of reading material for children by all the agencies involved;
- That 10 per cent of the annual education budget of the governments be used to purchase books for libraries.

These goals are to be achieved by using formal, non-formal, and open channels of learning.. Rural libraries should become the focal point for postliteracy and continuing educational programmes. Publishers, voluntary organizations, and school library programmes undertaken as part of the "Operation Blackboard Scheme" of the National Education Policy on Education, 1986 were given assistance. The following five libraries were regarded as national importance and may be stated in a very brief manner.

National Library, Kolkata

National Library, Kolkata was established in 1836 in the name of Calcutta Public Library. It was not a Government institution running on a proprietary basis. The then Governor General, Lord Metcalf transferred 4,675 volumes from the library of the College of Fort William to the Calcutta Public Library. This and donations of books from individuals formed the nucleus of the library. Prince Dwarkanath Tagore was the first proprietor of the Calcutta Public Library.

Both the Indian and foreign books, especially from Britain, were purchased for the library. In the report of 1850 we find that the library started collecting books in Gujarati, Marathi, Pali, Ceylonese and Punjabi. The Government of Bengal and North Western Provinces regularly made by individuals as well as donations. The Calcutta Public Library had a unique position as the first public library in this part of the country. Such a well-organized and efficiently run library was rare even in Europe during the first half of the 19th century. Because of the efforts of the Calcutta Public Library, the National Library has developed rare books and journals in its collection. The Imperial Library was formed in 1891 by combining a number of Secretariat libraries.

Of these, the most important and interesting was the library of the Home Department, which contained many books formerly belonging to the library of East India College, Fort William and the library of the East India Board in London. But the use of the library was restricted to the superior officers of the Government. Lord Curzon, the then Governor General of India, was the person who conceived the idea of opening a library for the use of the public. He noticed both the libraries, Imperial Library and Calcutta Public Library, were under-utilized for the want of facilities or restrictions.

So, he decided to amalgamate the rich collection of both of these libraries. He was successful in effecting the amalgamation of Calcutta Public Library with the then Imperial Library under certain terms. The library, called Imperial Library, was formally opened to the public on 30th January 1903 at Metcalf Hall, Kolkata. The aims and objectives of the Imperial Library, well defined in a Notification in the 'Gazette of India' *as ' It is intended* that it should be a library of reference, a working place for students and a repository of material for the future historians of India, in which, so far as possible, every work written about India, at any time, can be seen and read. John Macfarlane, the Asst.

Librarian of the British Museum, London, was appointed as the first Librarian of the Imperial Library. After his death, the famous scholar and linguist Harinath De took over the charge of the library. After his death J. A. Chapman became the librarian. Mr. Chapman showed keen interest in the affairs of the library and worked hard to improve its status. After his retirement, Khan Bahadur M.A. Asadulla was appointed as the librarian and he continued as the librarian till July 1947.

The policy of acquisition broadly adhered to by the Imperial Library was enunciated by Lord Curzon in his speech at the opening ceremony of the library, "The general idea of the whole Library is that it should contain all the books that have been written about India in popular tongues, with such additions as are required to make it a good all-round library of standard works of reference."

After the independence the Government of India changed the name of the Imperial Library as the National Library, with an enactment of the Imperial Library Act 1948 and the collection was shifted from the Esplanade to the present Belvedere Estate. On 1st February 1953 the National Library was opened to the public, inaugurated by Maulana Abul Kalam Azad. Sri B.S. Kesavan was appointed as the first librarian of the National Library.

The reviewing Committee in its report of 1969 suggested that the following should be the basic features of the National Library; Acquisition and conservation of all significant printed materials produced in the country to the exclusion of ephemera:

- Collection of printed materials concerning the country wherever published and also acquisition of photographic record of such materials that are not available within the country;
- Acquisition and conservation of manuscripts having national importance;
- Planned acquisition of foreign materials required by the country;
- Rendering of bibliographical and documentation service of retrospective materials, both general and specialized;
- Acting as a referral centre purveying full and accurate knowledge of all sources of bibliographical activities;
- Provision of photocopying and reprographic services; and
- Acting as the centre for international book exchange and international loan..

Khuda Bakhsh Oriental Public Library, Patna

Khuda Bakhsh Oriental Public Library, Patna was open for the public in October 1891 with 4000 Oriental manuscripts. Maulvi Khuda Bakhsh donated his entire collection to the nation by a deed of trust. Acknowledging the immense historical and intellectual value of its rich and valued collection, the Govt. of India declared the Library as Institution of National Importance by an act of Parliament in 1969. The Library is now fully funded by the Ministry of Culture. This autonomous institution is being governed by a Board with the Governor of Bihar as its ex-officio Chairman and Director is carrying the responsibility of dayto-day management of Library affairs.

Rampur Raza Library, Rampur

Rampur Raza Library, Rampur was founded by Nawab Faizullah Khan in 1774 AD. It was brought under the management of a Trust till the Government of India took over the library on 1 July 1975 under the Act of Parliament, which declared it as an institution of National importance. It contains very rare and valuable collection of manuscripts, historical documents, specimens of Islamic calligraphy, miniature paintings, astronomical instruments and rare illustrated works in Arabic and Persian languages besides 80,000 printed books. Nawab Faizullah Khan who ruled the state of Rampur, from 1774 to 1794, established the library with his personal modest collection kept in the Tosha Khana of his Palace. Now the Library occupies the position of an autonomous institution of national importance under Department of Culture, Government of India and is fully funded by Central Government. The Library has now attained an International status of higher studies.

Thanjavur Maharaja Serfoji's Sarasvati Mahal Library, Thanjavur

Thanjavur Maharaja Serfoji's Sarasvati Mahal Library, Thanjavur is one among a few medieval libraries existing in the world. It contains very rare and valuable collections of manuscripts, books, maps and paintings on all aspects of Art, Culture and Literature. The Encyclopedia Britannica in its survey of the Libraries of the world mentions this as "the most remarkable Library in India". The Library houses a rich and rare collection of manuscripts on art, culture and literature. Conceived and christened as the Royal Palace Library by the Nayak Kings of Thanjavur. And the Maratha rulers nourished it for intellectual enrichment.

In 1918 this Library was made as a public Library. A body constituted by the Government and financed by the Central and State Governments now administers the library. During the reign of Nayaks of Thanjavur, "Sarasvati Bhandar" was formed and developed. The Maratha rulers who captured Thanjavur in 1675 A.D. patronized the culture of Thanjavur and developed the Royal Palace Library till 1855 A.D. The Sarasvati Bhandar was situated within the Palace campus and the Manuscripts used for the purpose of reading by the Royal personages. Among the Maratha Kings, King Serfoji II, was an eminent scholar in many branches of learning and with great enthusiasm he took special steps for the enrichment of the Library.

It is a fitting tribute to the great collector Serfoji that the Library is named after him. Till the survival of the last Maratha Queen, the Library was the Palace property. After that, the Library together with the Palace properties formed the subject of litigation in Civil Courts. The Royal Family members voluntarily came forward to delete this Library from the suit properties formed an Endowment and dedicated this Library to the public with one lakh rupees for its maintenance and upkeep. The Government of Madras in their G.O. Ms. No.1306 Home dated 5th October 1918, took possession of the Library under the Charitable Endowment Act and framed scheme for the Library management.

In 1983, the Library was declared as an Institution of National Importance. The Government of Tamil Nadu abolished the Five Member Committee of administration and made it as a Registered Society as per G.O. 209 (EST) dated 1-2-83. The Society was constituted and got registration on 9-7-1986 under the Tamil Nadu Registered Societies Act of 1975. The Society consists of ex-officio members of Central and State Governments, nominated Scholars, Member from the Royal family and the Director of the Library. The Hon'ble Education Minister of the Government of Tamil Nadu is the ex-officio Chairman of this society.

Harekrushna Mahtab State Library, Bhubaneswar

Harekrushna Mahtab State Library, Bhubaneswar was conceived during 1st Five Year Plan under the advice of Government of India and was completed in 1959, enshrined within a beautiful land of 3 acres in a prime location of Capital City of Bhubaneswar. In 1967, it was named as Gandhi Bhawan commemorating birth centenary of Mahatma Gandhi, the father of the nation. In 1987 it was renovated and entire space of the four storied building was utilized for the functioning of two Libraries *i.e.* State Library for the entire State of Orissa and another Public Library for Bhubaneswar City.

In 1987, Government decided to rename the State Library and the Public Library as Harekrushna Mahtab State Library and the Bhubaneswar Public Library respectively. The former is a Reference Library and lending of books is not permitted whereas the latter is a Lending Library for the public of Bhubaneswar City. These two Libraries have managed to function over the limited space. Total readers seats available are about 350 against the present demands of 600-700 readers per day.

LIBRARY LEGISLATION IN INDIA

Since the beginning, the public libraries served as the local information centers making the source of knowledge readily available to the public. The local community from the local fund or individual munificence could not achieve the services of a public library. Public leaders, scholars and learned societies have realised that the only way to establish and develop a public library system is through legislation.

The UNESCO Public Library Manifesto, 1972 stated that, "The public library should be established under the clear mandate of law", which is substantiated by the IFLA/UNESCO Public Library Manifesto 1994 as;

- "The public library shall in principle be free of charge. The public library is the responsibility of local and national authorities. It must be supported by specific legislation and financed by national and local government. It has to be an essential component of any long-term strategy for culture, information provision, literacy and education".

Libraries are recorded under the Article 246 of Indian Constitution, Seventh Schedule List II of State List No.12 and the Indian Constitution Act, 1956, *"Libraries, museums and other similar institutions controlled or financed by the State; ancient and historical monuments and records other than those to be of national importance."* Provision of public library service is the responsibility of the State Government as the subject matter of libraries is relatable to entry 12 of the State List in the Seventh Schedule to the Constitution of India. Dr. S R Ranganathan regarded as the pioneer of library legislation in India. "The concept of legislation for libraries is a contribution of S R Ranganathan to Indian public libraries". He made library legislation obligatory for the implementation of the second law of library science, "Every reader his/her book". Ranganathan the second law can be properly carried out only by legislation.

Dr. S R Ranganathan strived a lot for library legislation and prepared different library bills for the Indian Union and constituent states; such as;

- Model Library Act for constituent states of India;
- Bengal;
- Bombay;
- Central Province and Berar;
- Old Madras state which later became Act in 1948;
- United Province;
- Cochin;
- Travancore;
- Union Government;
- Madhya Pradesh;
- Union and Constituent States;
- Constituent States;
- Union;
- West Bengal;
- Kerala;
- Uttar Pradesh;
- Mysore which became Act in 1965;
- Assam;
- Gujarat and Model Library Bill.

Public libraries also considered as community information centers providing access at local level to a wide range of knowledge and information for the benefit of the individual and society as a whole. To ensure sustained development and information network services public libraries should be based on legislation.

"Public library legislation may be in various forms depending upon the government structure. It can be simple, allowing the establishment of public libraries but leaving standards of service to the level of government directly responsible for the library, or more complex, with specific detail on what services should be provided and to what standard".

But no British Government passed library Act for creation of public library system in Indian states.. There have been different efforts to work out library legislation models in India. In the pre-independent and post-independent of India, there have been five models of public library bills suggested by experts and national level professional associations and organizations.

MODEL PUBLIC LIBRARIES ACT OF DR. S R RANGANATHAN

The first Model Public Libraries Acts was prepared by Dr. S R Ranganathan in 1930 and revised in 1957 and 1972. It was discussed at the

First All Asia Educational Conference held at Banaras during 26-30 December 1930. It was introduced in West Bengal Legislature in 1931 and in Madras Legislature in 1933. The Bill could not be passed due to financial clauses on library grant, library cess etc.

Salient features of final version are:

- Establishment of public libraries in city, rural and other areas;
- Constitution of State Library Authority *i.e.* Minister of Education;
- Constitution of State Library Committee as an advisory body of the State Library Authority;
- Constitution of Local Library Authority for each city and one for each district;
- State Library Authority, Government and Local Library Authority may determine library rate in such a manner and may determine collection of library cess from time to time.

MODEL PUBLIC LIBRARIES BILL OF MINISTRY OF EDUCATION

The Government of India, Ministry of Education appointed an Advisory Committee for Libraries in 1957, under the Chairmanship of Shri K P Sinha, former Director of Public Instruction, Bihar. This committee recommended the need for library legislation for each state. As a follow-up action of the Advisory Committee, the Ministry of Education, Government of India appointed a committee under the Chairmanship of Dr. M D Sen. The Committee drafted Model Public Libraries Bill in the year 1963.

The salient components of this Bill are:

- Constitution of State Library Authority as an apex body to advise the Government in the matter of library developments;
- Constitution of State Library Directorate for direction and controlling of library services;
- Constitution of District Library Committee in each district;
- Treatment of employees as government servant;
- Collection of library cess at the rate of 6 paise per rupee on house tax and property tax.

MODEL PUBLIC LIBRARIES BILL OF THE PLANNING COMMISSION

The Planning Commission, Government of India, constituted a 'Working Group on Libraries' in 1964 to plan and advice on the development of Libraries during the Fourth Five Year Plan. The Working Group recommended a Library Development Scheme to be implemented during the Fourth Plan period with a financial commitment of Rs.309 million, which was appended by Model Public

Libraries Bill and submitted its report in 1965. Bill was not considered even by a single state.

The Bill included the following features:

- Establish, maintain, develop and integrated adequate public library service in the state;
- Constitution of Committee of Experts to prescribe the standards of service;
- Constitution of State Library Council to advise the government for the promotion and development of library service;
- Establishment of State Library Directorate to control, direct and supervise library system in the state;
- Establishment of State Central Library, State Regional Libraries and District Libraries;
- Treatment of employees in the system of State Government Servants
- Government shall be the financial source and shall maintain the public library system in the state.

MODEL PUBLIC LIBRARIES BILL OF INDIAN LIBRARY ASSOCIATION

The Indian Library Association (ILA) formed in 1933, has keen interest in library legislation. The ILA discussed library legislation at its various seminars organized in 1964, 1978 and 1981. Consequently, ILA Council at its meeting held on 23 June 1989, keeping in view of the developments and experiences gain from the existing Acts, resolved to prepare a Model Library Bill.

Accordingly, as asked by ILA, Dr. Velaga Venkatappaiah, Chairman, Central Sectional Committee on Public Libraries of the ILA prepared a Model Public Library Bill. ILA accepted the draft Bill with minor changes at its National Seminar on Public Library Legislation in 1990 at the final product of the Model Public Libraries Bill was published in 1991.

The Bill was circulated to all the states and union territories but few states reacted favourably to the Bill. This Model Bill was again discussed in a National Seminar on Library Legislation and revised as the Model State Public Library and Information Service Act in 1995. In view of emergence of Information Technology at all levels, the model act was again revised in 2000.

The important components of this Bill are:

- State Library and Information Service, based on a State Policy;
- Constitution of State Library Authority at the apex level with Minister of Libraries as Chairman as policy making and executive body;
- Establishment of Directorate of Public Libraries for directing, controlling and supervising;

- Constitution of City, District Library Authority for rendering service from district to village level;
- Provision for network of Public Library and Information Services from state to village level;
- Constitution of State Library and Information Service;
- Collection of Library cess on house tax and property tax, entertainment tax, professional tax, vehicle tax, etc.;
- Constitution of State Boards for education, book production, co-ordination, etc.;
- Accountability of public expenditure and services.

MODEL UNION LIBRARY ACT

The Government of India appointed a committee to explore the possibilities to establish a National Central Library at New Delhi in 1948. Dr. S R Ranganathan, a member of the committee drafted a Library Development plan in 1950 with a 30-year programme and a draft Library Bill for the states and Union Public Library Act.

This was revised in 1959 and again in 1972. However, libraries falls under the state list of the constitution and it may not be possible to pass Bill as a Union Act, unless and until the constitution is suitably amended for this purpose.

The main features of this model Act are:

- Constitution of a National Library Authority;
- Establishment of national central libraries;
- Constitution of National Library Committee as an advisory body to the National library Authority;
- Constitution of National library fund;
- Amendment to the delivery of Books and Newspaper Act, 1954.

The IFLA/UNESCO Public Library Manifesto 1994 reads that, "The public library is the local center of information, making all kinds of knowledge and information readily available to its users". Public libraries, to become an enthusiastic source of information and knowledge for the local community, needs certain forms of developments in terms of infrastructure, collection and the trinity of library as well. It cannot survive by the local contributions and dedication alone, but through the support of government.

"The pubic library, as a democratic institution operated by the people for the people, should be established and maintained under the clear authority of law; supported wholly or mainly from public funds; open for free use on equal terms to all members of the community regardless of occupation, creed, class or race". Efforts have been going on well under the initiatives of professional associations and learned societies in this context. "In India, the post independence era was favourable to the establishment of public libraries based on legal basis"..

STATES WITH LIBRARY LEGISLATION

During the last six decades, 14 Public Library Bills were enacted in different states of India, such as:

- *Tamil Nadu:* The Tamil Nadu Public Libraries Act 1948;
- *Andhra Pradesh*: The Andhra Pradesh Public Libraries Act 1960;
- *Karnataka:* The Karnataka Public Libraries Act 1965;
- *Maharashtra*: The Maharastra Public Libraries Act 1967;
- *West Bengal:* The West Bengal Public Libraries Act 1979;
- *Manipur:* The Manipur Public Libraries Act 1988;
- *Kerala*: The Kerala Public Libraries Act 1989;
- *Haryana:* The Haryana Public Libraries Act 1989;
- *Mizoram:* The Mizoram Public Libraries Act 1993;
- *Goa:* The Goa Public Libraries Act 1993;
- *Orissa*: Orissa Public Libraries Act, 2001;
- *Gujarat:* Gujarat Public Libraries Act, 2001;
- *Uttaranchal:* Uttaranchal Public Libraries Act, 2005.
- *Rajasthan:* Rajasthan Public Libraries Act, 2006

Tamil Nadu

Tamil Nadu is the first state that enacted Public Libraries Act in independent India. It came into force with effect from 1 April 1950. The objectives of the Act are contained in its Preamble as, 'An act to provide for the establishment of public libraries in the province of Tamil Nadu and the organization of comprehensive rural and urban Library Service therein". It has 19 sections.

The salient features of this Act are given below:

- This Act facilitates establishment of Public Libraries in the State.
- Constitution of State Library Committee for the purpose of advising the government on such matters relating to libraries.
- Provision for appointment of Director of Public Libraries to control, direct and supervise public libraries.
- Constitution of Local Library Authorities, one for the City of Madras and one for each district.
- Every Local Library Authority shall levy in the area a library cess in the form of a surcharge on property tax or house tax at the rate of six paise per rupee.
- The Government shall contribute Library Fund to each of the Local

Library Authority, except the City of Madras, to the amount of library cess collected.

- The Act amended Sec.9 of the Press and Registration of Books Act, 1867, Central Act XXV of 1867 to the effect that every printer shall deliver five copies of each book to the State Government out of which four will be deposited in the State Central Library, Madras.

Tamil Nadu was very rich in public libraries. The Connemara Public Library was opened for the public in 1896 and became the State Central Library from 1 April 1950. There is a tremendous growth and development of public libraries since an enactment of Tamil Nadu Public Libraries Act 1948 being the first state in India with Library Legislation.

As on March 1998, the state has public library service units, as–1 State Central Library, 29 District Central Libraries, 1548 Branch Libraries, 506 Village Libraries, 649 Part-time Libraries, and 8 Mobile Libraries. The Department of Public Libraries has been offering extension services, like–Mobile Library Service, Home Delivery Service, Library Service for Children, Library Service for Police Personnel, Library Service for state workers and remote settlers in the hills, Hospital Library Service, Rural Library Service, Part-time Library Service, Library Service for Students, Library Service for research scholars and Library Service for competitions for various civil services.

Andhra Pradesh

The state of Andhra Pradesh was formed in 1956, comprising Andhra areas of composite Madras state and Telengana area of Hyderabad area, whereas Madras Public Libraries Act in force in Andhra area. To solve administrative problems on two acts in operational in one state; both the acts were amalgamated, modified and up-to-date as Andhra Pradesh Public Libraries Act 1960.

It received the Governor assent on 18th. February 1960. Andhra Pradesh is the second state that has enacted Public Libraries Act in independent India. Its Preamble reads that, "*An Act to* consolidate and amend the laws relating to the establishment and maintenance of Public Libraries in the State of Andhra Pradesh and matters connected therewith".

It has seven chapters. Important features of this Act are as below:

- Constitution of 'The Andhra Pradesh Granthalaya Parishad', as a corporate body, having perpetual succession and power to the provisions of this Act.
- Constitution of Directorate of Public Libraries to direct, supervise and control Public Library System.
- Constitution of Zilla Granthalaya Samastha, one for the City of Hyderabad, one for the district of Hyderabad and one for each districts.
- Provision to collect library cess by every Zilla Granthalaya Samstha

in its area as surcharge on property tax or house tax up to eight paise per rupee.

- The accounts of Zilla Granthalaya Samstha shall be open to inspection.
- Provision of Government Grant-in-aid to private libraries.
- Provision for constitution of a Library Service for the Zilla Granthalaya Samstha for the appointment of Librarians.

Andhra Pradesh is one of the leading states in India for the promotion of library services in India. It is the second in India with Public Libraries Act in 1960.

The structure of public library services can be classified into three categories consisting of:

- *Government Libraries:* 1 State Central Library, 6 Regional Libraries, and 1 Mobile Library,
- *Zila Grandhalaya Samstha Libraries:* 23 District/City Central Libraries, 1448 Branch Libraries, 355 Village Libraries, 3 Mobile Libraries, and 576 Book Deposit Centers,
- *Aided Libraries:* 1238 Gram Panchayat Libraries, 37 Cooperative Society Libraries, and 680 Private Libraries.

Karnataka

Karnataka is the third state in an independent India that have enacted Public Libraries Act. The objective of this Act can be seen in its Preamble that reads, '*An* Act to provide for the establishment and maintenance of Public Libraries and the organization of a comprehensive rural and urban library service in the State of *Karnataka* '.

Important features of this Act are given below:

- Constitution of State Library Authority to meet twice in a year, Minister of Public Libraries as its Chairman and State Librarian as *ex-officio* Secretary.
- Provision for creation of an independent Department of Public Libraries with a profession as its head, to supervise, direct and control library services.
- Provision for the establishment of State Library as apex of public library system in the state.
- Constitution of Local Library Authority, City Library Authority and District Library Authority.
- Provision for setting up of Advisory Library Committee for Branch and Village Library Services.
- Collection of library cess on tax on lands and buildings.
- Additional sections in State Central Library

- State Bureau of Copyright Collection
- State Library for the Blind
- State Bureau of Inter Library Loan
- State Bibliographical Bureau
- State Bureau of Technical Service.

Karnatàka is the third state in India that enacted Public Library Bill in 1965. The Belgaum Native General Library, established in 1848 by M.J.D.Invararity, was regarded as the first library started in Karnataka state. There were other seven libraries or reading rooms in Belgaum, namely, Library at Chikkodi established in 1886, Nippani Library in 1875, Gokak Library in 1865, Athani Library in 1865, Sampagaon Library in 1866, Khanapur Library in 1868, and Saundatti Library in 1870.

The existing public libraries in Karnataka are-1 State Central Library, 1 Indira Priyadarshini Chidren's Library, 1 Public Technical Library, 27 District Central Library, 19 City Central Library, 14 Mobile Libraries, 490 Branch Libraries, 107 Service Stations, 31 Reading Rooms, 5766 Gram Panchayat Libraries, 21 Aided Libraries, 200 Slum Libraries and 600 Reading Rooms in Slum Areas.

Maharashtra

Consequent upon the constitution of Maharashtra state, The Maharashtra Public Libraries Act, 1967 succeed Kolhapur Public Libraries Act 1945. The fourth state in an independent India that has enacted Public Libraries Act is Maharashtra state. Preamble of the Act read that, "To provide for the establishment, maintenance, organization and development of public libraries in the state of Maharashtra".

Important features of this Act are:

- Constitution of State Library Council. Minister for Education shall be the ex-officio President of the Council. The Council will advise the State Government on all matters connected with the administration of this Act.
- Constitution of a separate department of Libraries and the appointment of a professional Director;
- Establishment of Maharashtra State Library Service;
- Establishment of State Central library and a Divisional Library for each Division;
- Constitution of District Library Committee in each of the district. Chairman of the Education Committee of a Zilla Parishad in the district shall be ex-officio President of the Committee.
- Constitution of Library Fund by the State Government for carrying out the purpose of this Act. The State Government will contribute not less than a sum of twenty-five lakhs to the Library Fund every year.

The Birtishers started public libraries in Maharashtra after defeating Marathas in 1818 but no Indians were allowed membership of these libraries till 1830. Pioneer libraries estab-lished by Indian in Maharashtra were at Ahmednagar in 1838, Bombay in 1845, and Poona in 1848. In 1939, the government constituted a Library Development Committee to prepare a plan for public library development in the state of Bombay.

The report was implemented from 1955 to 1967. After an enactment of Maharashtra Public Libraries Act 1967, public library system was developed through voluntary organizations with grants from the government. As on 1998, Maharashtra has different categories of public libraries as–1 State Central Library, 6 Divisional Libraries, 31 District Libraries, 63 Taluka Grade A Libraries, 144 Taluka Grade B Libraries, 58 Taluka Grade C Libraries, and 3842 Recognized Libraries.

West Bengal

The West Bengal Legislature passed this Act and assent of the President was first published in the Calcutta Gazette, Extraordinary on the 7th January 1980. West Bengal enacted the Public Libraries Act in 1979 to become the fifth state of India with library legislation. Its preamble stated that, *"An Act to provide for the* establishment of Public libraries in the State of West Bengal and to regulate, guide, central, supervise and to grant recognition to the existing libraries in the State as also to provide for a comprehensive rural and urban library service in the State of *west Bengal"*.

Some of the important salient features of this Act are:

- Constitution of State Library Council for the purpose of advising the Government on the matters of public library services. Minister-in-Charge of Library Services shall be the Chairman of the Council;
- Constitution of the Department of Libraries to supervise and direct the maintenance of Public Libraries;
- Constitution of Local Library Authority for each district. The District Magistrate shall be the Chairman of the Local Library Authority. Provision for constitution of Executive Committee for Local Library Authority;
- The Government is empowered to appoint District Library Officers and District Librarians in districts. The Government, in consultation with the Local Library Authority may place a person in charge of a District Library to be called as District Librarian;
- Financial management of local libraries rests upon the Local Library Authority. Means of augmenting funds are:
- Contributions, gifts and income form endowments;
- Grants from the government
- Collection of Local Library Authority under the Act.

In 1780, Mr. John Andrews run a commercial library in Fort William and the first public library; Calcutta Public Library was established during the British period in 1836, which is now known as National Library. By 1900, there were 50 public libraries in Bengal.

The state government took up a seven tier library development scheme, which envisaged setting up of public libraries at different levels-State Central Library; District Library; Sub-Division/Area Library; Rural Library; Village Library; and Delivery Stations/Book Deposit Centers.

By 1996, West Bengal has one State Central Library, 22 District Libraries, 120 Sub-Divisional/Town Libraries, and 2276 Rural/Area/Primary Unit Libraries. There are also around 3000 non-governmental/non-sponsored public libraries. West Bengal is the fifth state in India with Library Legislation in 1979.

Manipur

Manipur is the sixth state in an independent India that has enacted Public Libraries Act in 1988. The preamble stated the objectives of this Acts as, "An Act to provide the establishment and maintenance of Public Libraries in the State of Manipur and matters connected therewith".

Salient features of this Act are given hereunder:

- Constitution of a State Library Committee, to advise the State Government on all matters arising under this Act and to exercise and perform such other powers and duties as may be prescribed.
- Constitution of a separate Department of Public Libraries under the Director, as its head.
- Constitution of District Library Authority for each district to supervise library services in the area of its jurisdiction.
- Provision to constitute Executive Committee and Sub-Committees of District Library Authority to enquire into and report or advice on any matters, which it may refer to them.
- Constitution of Library fund formed mainly with the contribution of the State Government.

Manipur is the sixth state in India with Public Library Acts in 1988. Manipur Club established in 1927 was changed over into Manipur Book Club/ Manipur Club Library and again changed into Jubabati Memorial Library in 1933. But the library had a setback during the Second World War.

Imphal Public Library, also known as Khwai Public Library was established in 1938 but was functioning till 1960 and later it was demolished in 1994. District Library and Children's Library-cum-Museun were merged on 26 August 1970 and came to be known as State Central library.. There are 9 District Libraries, 1 State Central Library, and 215 Libraries organized by Voluntary Organizations..

Kerala

Kerala Public Libraries Act, 1989 is also known as Kerala Granthasala Sanghom, 1989. Kerala enacted its pubic Libraries Act in 1989 to become the seventh state in India with library legislation. Preamble of this Act stated its objectives as, "*An Act* to consolidate and unify the library laws in the State and to provide for the recognition in the entire library system in the State of Kerala with a view to the development and maintenance of comprehensive rural and urban library service and for matters connected therewith or incidental hereto".

Important features of the Act are:

- Constitution of Kerala State Library Council with Executive Committee to advise the government on all matters connected with this Act and to supervise and direct all maters relating to library service in the state;
- Secretary of the State Library Council shall be the Chief Executive Authority of the State Library Council;
- Constitution of District Library Council to supervise, co-ordinate and control the Library service under its jurisdiction and to promote co-operation between libraries and cultural and educational institutions in the country;
- Constitution of Taluk Library Union, with the power to supervise, coordinate and control the library services in the Taluk and to give directions and advise to affiliated libraries in regard to their day to day function and management;
- The Government may make every year a grant to the State library council with a maximum of one per cent of the education budget of the State.
- The State Library Council shall maintain a fund called State Library fund. Library cess collected and grants of State and Central Government will be credited to the State Library fund.
- Transfer of Kerala Granthaala Sangham with its staff, assets, and liabilities to the State Library Council.
- Collection of Library Cess in the form of a surcharge on the building tax or the property tax at the rate of 5 paise for the whole rupee.

Christian missionaries started libraries in Kerala during the 19th century. The history of public library movement in Kerala started in 1829 with the establishment of Trivandrum Public Library. There are more than 5000 public libraries in Kerala now, one in every 8 square kilometers.

Public libraries can be grouped into four categories, as–Libraries directly run by the Government, Libraries run by the local bodies, Grant-in-Aid libraries affiliated to the Kerala Grandhasala Sangham, and Libraries run by the Local Library Authorities.

The Kerala Grandhasala Sangham was established in 1947 and was registered under Section 9 of the Travancore Company Act, 1939 and in 1948 the Government approved it as the Central Agency of the Libraries. It plays an incredible role for the promotion, development and encouraging the people of the state through library services. Kerala enacted Public Library Bill in 1989 to become the seventh state in India with Library Legislation.

Haryana

Haryana is the eighth state in India with library legislation. The preamble stated its objectives as, "An Act to provide for the establishment, maintenance and development of Public Libraries in the State of Haryana and for matters ancillary *thereto.*"

Some of the important features of this Act are:

- Constitution of State Library Authority to advise the Government on all matters for the promotion of library services in the State. Minister-in-charge of libraries will be the Chairman;
- Establishment of State Library Directorate to execute the programmes approved by the State Library Authority;
- Establishment of State Central library;
- Constitution of District Library in each district and Municipal/City/ Town library; Block library; Village library; and Smaller book deposit centers;
- Provision for three types of library funds, such as State Library Fund, District Library Fund, and City/Town/Block/Village Library Fund;
- Levy of Library cess in the form of surcharge on property tax and house tax as decided by the government from time to time;
- Provision to recognize state library associations, and co-operative institutions by the State Library Authority.

Before the creation of this separate state, some public libraries were already established, Guru Gobind Singh Municipal Library in 1926, Shri Parmeshwari Yuvak Librray in 1927, and Sri Bal Amar Samiti Library in 1932. A State Central Library was started in 1967 by th4 Government of Haryana. Besides it has started 12 District Libraries, 11 Sub-Divisional Libraries and 11 Municipal Libraries.

Many philanthropic trusts and local bodies/organizations had also established public libraries, which took active role in the promotion of reading habits and library services in the state. The Haryana Library Association was founded in 1967. The Haryana Public Libraries Bill was passed in 1989 and independent Directorate of Libraries was established in January 1993. Mobile library services to reach the interior of the remote villages with reading facilities were started and the people are very much encouraged for the development of libraries at villages and panchayat levels as a social education center and community information center as well.

Mizoram

Mizoram is the ninth state of India to have library legislation. Preamble of this Act stated its objective as, "An Act to provide for the establishment, maintenance and development of comprehensive public libraries system in the State of Mizoram".

Important features of this Act are:

- Constitution of State Library Council to advise the Government on all matters relating to libraries and also in regard to promotion and development of libraries in the State;
- Constitution of the Department of Public Libraries to control and supervise the public library system in the State;
- Constitution of State Library, District Library, Sub-Divisional Library and Village Libraries;
- Provision of grant-in-aid to recognized libraries;
- No library cess. All expenses shall be made from the Government funds.

Goa

Goa is the tenth state to have library legislation in India. Preamble of this Act stated that, "An Act to provide for the establishment, maintenance and development of Public Libraries in the State of Goa and for the matters ancillary hereto".

Important salient features of this Act are:

- Constitution of State Library Council with the Minister-in-charge a the Chairman to advise the Government on all matters arising under the Act;
- Constitution of State Library Directorate for controlling and directing the public library system in the State;
- Organization of State Library, District Library, Taluk Library, and Village library;
- Creation of Public Library employees similar to the employees of State Government;
- Recognition of one State Library Association as co-operating institution;
- State library fund from different sources, *viz.* Government contribution, Government Grants, and any other contribution from the public;
- Levy of Library Cess in the form of a surcharge on Indian Made Foreign Liquor at the rate of 50 paise per bulk litre of beer.

Under the order of the Viceroy, *Dom Manuel de Portugal e Castro*, a public library, *Publica Livraria* was opened and attached to *Academia Militar* in 1832 and it was named as *Bibliotheca Nacional de Goa* in 1959 and came under the administration of Education and Health Services department.

The Government of Goa constituted a State Level Expert Committee in 1978 and State Library Advisory Board in 1983 for the development of library services in the state. The public libraries of Goa can be categorized into five levels, as State Library, Taluka Libraries, Village Libraries, Government Aided Libraries, and Municipal Libraries. Goa is the tenth state in India with Public Library Act in 1993.

Orissa

The establishment of Diamond Jubilee Library at Kendrapara in 1897 and at Baripada in 1898 started the development of public library and followed by establishment of other libraries in the state. Three Government functionaries, Department of Information and Public Relations, Department of Sports and Culture, and Department of Housing and Urban Development operated public libraries in the state for some times.

In 1975, the Department of Cultural Affairs, Government of Orissa took complete charge of Public Libraries from the Department of Education. There is one State Library, 13 District Libraries, 4 Sub-Divisional libraries, 6 Ex. District Board Libraries, and 4 Memorial Hall Libraries.

Gujarat

Objective of Gujarat Public Libraries Act provided in its preamble is to provide for the promotion and development of public libraries in the State of Gujarat and for that purpose to constitute State Library development Council and for the matters connected therewith or incidental thereto.

Important features of this act are:

- Constitution of State Library Council with Minister–in-charge of Libraries as its Chairman;
- Establishment of Public Library Department with Director as its head of office;
- Establishment of District and Taluka Libraries at the headquarters of taluka;
- Constitution of District and Taluka Library Advisory Committee;
- Formation of State Library Development Fund;
- Recognition of libraries run by voluntary organi-zations.

The first considered public library in Gujarat was called, "Himabhai Institute of Library" established in 1849 in Ahmedabad. Other pioneer public libraries are Andrews Library established in 1850, Lang Library in 1857, Lakhajirao Pusthakalaya in 1868, Bhagavatsihji Library in 1884, State Library in 1865, Barton Library in 1882, Takhsinhi Library in 1877, and Victoria Jubilee Library in 1891.

There are 2 State Central libraries, 18 District Libraries in all the districts, 45 Taluka Libraries, 129 Mahila Libraries run by voluntary organizations, more than 300 Book Service Centers and Mobile Library service.

Uttaranchal

Uttaranchal is the 27th state of Indian Union, separated from Uttar Pradesh and coming into existence on 9.11.2000. The state comprises ten districts, namely Uttarkashi, Dehradun, Tehri Garhwal, Chamoli, Pithoragarh, Nainital, Uddam Singh Nagar, Pauri Garhwal and Hardwar. Public Libraries within these districts were automatically came under the Uttaranchal administration.

The state literacy rate is 72.28%. The state government is very interested to serve the people through public libraries and the Uttaranchal Public Libraries Bill was enacted in 2005 to become the thirteenth state in India with Library legislation. Some of the well established libraries by the state government of Uttar Pradesh were taken over while coming up into existence.

Rajasthan

Libraries were established in Rajasthan as early as 14th. Century and maintained in the form of *Pothi-Khanas* consisting rich collections of manuscripts on different disciplines. Rana Kumbha's Saraswati Bhandar Library was established in 1448. Raja Man Singh established library, *Pothi-Khana* in 1592 by keeping rare and important manuscripts.

Pioneer Public Libraries were established in Bharatpur in 1907, Sikar in 1908, Kota in 1910, Fatehpur in 1910, and Jodhpur in 1915. There are 5 Divisional libraries, 24 District Libraries, and 8 Tehsil Libraries with 600 Book Deposit Centers on 15 August 1956. Mobile van was also provided to Division Libraries to supervise library services in the state.

STATES/UTS WITHOUT LIBRARY LEGISLATION

Public library systems and services of Indian states and Union Territories are highlighted hereunder.

Arunachal Pradesh

Arunachal Pradesh, formerly known as North East Frontier Agency, introduced library service since 1950s. During the Seventh Five Year Plan period, the state government took up the scheme of developing libraries in the state and set up a number of libraries at block and circle levels. Mobile library system was introduced in the state capital. The state has six categories of library, such as–1 State Library, 2 Branch Libraries, 13 District Libraries, 2 Sub-Divisional Libraries, 20 Block Libraries, and 45 Circle Libraries.

Assam

In 1865, George Williamson, a tea-planter of Golaghat bequeathed 10,000 pounds for the purpose of educational and set up of libraries in Assam and the government taken up as an experiment measure to established public libraries at the initiatives of British government in 1902-1903 at Dhubri, Guwahati, Nagaon, Jorhat, Tezpur, Shillong, Sibsagar, Goalpara, Dibrugarh, Hailakandi, etc. and then handed over to the Local Boards.

The people were awakened and established rural libraries in some areas. The Assam Library Association came into existence in 1938 and extended all possible help to established public libraries in different areas. The Central Library, established in 1954 at Shillong and the Assam Government Public Library established in 1903 was amalgamated in 1956 and renamed as the State Central Library.

In 1955, seven District Libraries were set up at Guwahati, Nagaon, Jorhat, Dibrugarh, Tezpur, Dhubri and Silchar. Book Mobile Service along with 70 Deposit Centers for Circulation of Books was organized to villages in 1959. Assam is running 1 State Library, 1 Branch Library, 22 District Libraries, 14 Sub-Divisional Libraries, and 1 Children Library.

Bihar

The ancient Educational and Cultural Centers like Nalanda, Vikramshala, Pataliputra and Taxila had magnificent libraries and Bihar Library Association was founded on 15 October 1936. The Association popularized importance of libraries and in 1937 prepared a Draft Scheme for the development of libraries in Bihar.

There is one State Central Library at Patna, having seven wings, *viz.*, State Reference Library, State Lending Library, State Library for Blind, State Bureau of Inter-Library Loan, State Bibliographical Bureau, State Bureau of Technical Service, and State Institute of Library Training and Research. At present, there is 1 State Central Library, 6 Divisional Libraries, 7 Special Libraries, 17 District Central Libraries, 2 State Libraries, 11 Sub-Divisional Libraries, 328 Block Libraries, and 4422 Village Libraries in Bihar.

The Library service is at the government level is under the control and supervision of the Commissioner of Education. In the state of Jharkhand area, there are 5 District Libraries, 4 Sub-Divisional Libraries and other Village Libraries are under the public library sector. The state of Jharkhand came into existence on 15 November 2000 by separating some areas of Bihar state.

Himachal Pradesh

Under the scheme of Integrated Library Service formulated by the Union Ministry of Education, a small library system was introduced in 1952. A State Central Library was established in Solan in 1959, and within two years sic District Libraries were opened. The State Central Library created four departments, namely, reference, Lending, Periodicals, and Children Section for the benefit of the readers. Membership registration is free of charge to all the residents of Himachal Pradesh.

It has 1 State Central Library, 11 District Libraries, 15 Community Central Public Libraries, and 101 Senior Secondary School Libraries in the state. The School Libraries are also used as public libraries after the school hours. Two Mobile units are set up in 1961 to cater the needs of the community particularly in the rural areas of the state.

Jharkhand

The state of Jharkhand, separated from Bihar, is having 18 public libraries established by the state government.

These public libraries may be classified into four groups as below:

- Three State Public Libraries, one each at Ranchi, Chaibasa, Dhanbad and Dumka.
- One Divisional Library at Hazaribagh;
- Five District Libraries, one each at Gumla, Lohardaga, Daltonganj and Godda; and
- Eight Sub-Divisional Libraries, one each at Garhwa, Lahetar, Pakur, Simdega, Chatra, Sahebganj, Saraikela, and Khunti..

The library building are, generally, not functional to cater more readers at a time. Furniture is inadequate and water supply system is poor. No electricity connection was available to some of them due to non-payment of bills. Collection and subscription of periodicals/newspapers are not adequate to serve the library users as well.

Jammu and Kashmir

The state is divided into 14 districts. The Christian missinaries started education. Until 1947, the state has only two public libraries, namely, Sri Pratap Singh Library in 1893 in the city of Srinagar and Sri Ranbir Singh Library in Jammu. The state government establishes the department of public Libraries in 1961 for the establishment and promotion of public library services in the state. The state has 2 Central Libraries, one each in the province of Jammu and Kashmir, 14 District Libraries, 51 Tehsil Libraries, and 18 Block Libraries.

Madhya Pradesh and Chhattisgarh

The state of Madhya Pradesh including Chhattisgarh lies in the heart of the country came into existence on 1 November 1956. Madhya Pradesh was divided into two states, *viz.*, Madhya Pradesh and Chhatisgarh on 1 November 2000; hence the state of Chhattisgarh came into existence. It has 5 Regional Libraries in Bhopal, Gwalior, Jabalpur, Rewa, and Indore, 42 District Libraries, 6 Information Centers, 80 Private Public Libraries, and 15800 Gram Panchayat Libraries. The Madhya Pradesh Library Association was formed in 1957.

Meghalaya

Meghalaya has taken up the State Library of Assam established in Shillong in 1903 as its State Central Library. It has one State Central Library, four District Libraries, and Libraries run by voluntary organizations in different localities. The Meghalaya Library Association was established in 1994.

Nagaland

Nagaland has established a State Central Library at Kohima in 1981 functioning under the Directorate of Art and Culture. It offers computer facilities and reprographic services to its readers. There are eight District Libraries and four of them have completed computerization. 330 Rural libraries are registered under the department of Art and Culture.

Punjab

The first public library in Punjab, known as Punjab Public Library was established at Lahore in 1884. Other pioneer libraries are Dyal Singh Public Library was established at Lahore in 1896 through a trust created in the name of Dyal Singh, Sir Ganga Commercial Public Library established in 1923, and Dwarka Das Public Library at Lahore in 1921.

Pioneer Municipality Libraries in the state were established in Ludhiana in 1878, Lahore in 1884, Patiala in 1897, Amritsar in 1900, Kapurthala in 1904, and Sangrur in 1912. There are 2 State Central Libraries at Chandigarh and Patiala, 14 District Libraries, and 97 Municipal Libraries. Dr. A.C.Wooner founded the Punjab Library Association in 1915 at Lahore. The Association organize training, seminar, conferences and also publish some library literatures.

Sikkim

Sikkim public libraries came into existence under the influence of academic libraries in the state. After 1975 the Government of Sikkim realised the importance of public libraries and has started a few libraries but public libraries have not made much progress in a systematic way. All the four districts have a separate District Library at the district headquarters. These libraries were controlled, supervise and administered by the Cultural Department of the Government of Sikkim.

Tripura

From the nucleus of "Ujjayanta Palace Library", the then Maharaja Birchandra Manikya established a library in the Royal Palace in the year 1896 in Agartala was called as "Birchandra Library" and declared open to the public. This library was taken over by the government in 1953 and named as Birchandra Public Library and from 1977; it was designated as a State Central Library and renamed as Birchandra State Central Library.

Libraries are look after by the Government of Higher and Technical Education and at present the position of public library in Tripura is–1 State Central Library, 3 District Libraries, 7 Sub-Divisional Libraries, 10 Block Level Public Libraries, 2 Rural Libraries, and 1 Children Library. The departments of Social Education and Panchayat Raj also run some public libraries in the state.

Uttar Pradesh

Uttaranchal state came into existence on 9 November 2000 separating some areas from the state of Uttar Pradesh. Some libraries were established in the early days, such as, Raza Library, Rampur in 1750, Allahabad Public Library, Allahabad in 1763, Maulana Azad Library, Aligarh in 1877, Bharati Bhawan Library, Allahabad in 1889 and Lyall Library, Aligarh in 1899. The state has a State Central Library at Allhabad, 69 District level libraries, 62 other prominent public libraries run by voluntary organizations..

Andaman and Nicobar Island

Andaman and Nicobar Island, one of the Union Territories of India, have never experienced the services of libraries until a small library was set up in the cellular jail in the early 1930s. The prisoners were allowed to read books, newspapers and magazines in this library. The Government took initiatives in establishing school libraries. In 1957 an Information Centre was set up at Port Blair. In 1964, this Information Centre was converted into District Library and later on considering the public interest the District Library was enlarged and reorganized into the State Library in 1977. Library service is under the Department of Education and financed by the Andaman and Nicobar Administration and the department came forward with an idea of spreading education through the libraries. At present, there is 1 State Central library, 1 State Library, 2 District Libraries, 12 Zonal Libraries, and 3 Public Libraries..

Dadra and Nagar Haveli

In the Union Territory of Dadra and Nagar Haveli, there is a State Central Library at the capital city Silvasa and Public Library, known as Central Libariy at Naroli, Kanvel, Randha, Kilvani, Dapido, Amoli, Dushni and Mandoni. The Central Library at Silvasa and Naroli were established in 1954 and 1965 respectively.

Central Libraries at Silvasa, Dadra and Kanvel are functio-ning in their own buildings whereas the remaining libraries were in a rented building and primary schools. There are no public libraries run by voluntary organizations in this Union Territory. The library services were under the control and supervision of the Director of Education..

Daman and Diu

The Assistant Director of Education under the control of the Department of Education supervises library services in the Union Territory of Daman and Diu. There are 3 Municipal Libraries at Moti Daman, Nani Daman, and Diu. Establishment of a Central library, 2 District libraries, and 1 Mobile Library is under consideration..

Lakshadweep

There was no library service in this Union Territory before independence. The first public library was established at Karavati in 1951. However, the island has the apex library of this Union Territory established in 1958 as Freedom Fighters Central Library, which was subsequently named as Lakshadweep Central Library.

It has well organized public library system in which Lakshadweep Central Library serves as the State Central Library and each of the ten constituent inhabited islands Androtti, Amini, Agatti, Bitta, Chetlat, Kadmat, Kalpeni, Karavatti, Kilton, and Minicoy is provided with a public library by the Administration of Lakshadweep. These libraries were earlier known as Reading Room-cum-Library.

Library services are looked after by a Library Development Officer who performs the supervision function under the overall control of the Director of Social Welfare and Culture. To develop and sustain library movement, the administration has constituted a state level committee known as 'Lakshadweep State Library Committee' in 1994 comprising 10 members including Library Development..

Pondicherry

The history of Library in Pondicherry began with the establishment of a '*Bibliotheque Publique*' in 1827 with a modest stock of books collected from several Government establishments functioning in this region. The British Indian Government also donated some books to this library from time to time. It was renamed as '*Romain Rolland Library*' in 1967 after the French scholar Romain Rolland. The General Assembly, in 1892, authorized the opening of the library at Karaikal and constituted a Commission to advise the administration on measures to be taken for the development of the Library.

The Library was originally named as '*Bibliotheque Coloniale*'. This library was renamed as '*Bibliotheque Publique*' in 1952 and subsequently categorized as Regional Library and called as Government Public Library. The first library was actually started by the 'Association of Old Students' in 1918 at Mahe. The Old Boys Association donated all the books and furniture of Mahe Public Library. In 1964, the Union Territory Administration has evolved a policy of opening Branch Libraries at rural areas of the territory and the number of Branch Libraries opened in four regions are, 46 in Pondicherry region, 14 in Karaikal region, 3 in Mahe region, and 2 in Yanam region. The Director of Education from 1954 to 1991 controlled the library services. Since 1991,

Director of Art and Culture is the head of the Library services. There are three Assistant Library and Information Officers to look after the library services under the Director of Art and Culture..

National Capital Territory of New Delhi

Before the independence, Delhi was very poor in library services, particularly in public libraries, due to political structures, lack of educational facilities, and attitude of the authorities. Harding Library was established in 1862 and housed in a portion of the Town Hall.

In 1942, Delhi Municipal Committee changed the name of the library to the Harding Municipal Public Library, which was further rechristened in 1970 as the Hardayal Municipal Public Library after the famous freedom fighter and intellectual Lala Hardayal. The British Council Library and American Information resource Centre are also being developed for the public and function with the latest technology which enrich public library services in Delhi. Marwari Seth Kedar Nath Goenka in the Chandi Chawk area of Delhi set up the Marwari Library, the first of any type founded through community awareness in Modern India, in 1915.

Under the UNESCO's Pilot Project, the Ministry of Education, Government of India, founded Delhi Public Library in 1951. It was very much developed and became one of the depository libraries in India. The Delhi Public Library consists of the Central Library, Zonal Libraries, Branch Libraries, and Sub-Branch Libraries in addition to the Community libraries, Resettlement Colonies libraries, Sports libraries, and an adequately good network of Mobile Library Services to link up the remote urban and rural areas spread over the Union Territory of Delhi.

CONTRIBUTION OF RAJA RAMMOHUN ROY LIBRARY FOUNDATION

1972 was a significant year in the history of library movement in India. The country was celebrating the silver jubilee of its independence from the British Administration in 1972. Coincidentally it was an International Book Year with the slogan of 'Books For All' emphasizing promotion of reading habits among the masses. Not only that, it was the auspicious occasion of the bicentennial birth anniversary of an Indian social reformer, who stressed the need of modern education for the development of the nation.

In this august year, Raja Rammohun Roy Library came into being in May 1972. It is the nodal agency of Government of India to support public library services and systems and promote public library movement in the country. Raja Rammohun Roy Library Foundation is an autonomous organization, established and sponsored by the Department of Culture, Government of India. It is registered under the West Bengal Societies Registration Act, 1961. Its headquarters is located at Kolkata. In view of the expanding activities, the

Foundation has opened zonal offices under the Assistant Field Officers for monitoring the impact and implementation of the assistance rendered by the Foundation such as-Eastern Zonal Office at Calcutta; Northern Zonal Office at New Delhi; Southern Zonal Office at Chennai and Western Zonal Office at Mumbai.

Objectives

Raja Rammohun Roy Library Foundation is a national agency for the promotion of library services in general and public library services in particular. The main objective of the Foundation is to promote and support public library movement in the country by providing adequate library services and by developing reading habits all over the country with the active cooperation of State Government and Union Territories and of Voluntary Organizations operating in the filed of library services, cultural activities, adult education and the like.

Objectives of the Foundation may be listed as below:

- To promote library movement in the country;
- To enunciate a national library policy and to help build up a national library system;
- To provide financial and technical assistance to libraries;
- To provide financial assistance to organizations, regional or national engaged in the promotion of library development;
- To publish appropriate literature and to act as a clearing house of ideas and information on library development in India and abroad;
- To promote research in problems of library development;
- To advise the government on all matters pertaining to the library development in the country; and
- To propagate the adoption of library legislation in the country.

Assistance Programme

The Foundation promotes public library services rendering book and financial assistance to the public libraries under different schemes of assistance. The scheme of assistance is of two types, *viz.*, Matching and Non-Matching schemes.

Matching Schemes

Assistance under Matching Scheme is given from the resources shared on matching basis with the States/Union Territory Administrations on the basis of developed states 50;50; developing and lagging states 60;40 and North-Eastern States 90;10. This revised matching scheme is effective from 2005.

The Matching assistance can be given to achieve its main objectives for:

- Assistance towards building up of adequate stock of books and reading materials.

- Assistance towards development of rural book deposit centers and mobile library services.
- Assistance towards organization of seminars, workshops, training courses and book exhibition.
- Assistance towards storage and display of books including reading room furniture.
- Assistance to public libraries below district level for increasing accommodation.
- Assistance to public libraries below State Central Libraries to acquire TVcum-VCP sets for educational purposes/Computer for library application.
- Assistance towards Networking of Public Libraries.

Non-Matching Schemes

The Foundation fully gives assistance under this scheme from his own resources to implement its objectives for:

- Assistance towards building up of adequate stock of books through central selection.
- Assistance to voluntary organizations providing public library Services
- Assistance to children libraries or children's section of general public libraries including women section and senior citizen section.
- Assistance to public libraries towards celebration of 50 years, 100 years and 125 years.
- Assistance towards collection and compilation of library statistics through official and non-official agencies.
- Assistance to centrally sponsored libraries.
- Assistance towards organization of seminars/conferences by national level library organizations.
- Assistance towards establishment of children's corner.

Promotion of* District Youth Resource Centres *(DYRCs)

The development of DYRCs is being made commensurate with the decision of the inter Ministerial Steering Committee constitutes for the purpose with the representative from Ministry of Sports and Youth Affairs, Ministry of Culture, Raja Rammohun Roy Library foundation and Nehru Yuvak Kendra Sanghatana.

The DYRCs are assisted for the following purpose:

- Towards building up adequate stock of books.
- Towards acquiring storage materials and library furniture.
- Towards construction of library building.
- Towards acquisition of computers with accessories.

Promotional Activities

RRRLF has undertaken a number of promotional activities for qualitative improvement of library services. It is associated and interacts with different national and international library professional associations like IFLA, ILA, IASLIC and different state level library associations.

Some of the promotional activities taken up by the Foundation for the qualitative improvement of library services may be given as below:

- It organizes seminars and conferences on the topics related to the development of public libraries in India.
- It plays a major role in the preparation of National Policy on Library and Information Systems and also issued guidelines on public library systems and services.
- It instituted 'RRRLF Fellowship' to eminent men and women in the field of library services who have contributed significantly to the library movement particularly, public library movement in the country through active involvement in the movement, organizational initiative, intellectual leadership or are dedicated to the propagation of the reading habit among the mass. Fellowship carries a cash award of ₹25, 000/-besides a plaque and a citation detailing the services rendered by the Fellow in the country.
- 'RRRLF Best Library Award' for the Best State Central Library in India. The Award carries a Citation and a cash incentive of ₹1 lakh.
- 'RRRLF Best District Library Award' in each of the six regions. The Award carries a Citation and cash incentive of ₹50,000/-.
- The Foundation instituted 'RRRLF Best Rural Library Awards' one for each state since 2005.
- 'Raja Rammohun Roy Award' was introduced annually to the best contributor of an article covering the area of development of Public Library Systems and Services or suggesting measures for the promotion of reading habits.

Research Cell and Special Library

A research cell along with a special library on Library and Information Science and statistics unit supported by a computer unit are providing necessary input to its various activities. About 5000 important books and journals on Library and Information Science and allied fields have been acquired in the library.

Besides carrying on Research Projects on public library or allied subject, the Research Cell renders advisory and consultancy services whenever required. It has prepared and published a report on loss of books in libraries for the Government of India.

Publications

The Foundation has brought out many useful publications for the promotion and development of public library services in the country.

Some of its significant publications are;

- Indian Libraries; Trends and Perspectives
- Raja Rammohun Roy and the New Learning
- Directory of Indian Public Libraries
- RRRLF Newsletter
- Granthana-Indian Journal of Library Studies
- Annual Report
- Books for the Millions at their Doorsteps..

Modernization Programme

The Foundation is taking steps to meet the new technologies of information for the promotion of library services. It has a Computer Section for building-up data bank of Public Libraries for the country. This section is planned to give information storage, retrieval and data processing support for all the application areas. It has keen interest with enthusiasm to computerized state libraries in India. It gave computers to the state and district libraries to carry out Foundations' zeal to computerize such libraries. The work is going on to computerized shortly.

NATIONAL POLICY ON LIBRARY AND INFORMATION SYSTEM

John Martin said, "Policy is a statement of a specific goal or goals which are to be achieved, or to be pursued; a statement of the means by which realization of the goals will be brought about; an assignment of the responsibilities for implementation of the means, and a set of rules or guidelines regulating the activity". National Policy on Library and Information Science is to "provide a framework for properly planned and co-coordinated development of library and information structure in a country, resulting thereby in an enhanced and user-oriented information services to its user population".

The need for the formulation of National Policy on Library and Information Systems was brought to the notice of the Government of India by Indian library profession since 1950s by Dr. S.R.Ranganathan and in the recommendations of the Library Advisory Committee Report, 1958. Afterwards, professional organizations, like RRRLF, NISSAT and National Library urged upon the Government the necessity of enunciating such policy. The matter was discussed in the annual conference of IASLIC in 1979 at Roorkee and ILA in 1984 at Jaipur. Consequently, Indian Library Association submitted a draft policy statement to the Government in 1985. The Planning Commission Working Group in its report *Modernization of Library Services and Informatics for the 7th Five-Year Plan* emphasized the need of such policy.

The Raja Rammohun Roy Foundation, after nine years of its inception, took up the task in 1981 and after careful deliberations submitted a Draft National policy on Library and Information Systems to the government in July 1984.

On the basis of the draft policy submitted by the Raja Rammohun Roy Library Foundation and Indian Library Association, the Government of India, Ministry of Human resources Development, Department of Culture, set up a Committee in October 1985 under the Chairmanship of Professor D.P.Chattopadhyaya for the formulation of a National Policy on Library and Information Systems and the final report was submitted in May 1986 which includes:

- The Public Library system;
- The Academic Library System;
- Special Libraries and Information Systems;
- The National Library System and the Bibliographical Services;
- Manpower Development and Professional Status; and
- Modernization of Library and Information Systems.

Though the government has not adopted the recommen-dations as the official policy, but it serves as suggestive model for the development of libraries as a whole.

The recommendations under the Public Library System are as follows:

- The most important task before the government is to establish, maintain and strengthen the free public libraries in the country and enable them to work as a system.
- The main thrust in this area should go to the rural public library. A village or a village cluster with an adequate population should have a community library, which will also serve as an information center. Resources of different agencies engaged in the work of public health, adult education, local selfgovernment and such others may be pooled to build up this composite center.
- An important link should be established between the community library of the village and the village primary school. If the school does not have a library of its own, the community library should provide the children with an adequate book-corner.
- The community library should also importantly cater for adult education and make adequate audio-visual aids available to attract the illiterate villagers.
- The district library should serve as an apex library for each district with public libraries at city, town and village levels constituting important components in the district library system. In addition to

the usual services to be rendered by it, it should also provide for learning facilities and recreation for the handicapped. Wherever possible, district libraries and comparable city public libraries should provide literature in Braille. The district library and branch libraries should also arrange mobile and circulating library services within its area wherever it is necessary and feasible. Special services should be rendered to hospitals, prisons, and the infirm in their homes.

- Libraries for special groups should be built in areas of tribal concentration or minority communities to develop their distinctive cultures. The government will provide all encouragement for such communities to develop their own libraries through voluntary effort.
- Each public library should have a section for children and, in addition, separate libraries for children with attractive books and audio-visual supporting materials should be established wherever possible.
- The district library will take the leadership in establishing linkages between all other public libraries of the district and work towards resource sharing within the area.
- The key role of public libraries as chief sustaining agencies of distance education should be recognized and they should be adequately equipped with the relevant resources for this purpose.
- All the libraries within a state should form part of a network extending from the community library of the village through intermediary levels to the district and to the State Central Library. This State network should eventually connect with the national level.
- The role of the State Central Library is crucial in networking and the establishment of uniform library procedures within the States. The State Central Library/Directorate of Public Libraries has to perform as the coordinating agency for public libraries in the State.
- To bring about the development of the public libraries in a State it is vital that each State enact its own library legislation. The Central Government should revise the Model Public Library Bill, which it has already prepared, in the light of experience gained in recent years and urge upon the States the importance of enacting such legislation. Finances for library development should be found by each State either from its general revenues or from local taxation.
- The Central Government should assist the State in the development of public libraries in a larger way than it has done so far. The Raja Rammohun Roy Library Foundation as the national agency for co-coordinating and assisting the development of public libraries be suitably strengthened enabling it to discharge its responsibilities effectively.

NATIONAL KNOWLEDGE COMMISSION

National Knowledge Commission was set up by the Prime Minister of India, Manmohan Singh to prepare a blueprint to tap into the enormous reservoir of our knowledge base so that our people can confidently face challenges of the 21st. Century. The Commission has a designated time frame of three years from 2nd. October 2005 to 2nd. October 2008.

The Commissions' Terms of References are:

- Build excellence in the educational system to meet the knowledge challenges of the 21st. century and increase India's competitive advantage in fields of knowledge.
- Promote creation of knowledge in Science and Technology laboratories.
- Improve the management of institutions engaged in Intellectual Property Rights.
- Promote knowledge applications in Agriculture and Industry.
- Promote the use of knowledge capabilities in making government an effective, transparent and accountable service provider to the citizen and promote widespread sharing of knowledge to maximize public benefit.

The Commission headed by Mr. Sam Pitroda as its Chairman and there are other 5 members, who are renowned persons in different fields of knowledge. It is a high-level advisory body to the Prime Minister of India, with a mandate to guide policy and generate reforms. The Commission is the world's first body of its kind.

The prime focus of the Commission is on five key areas of the knowledge paradigm, such as:

- Access
  - Literacy
  - Language
  - Translation
  - Libraries
  - Networks
  - Portals
- Concepts
  - School Education
  - Vocational Education
  - Higher Education
  - Medical Education
  - Legal Education
  - Management Education
  - Engineering Education
  - Open and Distance Education

- Creation
  - Science and Technology
  - Intellectual Property Rights
  - Innovation
  - Entrepreneurship
- Application
  - Traditional knowledge
  - Agriculture
- Services
  - E-governance

Besides the Working Group on Libraries, other four Committees were set up with specialists and professionals in different areas of Libraries under the Chairmanship of Mrs. Kalpana Dasgupta.

Such Committees are:

- Committee on database creation and networking;
- Committee on private collections;
- Committee to set standards and modalities for collection development, systems and services;
- Committee on staffing pattern and staff requirement of libraries.

Terms of References of the Working Group on Libraries are given below:

- To redefine the objectives of the country's Library and Information Service sector;
- To identify constraints, problems and challenges relating to the sector;
- To recommend changes and reforms to address the problems and challenges to ensure a holistic development of information services in all areas of national activity;
- To take necessary steps to mobilize and upgrade the existing library and information systems and services, taking advantage of the latest advances in Information Community Technology;
- To explore possibilities for innovation and initiate new programmes relevant to our national needs, especially to bridge the gap between the information rich and the information poor within society;
- To suggest means of raising standards and promoting excellence in Library and Information Science education including re-orientation and training of working professionals;
- To assist in setting up facilities to preserve and access to indigenous knowledge and the nation's cultural heritage;
- To set up adequate mechanisms to monitor activities for securing the benefits of acquisition and application of knowledge for the people of India;
- To examine any other issues that may be relevant in this context..

The Notional Knowledge Commission's Working Group on Libraries, after consultations of more than 20 state representatives and NGOs and many more interest groups and professionals in the field, ready its first recommendations for submission to the nation.

Moreover, the Commission submitted its first recommendations to the Prime Minister in December 2006 on the following areas:

- Libraries
- Translation
- Language
- Knowledge Networks
- Right to Education
- Vocational education
- Higher Education
- National Science and Social science Foundation
- E-governance.

The Commission argued Libraries as Gateways to knowledge and continued that a "Library is not a building stacked with books-it is a repository and source of information and ideas, a place for learning and enquiry, and for the generation of thought and the creation of new knowledge. Public libraries in particular have the potential to bridge the gap between the 'information poor' and the 'information rich' by ensuing that people from all sectors and settings of society and the community across India have easy access to knowledge seek".. The Commission clearly incorporated roadmap for the execution of its recommendations on libraries under different points of consideration. It gave a Library Charter that is incorporated below.

Recognising that the library's objectives are to:

- Disseminate knowledge as widely as possible;
- Serve as a major vehicle to facilitate creation of new knowledge;
- Facilitate optimal use of knowledge by all sectors, such a government, industry, rural sector and civil society;
- Ensure that people from all sectors and all parts of the country have easy access to knowledge relevant to their needs, in their own language.

The library undertakes to:

- Serve as local center of information and a gateway to national and global knowledge providing fair access to knowledge and information to as many as users as possible;
- Offer an inviting and attractive physical space with clean drinking water and toilet facilities;
- Offer proactive services to its user communities;
- Ensure that users are treated with courtesy and respect by library staff;

- Pay attention to the needs of children, women, senior citizens and the physically challenged;
- Optimize its potential to provide access to information and knowledge to all;
- Help users developed information skills to make optimum use of resources;
- Improve its collections and services on continuing basis in consultation with users;
- To work more effectively and efficiently by undertaking every activity in a professional manner;
- To bridge the gap between the information poor and the information rich.

The Commission is organizing discussion forum at different areas for the preparation of its final report, which is expected to be submit to the nation within its stipulated time.

LIBRARY ASSOCIATIONS

The term 'association' is used to denote a group or body of individuals or institutions associated with a common purpose revolving generally for the two main purposes, viz.,:

- Advancement of the service oriented goals of the association, and
- Protection of the interests of the members.

Association may be of different kinds with different objectives and categories, professional or non-professional. However, by considering its nature, Pandey S.K.Sharma defined library associations as 'a group or body of libraries or librarians and users of libraries formed with the common purpose of advancement of library profession including service and also for protection of interests of the members including raising their capabilities to serve more effectively'.

There are more than seventy professional organizations and associations at state level in India. William A Borden went to Baroda in 1910 at the invitation of Maharaja Sayajirao Gaekwar of Baroda and organized the first professional organization of librarians in the country, the Baroda Library Club in 1912. Other professional associations came up afterwards and some of the national level associations worth to be mentioned for their contributions in public library developments in the country.

NATIONAL LIBRARY OF INDIA

The National Library of India at Belvedere, Kolkata, is the largest library in India by volume and India's library of public record. It is under the Department of Culture, Ministry of Tourism and Culture, Government of India. The library is designated to collect, disseminate and preserve the printed material produced in India. The library is situated on the scenic 30 acre Belvedere Estate, in Kolkata. The Library is the largest in India, with a collection in excess of 2.2 million books.

AIMS

- Acquisition and conservation of all significant national production of printed material, excluding ephemera.
- Collection of printed material concerning the country, no matter where it is published, and as a corollary, the acquisition of photographic records of such material that is not available with in the country
- Acquisition and conservation of foreign material required by the country.
- Rendering of bibliographical and documents services of current and retrospective material, both general and specialised.
- Acting as a referral centre purveying full and accurate knowledge.

HISTORY

The Calcutta Public Library

The history of the National Library began with the formation of Calcutta Public Library in 1836. That was a non-governmental institution and was run on a proprietary basis. People contributing ₹300 in subscription became the proprietors. Prince Dwarkanath Tagore was the first proprietor of that Library. ₹300 at that time was a significant amount, so poor students and others were allowed free use the library for some period of time. Lord Metcalfe, the Governor General at that time, transferred 4,675 volumes from the library of the College of Fort William, Calcutta to the Calcutta Public Library. This and donations of books from individuals formed the nucleus of the library. Both Indian and foreign books, especially British, were purchased for the library. Donations were regularly made by individuals as well as by the government.

The Calcutta Public Library had a unique position as the first public library in this part of the world. Such a well-organized and efficiently run library was rare even in Europe during the first half of the 19th century. Because of the efforts of the Calcutta Public Library, the present National Library has many extremely rare books and journals in its collection.

The Imperial Library

Built after the model of the Town Hall at Ypres. A fine example of the Public Buildings in Calcutta.The Imperial Library was formed in 1891 by combining a number of Secretariat libraries in Calcutta. Of those, the most important and interesting was the library of the Home Department, which contained many books formerly belonging to the library of East India College, Fort William and the library of the East India Board in London. But the use of the library was restricted to the superior officers of the Government.

Amalgamation of the Calcutta Public Library and Imperial Library

In 1903, Lord Curzon, the Governor-General of India, conceived the idea of opening a library for the use of the public. He noticed both the libraries—Imperial Library and Calcutta Public Library were under-utilized because of limited access and lack of amenities. He decided to amalgamate the rich collection of both of these libraries. The new amalgamated library, called Imperial Library, was formally opened to the public on January 30, 1903 at Metcalfe Hall, Kolkata.

Metcalfe Hall had earlier been the residence of the Governor-Generals Wellington, Cornwallis and Warren Hastings:

- "It is intended that it should be a library of reference, a working place for students and a repository of material for the future historians of India, in which, so far as possible, every work written about India, at any time, can be seen and read."—*The Gazette of India*

Declaring the Imperial Library as the National Library

After Independence the Government of India changed the name of the Imperial Library to the National Library, with the enactment of the Imperial Library Act, 1948, and the collection was shifted from the Esplanade to the present Belvedere Estate. On February 1, 1953, the National Library was opened to the public, inaugurated by Maulana Abul Kalam Azad. B. S. Kesavan was appointed the first Librarian of the National Library.

Discovery of Hidden Chamber

In 2010, the Ministry of Culture, the owner of the library, decided to get the library building restored by the *Archaeological Survey of India* (ASI). While taking stock of the library building, the conservation engineers discovered a previously unknown room. The ground-floor room, about 1000 sq. ft. in size, seems to have no opening of any kind. The ASI archaeologists tried to search the first floor area for a trap door, but found nothing.

Since the building is of historical and cultural importance, ASI decided to bore a hole through the wall instead of breaking it. There was speculations about the room being a punishment room used by Warren Hastings and other British officials, or a place to store treasure. After six months of study, it was determined to be not a room at all, but merely "a block stuffed with mud, perhaps constructed by the British architects to strengthen the base of the building."

COLLECTION

Indian Languages Collection

The National Library receives books and periodicals in almost all Indian languages. These are received under the Delivery of Books and Newspapers Act 1954. Language divisions acquire, process and provide reading materials in all major Indian languages. Hindi, Kashmiri, Punjabi, Sindhi, Telugu and Urdu language divisions maintain their own stacks. Other language books are stacked in the Stack division.

Language divisions are also responsible for answering reference queries. The library has separate Indian language divisions for Assamese, Bengali, Gujarati, Hindi, Kannada, Kashmiri, Malayalam, Marathi, Oriya, Punjabi, Sanskrit, Sindhi, Tamil, Telugu and Urdu. Sanskrit language division also collects and processes Pali and Prakrit books. English books published in India are collected under D.B. Act.

Assamese Language Collection

In1963, a separate division was established in the National Library to collect and process Assamese books. At present the division has 12,000 books. This collection has some works published between 1840 and 1900. Some of the important publications are Asamiya Larar Mitra by Anandaram Dhekiyal Phukan, Larabodh Byakaran by Dharmeswar Goswami, Prakrit Bhugol by Lambodara Datta and several volumes of Sri Sankardev's Kirattan, Gunamala, Srimad Bhagavad, Bargit, Rukmini Haran Nat, and Ankiyanat. Volumes of the periodical Arunodoi are also available in the collection.

Bengali Language Collection

The library has 85,000 books in its Bengali collection. The collection contains very rare and valuable books as well as periodicals published from the last quarter of the 18th century. Early Bengali plays and novels are well represented. The collection has many rare items such as the manuscripts of Sarat Chandra Chattopadhaya, Bibuti Bhushan Bandao-padhaya, Jibanananda Das and Bisnu De.

154 letters of Netaji Subhas Chandra Bose written to his nephew Sri Asok Nath Bose and letters to Sarat Chandra Bose are also available in the collection. The collection has the complete set of Rabindranath Tagore's works, except a few of his early works. This includes 190 first editions of Tagore's works.

Some of the rare and important works in this collection are: A Grammar of the Bengal Language by Nathaniel Brassey Halhed, which is the earliest printed book in Bengali, Henry Forster's A Vocabulary in Two parts, English and Bangalee, William Carrey's Dialogues, Intended to Facilitate the Acquiring of the Bengali Language, Ram Ram Basu's Raja Pratapaditya Charitra, Mrityunjay Vidyalankar's Batris Simhansan, Ramayana translated by Krittibas and published in five volumes, Mahabharat translated by Kashi Ram Das, Chandicharan Munshi's Tota Itihas, Jayanarayan Ghosal's Sri Karunanidhanavilasa, William Carey's Dictionary of the Bengali Language, 2 volumes. There are 400 titles of Bengali periodicals including many rare 19th century periodicals such as Digdarshan first Bengali monthly and the first issue of Samachar Darpan—the first Bengali weekly.

Gujarati Language Collection

The library has 37,000 Gujarati books. 1100 of them are titles published prior to 1900. This collection also has 30 albums of paintings by Kanu Desai published between 1936 and 1956. Ancient Jaina miniature paintings are well reproduced in Sri Jaina Chitravali, Sri Jaina Chitra Patavali and other valuable books edited by Sarabhai Nawab.

The authentic editions of the poetic works of medieval Gujarati poets such as Narsinh Meheta, Mirabai, Premanand and Symal Bhat are also part of the holdings. The rare titles include Robert Drummond's Illustrations of Grammatical Parts Guzerattee, Maratta and English Languages, translations of Aesop's Fables by Bapushastri Pandya Raykaval, Edalji Patel's Suratani Tavarikh and Jnana Chakra—a Gujarati encyclopaedia in 9 volumes.

Hindi Language Division

Hindi is one of the official languages of India. The collection building of Hindi books has been continuing since the time of the Imperial Library, and a separate division was established in 1960. At present 80,000 Hindi books are in the library collection. The collection has rare works published during the last decades of the 18th Century. Many of the publications published by Lulloo Lal, the first printer, publisher and writer of Kolkata, are represented in this collection.

The following rare books published by Lulloo Lal are in the library: Braja Bhasha Grammar, Lataife Hindi, Rajaniti, and Prem Sagur. In addition, the library has The Oriental Linguist with an Extensive Vocabulary English and Hindoostanee and Hindoostanee and English by John B. Gilchrist, Hindi-Roman Orthoepigraphical Ultimatum by John B. Gilchrist, Rajneeti by Narayana Pandit, Sudamacaritra by Haldhara Dasa, Raga Kalpadruma, Baital Pachisi by Duncan Forbes, Dictionary of Hindee and English by J. T. Thompson, Yavan Bhasa ka Vyakaran by Hooper William, Siva Simha Saroja by Siva Simha Senagar, Hindi Pradipa edited by Balkrishna Bhatt, Brief Account of the Solar System in Hindi, and a microfilm copy of Bal Bodhini—a monthly journal for women edited by Bharatendu Harischandra. There are also about 1200 rare first issues of important journals.

Kannada Language Collection

A separate Kannada division was set up in 1963 in the National Library.

In 1960, the library purchased the personal collection of H. Channakeshava Ayyangar. It consists of 1300 books published between the last two decades of the 19th century and the first three decades of the 20th century. An important contribution towards building the collection was the efforts of G. P. Rajaratnam, a noted Kannada author.

Immediately after the enactment of the D.B. Act, Rajaratnam toured the erstwhile Mysore state to create awareness among the publishers about the Act. He collected about 1500 books without any expense to the library. The Kannada collection in the library is particularly useful for the study of the cultural history of Karnataka. At present there are 32,000 Kannada books in the library.

Kashmiri Language Collection

The Kashmiri division was formed in 1983. Currently the library has 500 Kashmiri books. Some of the important items in this collection are Muhammad Yusuf Teng's Shirin Qalm, Wiyur edited by Ghulam Muhammad Rafiq, Ghulam Nabi Khyal's Akah Nandun, Nurnama and compiled by Muhammad Amin Kaim, Fazil and Kashmiri's Krishna Lila.

Malayalam Language Collection

The Malayalam division was established as a separate division in 1963, with around 5000 books. Now the collection has 34,500 books. The earliest printed book, Centum Adagia Malabarica, a Latin translation of Malayalam proverbs, dates back to 1791. The Latin translations are printed alongside the Malayalam originals.

Rare and old books include Robert Drummond's Grammar of the Malabar Language, Dr Gundart's Malayalam-English Dictionary Vartamanapu-stakam by Parammachkal Govarnno-doracchan, Appu Nedungadi's Kundalata and Chantu Menan's Indulekha. Apart from these, many works representing earlier periods are part of this collection. A few of these are Ramacaritam, works of Niranam, Cerussery's Krishnagatha, Vatakkan Pattukal, Ezuttachan's Adhyatama Ramayana, Ramaprattu Variyar's Kucelavrtam, and Kuncan Nampyar's Tullol.

Marathi Language Collection

The Marathi division was established in 1963 with a collection of 8900 volumes. The division now has 37,000 books in its collection. In 1954 the National Library purchased the library of the Bengal Nagpur Railway Indian Institute, Kharagpur, which had a good number of Marathi books. Sir Jadunath Sarkar collection also has about 350 Marathi books, mostly on the history of the Marathas. The division has many rare and old Marathi publications. These include William Carey's A Grammar of the Mahratta Language and Dictionary of the Maharatta Language, Simhasana Battisi, Raghuji

Bhonsalyaci Vanshavali, Vans Kennedy's A Dictionary of Maratta Language, Nava Karar, A Short Account of Railways by K. Bhatwadekar, Charles Hutton's Bijaganit, Tukaram's Abhangachi Gatha edited by Vishnu Parashuram Pandit and Shankar Pandurang Pandit, Itihasaprisiddha Purushanche va Striyanche Povade edited by H. A. Acworth.

Oriya Language Collection

A separate Oriya division was established in 1973. The Imperial Library had only 133 books; later the collection was increased to 425 books. Currently, the division has 19,500 books. The oldest publication available in the Oriya collection dates back to 1831. It is Rev. Amos Sutton's Introductory Grammar of Oriya Language. Some of the other rarities in the collection are Jayadeva's Gitagovinda, translated by Dharanidhara, Amos Sutton's An Oriya Dictionary, 3 volumes, Dharmapustakara Adibhaya, and Purnacandra Odiabhasa Kosh, a lexicon of the Oriya language compiled by Gopalachandra Praharaj.

Punjabi Language Collection

A separate division for the acquisition and processing of Punjabi language books was established in 1974. Most of the works in this collection are of recent origin. There are a few old and rare Punjabi books, such as William Carey's A Grammar of Punjabee Language, Samuel Starkey's A Dictionary of English Punjabee, Geographical Description of the Panjab, Bhai Santosh Singh's Guru Paratap Suraj Granthavali and Gurudas Bhai's Vars.

Sanskrit, Pali and Prakrit Languages Collection

Sanskrit has a rich literature in many fields of knowledge. A separate division in the library collects and processes Sanskrit books. At present the division has over 20,000 Sanskrit books, printed in the Devanagari script. Almost all Indian language divisions possess Sanskrit works printed in their respective language scripts. The library also has a rich collection of Sanskrit works edited or translated with original scripts, in English and many other foreign languages. The collection attracts scholars from India and abroad. Apart from Sanskrit, books in Pail and Prakrit languages are also collected and processed by this division. At present the library has about 500 books in Pali and a comparable collection of books in Prakrit.

Sindhi Language Collection

Since 1957, the library has been building a collection of Sindhi books. At present the library has 2100 Sindhi books. Shah Abdul Latif's Shah Jo Rasalo and Shah Jo Sher are the rare items in this collection.

Tamil Language Collection

The Tamil division was formed in 1963. The division currently has 57,000 books. Apart from this, the library has 1000 Tamil books and 300 Tamil manuscripts in the Vaiyapuri Pillai collection. There are many rare and old works among the Tamil titles. Early printed Tamil books in the library include the Tamil Bible, John Philip Fabricius's A Malabar and English Dictionary, a Tamil translation of John Bunyan's Piligrim's Progress, and Caldwell's Comparative Grammar of DravidianLlanguages. The collection also includes standard editions of five great Sangam Classics.

Telugu Language Collection

The Telugu division was started in the National Library in 1963. The collection has a good number of old Telugu books published since the earlier decades of the 19th century. Some of the rarities in Telugu available in this collection are William Carey's Grammar of Telugu Language, C.P. Brown's A Vocabulary of Gentoo and English, Vakyavali, Catalogue of Telugu books in the British Library, London compiled by L. D. Barnett.

Urdu Language Collection

Like Arabic and Persian, the Urdu collection was substantial since the days of Imperial Library. Special collections such as the Buhar Library, Hidayat Husain collection, Zakariya collection and Imambara collection have some Urdu books and manuscripts. In 1968 a separate Urdu division was set up formed in the library. At present it has more than 20,000 books. Some of the oldest are Uklakhi Hindee or Indian Ethics, and Mir Muhamad Taki's Kulliuat-e-Mir.

English Language Collection

The National Library has an invaluable collection of books in the English language, because of the systematic development by Calcutta Public Library and the Imperial Library. Way back in 1848, an attempt was made to acquire journals issued by the foreign learned institutions.

Serious works were purchased in larger numbers than light literature. The same policy has been pursued in recent times. Although the library has English books and other reading materials in almost all subjects, the collection is especially rich in the humanities, British and Indian history and literature

Foreign Languages Collections

One of the aims of the National Library is to collect all the books published on India, anywhere in the world and in any language. At the same time it collects reading materials on other subjects in different languages for the use of the country. The Imperial Library had a good number of Arabic and Persian works and a few other foreign language books. In 1985 the European Languages Division was reorganized and five separate divisions were formed. These are East Asian Languages Division, Germanic Languages Division,

Romance Languages Division, Slavonic Languages Division,West Asian and African Languages Division. The foreign language works are mainly acquired through purchase, gift and exchange. The divisions mentioned are responsible for collection development, collection organisation and information dissemination to the readers in the respective languages. They also maintain their own stacks and provide reading facilities.

East Asian Languages Collection

A separate division collects, processes and preserves Chinese and other East Asian languages. At present the collection has 15,000 Chinese books and one thousand each in Japanese, Korean, Tibetan, Nepali and Thai languages.

Germanic Languages Collection

The Germanic Languages division was formed in the library in the year 1985. The division has books in German, Dutch, Norwegian and Swedish. But the largest number of books is in German. The division has book exchange agreements with seven Germanic language-speaking countries. Berliner Zeitung, a newspaper published from former East Germany is available in this collection.

Romance Languages Collection

Romance Languages division came into existence in 1985, along with other foreign languages divisions. Although the collection includes books and other materials in languages belonging to the Romance group, the largest number of books is in French, about 5000. About 2000 Romanian and a handful of books in Italian and Spanish are also available.

Slavonic Languages Collection

The collection has books in Slavonic languages, spoken in Russia, Poland, Bulgaria, the Czech Republic, Slovakia, former Yugoslavia and other countries and peoples of the region. It deals with reading materials in 28 languages. But the largest collection is in the Russian language. At present the division has 65,000 books.

West Asian and African Languages Collection

The Buhar Library may be considered the nucleus of West Asian and African languages collection. The division has a handful of books in other West Asian languages such as Hebrew and Amharic. The largest number of books is in Persian and Arabic, approximately 12,000 in Arabic and 12,000 in Persian. The collection includes the lexicons compiled and prepared by Indians authors of the past and edited by the 'native' scholars of the College of Fort William and European orientalists of the said college. The division also holds a large numbers of historical works published under the Bibliotheca Indica series of the Asiatic Society of Bengal in the 19th century. A large number of Arabic and Persian books and manuscripts can also be found in Sir Abdur Rahim Collection, Hidayat Husain Collection, Zakaria Collection and Imambara Collection. Sir Jadunath Sarkar Collection also has 200 Persian manuscripts. These manuscripts relate mainly to the later Mughal period and the early years of British rule.

Rare Books

The National Library has an impressive number of rare books and other reading materials. In 1973, a separate Rare Books division was established. At present the books published prior to 1860 are considered rare books, along with limited and first editions, books distinguished by their design, illustration or history, and a few other criteria. Along with rare books, manuscripts and microfilms of the library are also stacked in this division. The division also provides reading facilities to the users who wish to consult these items. At present the division has 4700 monographs, 3000 manuscripts and 1500 microfilms

Manuscripts

National Library has about 3600 rare and historically important manuscripts in different languages. These manuscripts are preserved separately along with other important and rare books in the Rare Books division.

Science and Technology Collection

Following the recommendations of the Reviewing Committee, the Science and Technology division was set up in 1972. The basic function of this division is to collect and disseminate the core material in science and technology. At present the division holds about 17,000 books and monographs and 800 current print periodicals. The division provides reading facilities and has an open access stack system.

Indian Official Documents

All the publications of Government of India, State Governments, Union Territories, Government Undertakings, Autonomous Bodies are collected, processed and preserved separately. A separate division for this purpose was established in 1972. The library owns a rich collection of Indian official documents from the days of the East India Company to the present.

The collection also includes the documents published by the Government of Great Britain relating to India. A good collection of Myanmarese documents and few documents of Aden, Sri Lanka, Persian Gulf Political Residency are also part of this collection. At present, the division holds around 4,90,000 documents.

Foreign Official Documents

The National Library is one of the repository libraries for United Nations Organisation and its agencies. Thus all the publications of UNO and its agencies are received by the library free of cost. These documents are processed and stacked separately. The library also receives publications of the governments of the United States of America, Great Britain, Canada, the Commonwealth nations, and the publications of the European Economic Committee. Almost all the volumes of the sessional sets of British Parliamentary papers since the beginning of the 19th century are available. Apart from the depositary copies, the library acquires selected foreign publications through purchase. At present the library has around 400,000 foreign official documents.

Newspapers and Periodicals

All the newspapers and periodicals in Indian languages are received and processed in their respective language divisions. But English newspapers and periodicals, both the Indian and foreign, are acquired and processed separately. A separate Serials division is responsible for acquiring and processing of English newspapers and periodicals. The library has a rich collection of late 19th and early 20th century newspapers and periodicals, but almost all of them are incomplete sets. There are catalogues for periodicals, newspapers and gazettes available in the library up to 1953.

Maps and Prints

The library has an extensive collection of maps from the 17th century onwards. Indian topographical sheets of earlier days and maps of natural resources, population, transport and communication systems, agricultural production, soil, vegetation and the geology of India form the major part of the collection. At present the library has 85,000 printed maps, 54 cartographic manuscripts, and 280 atlases

Microforms

The library has around 500 rolls of Microfilms and 1000 Microfiches. These are preserved in the Rare Books division. The Census of India is one of the most important and rare document available in the form of Microfiches...

CONSERVATION ACTIVITIES

One of the basic functions of the National Library is to conserve the printed heritage for future generations.

For this purpose the library has separate divisions for physical, chemical, reprographic and digital conservation:

- *Physical Conservation*: Books damaged by human error or by natural causes are mended, repaired and bound in the Binding division. Journals are bound by volume.

- *Chemical Conservation*: The Laboratory division of the library, established in 1968, is taking care of the chemical treatment of books. Advanced procedures of chemical treatment are adopted to restore brittle and damaged books. The library is in the process of developing non-chemical treatment system for the preservation of printed materials. An indigenously developed fumigation chamber is being used to destroy the eggs and larvae of insects and termites. Encapsulation is another method of preservation that has been developed by the library.
- *Reprographic Preservation*: Most of the 19th century newspapers, Arabic, Persian and Sanskrit manuscripts have already been microfilmed. 5000 rolls of microfilms are already produced so far by the Reprography division.
- *Digitisation*: The scanning and archiving of rare and brittle books and other documents on compact disc has started. English books and documents published before 1900 and Indian publications preceding 1920 are considered for digitisation. 9140 selected books in Indian and English languages have already been scanned and stored—a total of over 3.2 million pages.

ACADEMIC LIBRARY

An academic library is a library that is attached to academic institutions above the secondary level, serving the teaching and research needs of students and staff. These libraries serve two complementary purposes: to support the school's curriculum, and to support the research of the university faculty and students. The support of teaching requires material for class readings and for student papers. In the past, the material for class readings, intended to supplement lectures as prescribed by the instructor, has been called reserves.

In the period before electronic resources became available, the reserves were supplied as actual books or as photocopies of appropriate journal articles. Traditionally, one copy of a book was made available for each 10 students—this is practical for large classes only if paperback copies are available, and the books reused from term to term.

Academic libraries must decide what focus they take in collecting materials since no single library can supply everything. When there are particular areas of specialization in academic libraries these are often referred to as niche collections. These collections are often the basis of a special collection department and may include original papers, artwork, and artifacts written or created by a single author or about a specific subject.

ACADEMIC LIBRARIES IN INDIA: A PRESENT-DAY SCENARIO

Education aims to impart knowledge and makes good citizens. Libraries are the repositories of knowledge and form an integral part of education.

Libraries have a long history, starting with the chained and closed-access libraries of earlier times to the present-day hybrid, digital, and virtual libraries that use the latest technology for provision of information through various services.

Librarians have also changed from storekeepers who were concerned with protection of books against theft, mutilation, and pilferage, to that of information officers, navigators, and cybrarians who find themselves in the vast ocean of reading material and are busy in satisfying their clients who want anytime and anywhere information.

With the advent of computers, the nature of libraries has changed dramatically. Computers are being used in libraries to process, store, retrieve and disseminate information. As a result, the traditional concept of library is being redefined from a place to access books to one which houses the most advanced media including CD-ROM, Internet, and remote access to a wide range of resources.

Libraries have now metamorphosed into digital institutions. Gone are the days when a library was judged by its quantitative resources. Today, libraries are surrounded by networked data that is connected to a vast ocean of Internet-based services. Moreover, electronic resources relevant to the professions are developing at an unprecedented pace. Academic libraries are considered to be the nerve centres of academic institutions, and must support teaching, research, and other academic programmes. The situation in academic libraries of India is the same as that of academic libraries the world over; however, Indian libraries must provide maximum information with limited resources.

The Educational System of India

India has a large higher education system. The growth rate of educational institutions in India was very slow before independence in 1947. Today there are a total of 237 universities, including 116 general universities, 12 science and technology universities, 7 open universities, 33 agricultural universities, 5 women's universities, 1 language universities and 11 medical universities along with 12,600 colleges that provide education in all disciplines. The number of teachers is 3.1 million, and 7.8 million students are enrolled in higher education.

University Grants Commission (UGC)

UGC, established by an act of parliament in 1956, coordinates and monitors the higher education system in India and provides grants to the universities and colleges. Two hundred ninety four universities/institutions in the country are directly under the purview of UGC. It also advises the union and state governments on measures to university education. It frames rules and regulations for overall teaching and research at higher education. As a result, it also looks after the academic libraries, *i.e.*, sets various standards for library education, library staff, library services, etc. A number of committees have been set up by the UGC for the support of higher education in general and the library services in academic libraries in particular. UGC has also set up three information centres covering different disciplines—the *National Centre for Science Information* (NCSI) at Indian Institute of Science Bangalore, SNDT Women's University Mumbai, and National Social Science Information Centre at M.S. University at Baroda, to provide the document delivery services to students, teachers, and researchers.

Information and Library Network

The University Grants Commission has set up an autonomous Inter-University Centre in 1991 called INFLIBNET. It is involved in modernizing university libraries in India and connects them through a nation-wide high-speed data network. It promotes automation of libraries, develops standards, creates union catalogues of serials, theses, books, monographs and non-book materials; provides access to bibliographic information sources; creates database of projects, institutions, specialists; provides training, etc. Almost all academic libraries, especially university libraries, are members of INFLIBNET. It has also developed library automation software called SOUL (*Software for University Libraries*) and has distributed the same free of cost to its member libraries.

Other Networks

Besides INFLIBNET, a number of other national networks and various library networks have also been developed including:

- NICNET (National Informatic Center's network),
- INDONET,
- ERNET,
- CALIBNET,
- DELNET:
  - ADINET is associated with INFLIBNET,
  - DELNET with NIC and
  - MALIBNET with CFTRI.

A number of educational institutions are members of such networks. These networks, especially DELNET are engaged in compiling union catalogs, creating various databases of experts, providing training to library staff, ILL, online facilities, reference service, assistance in retrospective conversion, etc.

Library Consortia

Due to a financial crunch and the rising costs of journals, many Indian university and college libraries cannot subscribe to all the required journals and databases. To overcome this problem, libraries are forming consortia.

Some special libraries and organizations like the Indian Institute of Astrophysics Library, Inter-university Centre for Astronomy and Astrophysics Library, *National Centre for Radio Astrophysics* (NCRA) Library, Physical Research Laboratory (PRL) Library, Raman Research Institute (RRI) Library, Tata Institute of Fundamental Research (TIFR) Library, Council of Scientific and Industrial Research, Department of Atomic Energy, etc., have established consortia to share electronic access to journal literature. NISCAIR (formed by the merger of INSDOC and NISCOM) is developing a consortium for CSIR labs for accessing e-journals. Consortia in India are still a new concept that requires proper guidelines and methodologies. In a survey by UGC in 2001, it was noted that although 142 university libraries had computer and Internet facilities and were interlinked to INFLIBNET, they were subscribing to printed journals only.

In order to solve this problem, UGC launched a major initiative called UGC-INFONET that provides high speed Internet connections so as to have electronic access to professional literature including research journals, abstracts, review publications, and databases from all areas in science and technology, as well as in social sciences and humanities. Today, a number of professional journals are available over UGC-INFONET to all universities. The e-subscription initiative under UGC-Infonet is an important portal for sharing print as well as electronic resources amongst university libraries. INFLIBNET functions as a resource center with an aim to cater to the needs of its members for resources not accessible to them in electronic media or are available in print media.

INDEST Consortium

The Ministry of Human Resource Development (MHRD) has set up the "Indian National Digital Library in Science and Technology Consortium". The ministry provides funds required for the subscription to electronic resources for 38 academic institutions, including the Indian Institute of Sciences, Indian Institute of Technology, Regional Engineering Colleges, Indian Institute of Managements, and about 60 centrally-funded/aided government institutions through the consortium. The INDEST consortium is the most ambitious initiative so far in the area of engineering and technology disciplines. The primary objective of libraries is to organize and provide access to information, and it remains the same although the format and methods have changed drastically.

Under the present scenario of declining budgets and higher subscription costs of journals in India, it is becoming very difficult to meet the demands of library/information users. The only solution to the problem is the pooling and sharing of resources—print as well as electronic—by way of consortia. New technology has provided great opportunities for delivery of services within consortia. More and more libraries must unite, which of course requires a change in the attitudes, practices, and policies to get the maximum benefit.

SCHOOL LIBRARY

A school library is a library within a school where students, staff, and often, parents of a public or private school have access to a variety of resources. The goal of the school library media center is to ensure that all members of the school community have equitable access "to books and reading, to information, and to information technology." A school library media center "uses all types of media... is automated, and utilizes the Internet for information gathering." School libraries are distinct from public libraries because they serve as "learner-oriented laboratories which support, extend, and individualize the school's curriculum... A school library serves as the center and coordinating agency for all material used in the school."

Researchers have demonstrated that school libraries have a positive impact on student achievement. More than 60 studies have been conducted in 19 U.S. states and one Canadian province. The major finding of these studies is that students with access to a well-supported school library media programme with a qualified school library media specialist, scored higher on reading assessments regardless of their socio-economic statuses. In addition, a study conducted in Ohio revealed that 99.4% of students surveyed believed that their school librarians and school library media programmes helped them succeed in school. A report that reported similar conclusions was compiled by Michele Lonsdale in Australia in 2003.

HISTORY OF SCHOOL LIBRARIES

The later part of the 19th century marked the beginning of the modern American library movement with the creation of the American Library Association (ALA) in 1876 by a group of librarians led by Melvil Dewey. At these beginning stages of development, the school libraries were primarily made up of small collections with the school librarian playing primarily a clerical role.

1920 marked the first effort by the library and education communities to evaluate school libraries with the publication of the *Certain Report*, which provided the first yardstick for evaluating school libraries. School libraries experienced another major push following the launch of Sputnik in 1957, which forced the United States to re-evaluate its priorities for math and science education. As a result, the 1960s were one of the greatest periods of growth and development for school libraries due to an increased flow of money and support from the private sector and public funding for education. Most notable during this time was the *Knapp School Libraries Project* which established model school library media centers across the country. Hundreds of new school libraries were expanded and renovated during this time. Most recently, school libraries have been defined by three major guidelines documents: *Information Power* and *Information Power II*. Globally important mission statement is the Unesco School library Manifesto.

THE PURPOSE OF THE SCHOOL LIBRARY

The school library exists to provide a range of learning opportunities for both large and small groups as well as individuals with a focus on intellectual content, information literacy, and the learner. In addition to classroom visits with collaborating teachers, the school library also serves as a place for students to do independent work, use computers, equipment and research materials; to host special events such as author visits and book clubs; and for tutoring and testing.

The school library media center programme is a collaborative venture in which school library media specialists, teachers, and administrators work together to provide opportunities for the social, cultural, and educational growth of students. Activities that are part of the school library media programme can take place in the school library media center, the laboratory classroom, through the school, and via the school library's online resources.

THE SCHOOL LIBRARY COLLECTION

School libraries are similar to public libraries in that they contain books, films, recorded sound, periodicals, realia, and digital media. These items are not only for the education, enjoyment, and entertainment of the all members of the school community, but also to enhance and expand the school's curriculum.

STAFFING OF THE SCHOOL LIBRARY

In many schools, school libraries are staffed by librarians, teacher-librarians, or school library media specialists who hold a specific library science degree. In some jurisdictions, school librarians are required to have specific certification and/or a teaching certificate. The school librarian performs four leadership main roles: teacher, instructional partner, information specialist, and programme administrator. In the teacher role, the school librarian develops and implements curricula relating to information literacy and enquiry. School librarians may read to children, assist them in selecting books, and assist with schoolwork.

Some school librarians see classes on a "flexible schedule". A flexible schedule means that rather than having students come to the library for instruction at a fixed time every week, the classroom teacher schedules library time when library skills or materials are needed as part of the classroom learning experience. In the instructional partner role, school librarians collaborate with classroom teachers to create independent learners by fostering students' research, information literacy, technology, and critical thinking skills.

As information specialists, school librarians develop a resource base for the school by using the curriculum and student interests to identify and obtain library materials, organize and maintain the library collection in order to promote independent reading and lifelong learning. Materials in the library collection can be located using an *Online Public Access Catalog* (OPAC). This role also encompasses many activities relating to technology including the integration of resources in a variety of formats: periodical databases; Web sites; digital video segments; podcasts; blog and wiki content; digital images; virtual classrooms, etc.

School librarians are often responsible for audio-visual equipment and are sometimes in charge of school computers and computer networks. Many school librarians also perform clerical duties. They handle the circulating and cataloging of materials, facilitate interlibrary loans, shelve materials, perform inventory, etc.

RESEARCH LIBRARIES

A research library contains an in-depth collection of material on one or more subjects. A research library supports scholarly research and will generally include primary as well as secondary sources; it will maintain permanent collections and attempt to provide access to all necessary material. A research library is most often an academic or national library, but a large special library may have a research library within its special field and a very few of the largest public libraries also serve as research libraries. A large university library may be considered a research library; and in North America they may belong to the Association of Research Libraries.

A research library can be either a reference library, which does not lend its holdings, or a lending library, which does lend all or some of its holdings. Some extremely large or traditional research libraries are entirely reference in this sense, lending none of their material; most academic research libraries, at least in the U.S., now lend books, but not periodicals or other material.

REFERENCE LIBRARIES

A reference library does not lend books and other items; instead, they must be read at the library itself. Typically such libraries are used for research purposes, for example at a university. Some items at reference libraries may be historical and even unique. Examples of reference libraries include the British Library in London and the Bodleian Library at Oxford University. Many libraries contain a "reference section", which holds books, such as dictionaries, which are common reference books, and are therefore not lent out. Such references sections may be referred to as "reading rooms", which may also include newspapers and periodicals.

SPECIAL LIBRARIES

All other libraries fall into the "special library" category. Many private businesses and public organizations, including hospitals, museums, research laboratories, law firms, and many government departments and agencies, maintain their own libraries for the use of their employees in doing specialized research related to their work.

Special libraries may or may not be accessible to some identified part of the general public. Branches of a large academic or research libraries dealing with particular subjects are also usually called "special libraries": they are generally associated with one or more academic departments. Special libraries are distinguished from special collections, which are branches or parts of a library intended for rare books, manuscripts, and other special materials.

ARCHIVE, MUSEUM AND RECORDS MANAGEMENT

ARCHIVE

An archive is a collection of historical records, or the physical place they are located. Archives contain primary source documents that have accumulated over the course of an individual or organization's lifetime, and are kept to show the function of an organization. In general, archives consist of records that have been selected for permanent or long-term preservation on grounds of their enduring cultural, historical, or evidentiary value. Archival records are normally unpublished and almost always unique, unlike books or magazines for which many identical copies exist. This means that archives are quite distinct from libraries with regard to their functions and organization, although archival collections can often be found within library buildings. A person who works in archives is called an archivist.

The study and practice of organizing, preserving, and providing access to information and materials in archives is called archival science. When referring to historical records or the places they are kept, the plural form *archives* is chiefly used. Archivists tend to prefer the term "archives" as the correct terminology to serve as both the singular and plural, since "archive," as a noun or a verb, has acquired meanings related to computer science. The use of keeping official documents is very old.

Archeologists have discovered archives of hundreds of clay tablets going back to the IIIrd and IInd millennia BC in sites like Ebla, Mari, Amarna, Hattusas, Ugarit, Pylos. And these discoveries have been fundamental to know ancient alphabets, languages, literatures and politics. Archives were well developed by the ancient Chinese, the ancient Greeks, and ancient Romans. However, they have been lost, since documents were written on organic materials like papyrus and paper. On the contrary, many archives founded since Middle Age by churches, kingdoms and cities survive and often have kept their official status uninterruptedly till now. They are the basic tool for historical research on these ages. Modern archival thinking has many roots in the French Revolution. The French National Archives, who possess perhaps the largest archival collection in the world, with records going as far back as A.D. 625, were created in 1790 during the French Revolution from various government, religious, and private archives seized by the revolutionaries.

Users and Institutions

Historians, genealogists, lawyers, demographers, film-makers, and others conduct research at archives. The research process at each archive is unique, and depends upon the institution in which the archive is housed. While there are many different kinds of archives, the most recent census of archivists in the United States identified five major types: academic, business, government, non-profit, and other.

There are also four main areas of enquiry involved with archives:

- Material technologies,
- Organizing principles,
- Geographic locations, and
- Tangled embodiments of humans and non-humans.

These areas help to further categorize what kind of archive is being created.

Academic

Archives in colleges, universities, and other educational facilities are typically housed within a library, and duties may be carried out by an archivist. professors may also run a smaller archive. Academic archives exist to preserve and celebrate the history of their school and academic community. An academic archive may contain items such as the administrative records of the institution, papers of former professors and presidents, memorabilia related to school organizations and activities, and items the academic library wishes to remain in a closed-stack setting, such as rare books or thesis copies.

Access to the collections in these archives is usually by prior appointment only; some have posted hours for making enquiries. Users of academic archives can be undergraduates, graduate students, faculty and staff, scholarly researchers, and the general public. Many academic archives work closely with alumni relations departments or other campus institutions to help raise funds for their library or school. Because of their library setting, a degree certified by the American Library Association is preferred for employment in an academic archive in the United States.

Business

Archives located in for-profit institutions are usually those owned by a private business. Examples of prominent business archives in the United States include Coca-Cola, Procter and Gamble, Motorola Heritage Services and

Archives, and Levi Strauss and Co. These corporate archives maintain historic documents and items related to the history and administration of their companies. Business archives serve the purpose of helping their corporations maintain control over their brand by retaining memories of the company's past. Especially in business archives, records management is separate from the historic aspect of archives.

Workers in these types of archives may have any combination of training and degrees, from either a history or library background. These archives are typically not open to the public and only used by workers of the owner company, although some will allow approved visitors by appointment. Business archives are concerned with maintaining the integrity of their company, and are therefore selective of how their materials may be used.

Government

Government archives include those maintained by local and state government as well as those maintained by the national government. Anyone may use a government archive, and frequent users include reporters, genealogists, writers, historians, students, and people seeking information on the history of their home or region. Many government archives are open to the public and no appointment is required to visit. In the United States, *National Archives and Records Administration* (NARA) maintains central archival facilities in the District of Columbia and College Park, Maryland, with regional facilities distributed throughout the United States.

Some city or local governments may have repositories, but their organization and accessibility varies widely. State or province archives typically require at least a bachelor's degree in history for employment, although some ask for certification by test as well. In the UK the National Archives, formerly known as the Public Record Office, is the government archive for England and Wales. The National Monuments Record is the public archive of English Heritage. The National Archives of Scotland, located in Edinburgh, serve that country while the Public Record Office of Northern Ireland in Belfast is the government archive for Northern Ireland.

A network of local authority-run record offices and archives exists throughout England, Wales and Scotland and holds many important collections, including local government, landed estates, church and business records. Many archives have contributed catalogues to the national Access 2 Archives programme and online searching across collections is possible. In France, the French Archives Administration in the Ministry of Culture manages the National Archives which possess 406 km. of archives as of 2010 with original records going as far back as A.D. 625, as well as the departmental archives, located in the *préfectures* of each of the 100 *départements* of France, which possess 2,297 km. of archives, and also the local city archives, about 600 in total, which possess 456 km. of archives.

Put together, the total volume of archives under the supervision of the French Archives Administration is the largest in the world:

- In India the National Archives are located in New Delhi.
- In Taiwan the National Archives Administration are located in Taipei.

Most intergovernmental organisations keep their own historical archives. However, a number of European organi-sations, including the European Commission, choose to deposit their archives with the European University Institute in Florence.

MUSEUM

A museum is an institution that cares for a collection of artifacts and other objects of scientific, artistic, cultural, or historical importance and makes them available for public viewing through exhibits that may be permanent or temporary. Most large museums are located in major cities throughout the world and more local ones exist in smaller cities, towns and even the countryside. The continuing acceleration in the digitization of information, combined with the increasing capacity of digital information storage, is causing the traditional model of museums to expand to include virtual exhibits and high-resolution images of their collections for perusal, study, and exploration from any place with Internet connectivity.

Purpose

Museum purposes change from institution to institution. Some favour education over conservation, or *vice-versa*. For example, in the 1970s, the Canada Science and Technology Museum favoured education over preservation of their objects. They displayed objects as well as their functions. One exhibit featured a historic printing press that a staff member used for visitors to create museum memorabilia. Some seek to reach a wide audience, such as a national or state museum, while some museums have specific audiences, like the LDS Church History Museum or local history organizations.

Generally speaking, museums collect objects of significance that comply with their mission statement for conservation and display. Although most museums do not allow physical contact with the associated artifacts, there are some that are interactive and encourage a more hands-on approach. In 2009, Hampton Court Palace, palace of Henry VIII, opened the council room to the general public to create an interactive environment for visitors. Rather than allowing visitors to handle 500 year old objects, the museum created replicas, as well as replica costumes. The daily activities, historic clothing, and even temperature changes immerse the visitor in a slice of what Tudor life may have been

Management

The roles associated with the management a museum largely depends on the size of the institution, but every museum has a hierarchy of governance with a Board of Trustees serving at the top. The Director is next in command and works with the Board to establish and fulfill the museum's mission statement and to ensure that the museum is accountable to the public.

Together, the Board and the Director establish a good system of governance that is guided by various other documents such as an institutional or strategic plan, institutional code of ethics, bylaws, and collections policy. The *American Association of Museums* (AAM) has also formulated a series of standards and best practices that help guide the management of museums. Unfortunately, many small, local museums lack this guidance since accreditation with AAM requires a museum to operate on an annual budget of at least $25,000. A change in leadership may ultimately effect changes at the museum, as new directors commonly have new ideas for the institution they work for.

For instance, the Los Angeles County Museum of Art's Director and CEO, Michael Govan, has made great strides for the museum since he started in 2006. Undertaking elaborate building projects, acquiring large collections of objects, and creating new relationships with contemporary artists are just some of his accomplishments. While change and growth is often good for a museum, they should not reach outside the original mission statement of the institution.

Museum professionals Hugh H. Genoways and Lynne M. Ireland, "Administration of the organization requires skill in conflict management, interpersonal relations, budget manage-ment and monitoring, and staff supervision and evaluation. Managers must also set legal and ethical standards and maintain involvement in the museum profession." Various positions within the museum carry out the policies established by the Board and the Director. These positions include but are not limited to curators, collections managers/registrars, public programmers/educators, exhibition designers, and building operators.

These positions and all other employees should work together towards the museum's institutional goal:

- *Curator:* Research the collection and most often write the text labels for exhibitions. In larger institutions, there may be a curator assigned to each collection of objects the museum holds. Ex: Curator of Modern Art, Curator of Natural History, Curator of History, etc.
- *Collections Management/Registrar*: Responsible for the care and maintenance of all objects in the museum's collection, tracks movement of objects in and out of the museum on loan or on exhibition, records information about objects in databases-such as an object's provenance. Registrars oversee the accessi-oning process,

which formally accepts objects into the museum's collection with an accession number and detailed record. Collections Managers and Registrars uphold the Collections Policy, which guides what is and is not accepted into the museum collection.

- *Public Programmer/Educator:* Creates programmes for the public and designs interactives for exhibitions. This position also oversees volunteers and docents at the museum. Depending on the institution, educators may also research the collections and write text for exhibitions. Educators work with the Board, Director, and Curator to ensure that the needs of the public are met as laid out in the institution's mission statement.
- *Exhibition Designer*: Designs and installs the exhibition under the supervision of the curator and collections manager. They have the vital role of creating exhibition space that is navigable by the visitor.
- *Building Operators:* Oversee security and maintenance of the museum. In larger museums, building operators will work with Collections Managers to maintain appropriate levels of temperature and humidity which can affect the stability of the objects.

RECORDS MANAGEMENT

Records management, or RM, is the practice of maintaining the records of an organization from the time they are created up to their eventual disposal. This may include classifying, storing, securing, and destruction of records. A record can be either a tangible object or digital information: for example, birth certificates, medical x-rays, office documents, databases, application data, and e-mail. Records management is primarily concerned with the evidence of an organization's activities, and is usually applied according to the value of the records rather than their physical format.

In the past, 'records management' was sometimes used to refer only to the management of records which were no longer in everyday use but still needed to be kept-'semi-current' or 'inactive' records, often stored in basements or offsite. More modern usage tends to refer to the entire 'lifecycle' of records-from the point of creation right through until their eventual disposal.

- *The ISO 15489-1:* 2001 standard defines records management as " field of management responsible for the efficient and systematic control of the creation, receipt, maintenance, use and disposition of records, including the processes for capturing and maintaining evidence of and information about business activities and transactions in the form of records".
- *The ISO 15489-1:* 2001 defines records as "information created, received, and maintained as evidence and information by an organization or person, in pursuance of legal obligations or in the

transaction of business". While there are many purposes of and benefits to records management, as both this definition highlights, a key feature of records is their ability to serve as evidence of an event. Proper records manage-ment can help preserve this feature of records.

It should be noted that the format and media of records is generally irrelevant for the purposes of records management. The ISO considers management of both physical and electronic records. Also, section DL1.105 of the United States Department of Defence standard DoD 5015.02-STD defines Records Management as "[t]he planning, controlling, directing, organizing, training, promoting, and other managerial activities involving the life cycle of information, including creation, maintenance, and disposal, regardless of media."

Practicing Records Management

A Records Manager is someone who is responsible for records management in an organization.

Section 4 of the ISO 15489-1:2001 states that records management includes:

- Setting policies and standards;
- Assigning responsibilities and authorities;
- Establishing and promulgating procedures and guide-lines;
- Providing a range of services relating to the manage-ment and use of records;
- Designing, implementing and administering specia-lized systems for managing records; and
- Integrating records management into business systems and processes.

Thus, the practice of records management may involve:

- Planning the information needs of an organization
- Identifying information requiring capture
- Creating, approving, and enforcing policies and practices regarding records, including their organi-zation and disposal
- Developing a records storage plan, which includes the short and long-term housing of physical records and digital information
- Identifying, classifying, and storing records
- Coordinating access to records internally and outside of the organization, balancing the requirements of business confidentiality, data privacy, and public access.
- Executing a retention policy on the disposal of records which are no longer required for operational reasons; according to organizational policies, statutory requirements, and other regulations this may involve either their destruction or permanent preservation in an archive.

Records management principles and automated records management systems aid in the capture, classification, and ongoing management of records throughout their lifecycle. Such a system may be paper based or may be a computer system, such as an electronic records management application.

Managing Physical Records

Managing physical records involves different disciplines and may draw on a variety of forms of expertise. Records must be identified and authenticated.

This is usually a matter of filing and retrieval; in some circumstances, more careful handling is required.

- *Identifying Records*: If an item is presented as a legal record, it needs to be authenticated. Forensic experts may need to examine a document or artifact to determine that it is not a forgery, and that any damage, alteration, or missing content is documented. In extreme cases, items may be subjected to a microscope, x-ray, radiocarbon dating or chemical analysis. This level of authentication is rare, but requires that special care be taken in the creation and retention of the records of an organization.
- *Storing Records:* Records must be stored in such a way that they are accessible and safeguarded against environmental damage. A typical paper document may be stored in a filing cabinet in an office. However, some organisations employ file rooms with specialized environmental controls including temperature and humidity. Vital records may need to be stored in a disaster-resistant safe or vault to protect against fire, flood, earthquakes and conflict. In extreme cases, the item may require both disaster-proofing and public access, such as the original, signed US Constitution. Civil engineers may need to be consulted to determine that the file room can effectively withstand the weight of shelves and file cabinets filled with paper; historically, some military vessels were designed to take into account the weight of their operating procedures on paper as part of their ballast equation. In addition to on-site storage of records, many organizations operate their own off-site records centers or contract with commercial records centres.
- *Circulating Records:* Tracking the record while it is away from the normal storage area is referred to as circulation. Often this is handled by simple written recording procedures. However, many modern records environments use a computerized system involving bar code scanners, or *radio-frequency identification technology* (RFID) to track movement of the records. These can also be used for periodic auditing to identify unauthorized movement of the record.
- *Disposal of Records:* Disposal of records does not always mean

destruction. It can also include transfer to a historical archive, museum, or private individual. Destruction of records ought to be authorized by law, statute, regulation, or operating procedure, and the records should be disposed of with care to avoid inadvertent disclosure of information. The process needs to be well-documented, starting with a records retention schedule and policies and procedures that have been approved at the highest level. An inventory of the records disposed of should be maintained, including certification that they have been destroyed. Records should never simply be discarded as refuse. Most organizations use processes including pulveri-zation, paper shredding or incineration.

Commercially available products can manage records through all processes active, inactive, archival, retention scheduling and disposal. Some also utilizes RFID technology for the tracking of the physical file.

Managing Electronic Records

The general principles of records management apply to records in any format. Digital records, however, raise specific issues. It is more difficult to ensure that the content, context and structure of records is preserved and protected when the records do not have a physical existence. This has important implications for the authenticity, reliability, and trust-worth-iness of records.

Much research is being conducted on the management of electronic records. The International Research on Permanent Authentic Records in Electronic Systems Project is one example of such an initiative. Based at the School of Library, Archival and Information Studies at the University of British Columbia, in Vancouver, British Columbia, Canada, the InterPARES Project is a collaborative project between researchers all across the world committed to developing theories and methodologies to ensure the reliability, accuracy, and authenticity of electronic records.

Functional requirements for computer systems to manage electronic records have been produced by the US Department of Defence, the National Archives of England and Wales and the European Commission, whose MoReq (Model Requirements for the Management of Electronic Records) specification has been translated into at least twelve languages and is used beyond the borders of Europe.

Development of MoReq was initiated by the DLM Forum, funded by the European Commission. Particular concerns exist about the ability to access and read electronic records over time, since the rapid pace of change in technology can make the software used to create the records obsolete, leaving the records unreadable. A considerable amount of research is being undertaken to address this, under the heading of digital preservation. The Public Record Office Victoria (PROV) located in Melbourne, Australia published the Victorian Electronic Records Strategy (VERS) which includes a standard for the preservation, long-term storage and access to permanent electronic records.

The VERS standard has been adopted by all Victorian Government departments. A digital archive has been established by PROV to enable the general public to access permanent records. Archives New Zealand is also setting up a digital archive.

Electronic Tax Records

Electronic Tax Records are computer-based/non-paper versions of records required by tax agencies like the Internal Revenue Service. There is substantial confusion about what constitutes acceptable digital records for the IRS, as the concept is relatively new. The subject is discussed in Publication 583 and Bulletin 1997-13, but not in specific detail. Businesses and individuals wishing to convert their paper records into scanned copies may be at risk if they do so. For example, it is unclear if an IRS auditor would accept a JPEG, PNG, or PDF format scanned copy of a purchase receipt for a deducted expense item.

Current Issues in Records Management

As of 2005, records management has increased interest among corporations due to new compliance regulations and statutes. While government, legal, and healthcare entities have a strong historical records management discipline, general record-keeping of corporate records has been poorly standar-dized and implemented. In addition, scandals such as the Enron/Andersen scandal, and more recently records-related mishaps at Morgan Stanley, have renewed interest in corporate records compliance, retention period requirements, litigation preparedness, and related issues. Statutes such as the US Sarbanes-Oxley Act have created new concerns among corporate "compliance officers" that result in more standardization of records management practices within an organization.

Most of the 1990s has seen discussions between records managers and IT managers, and the emphasis has expanded to include the legal aspects, as it is now focused on compliance and risk. Privacy, data protection, and identity theft have become issues of interest for records managers. The role of the records manager to aid in the protection of an organization's records has often grown to include attention to these concerns. The need to ensure that certain information about individuals is not retained has brought greater focus to records retention schedules and records destruction.

The most significant issue is implementing the required changes to individual and corporate culture to derive the benefits to internal and external stakeholders. Records manage-ment is often seen as an unnecessary or low priority administrative task that can be performed at the lowest levels within an organization. Publicised events have demonstrated that records management is in fact the responsibility of all individuals within an organization and the corporate entity. An issue that has been very controversial among records managers has been the uncritical adoption of Electronic Document and Records Management Systems.

One well known RM thinker, Steve Bailey, has stated:

- "As far as the average user is concerned, the EDRMS is something they didn't want, don't like and can't use. As such, its no wonder that so few users accept them–as one person once said to me "making me use an EDRMS is like asking a plasterer to use a hammer!
- "And now, finally, it is time to turn our eyes to the records management profession itself. In my opinion, we have come within a whisker of allowing our blind obsession with EDRMS to turn us into an intellec-tually-sterile, vendor-led profession. For the best part of a decade we have allowed others to do the thinking for us and have come to rely on EDRMS as our intellectual-crutch. But make no mistake about it, the blame for this rests squarely with us. Like children following the Pied Piper, we allowed ourselves to be so enchanted by the tune being played that we were led, without question or debate, wherever the tech-nology took us."

Another issue of great interest to records managers is the impact of social media, such as wikis, Facebook and Twitter, on traditional records management practice, principles, and concepts.

4

Public Library: Backdrop and Growth

INTRODUCTION

A public library is a library that is accessible by the public and is generally funded from public sources and operated by civil servants. There are five fundamental characteristics shared by public libraries. The first is that they are supported by taxes; they are governed by a board to serve the public interest; they are open to all and every community member can access the collection; they are entirely voluntary in that no one is ever forced to use the services provided; and public libraries provide basic services without charge. Public libraries exist in many countries across the world and are often considered an essential part of having an educated and literate population. Public libraries are distinct from research libraries, school libraries, and other special libraries in that their mandate is to serve the general public's information needs.

Public libraries also provide free services such as preschool story times to encourage early literacy, quiet study and work areas for students and professionals, or book clubs to encourage appreciation of literature in adults. Public libraries typically allow users to take books and other materials off the premises temporarily; they also have non-circulating reference collections and provide computer and Internet access to patrons.

SERVICES OFFERED

In addition to print books and periodicals, most public libraries today have a wide array of other media including audiobooks, e-books, CDs, cassettes, videotapes, DVDs, and video games, as well as facilities to access the Internet and inter-library loans.

Readers' advisory is a fundamental public library service that involves suggesting fiction and nonfiction titles. Public libraries may also provide other services, such as community meeting rooms, storytelling sessions for infants, toddlers, preschool children, or after-school programmes, all with an intention of developing early literacy skills and a love of books. In person and on-line programmes for reader development, language learning, homework help, free lectures and cultural performances, and other community service programmes are common offerings. One of the most popular programmes offered in public libraries are summer reading programmes for children, families, and adults. In rural areas, the local public library may have, in addition to its main branch, a mobile library service, consisting of one or more buses furnished as a small public library, serving the countryside according to a regular schedule. Public libraries also provide materials for children, often housed in a special section. Child-oriented websites with on-line educational games and programmes specifically designed for younger library users are becoming increasingly popular. Services may be provided for other groups, such as large print or Braille materials, Books on tape, young adult literature and other materials for teenagers, or materials in other than the national language.

California and Nevada now offer a new service called Link+. This new programme links county libraries across the two states, allowing patrons access to books their library may not have in their collection. Librarians at most public libraries provide reference and research help to the general public, usually at a reference desk but can often be done by telephone interview. As online discussion and social networking allow for remote access, reference is becoming available virtually through the use of the Internet and e-mail. Depending on the size of the library, there may be more than one desk; at some smaller libraries all transactions may occur at one desk, while large urban public libraries may employ subject-specialist librarians with the ability to staff multiple reference or information desks to answer queries about particular topics at any time during regular operating hours. Often the children's section in a public library has its own reference desk. Public libraries are also increasingly making use of web 2.0 services, including the use of online social networks by libraries. Public libraries in some countries pay authors when their books are borrowed from libraries. These are known as Public Lending Right programme.

DIGITAL DIVIDE

As more commercial and governmental services are being provided online, public libraries increasingly provide Internet access for users who otherwise would not be able to connect to these services. Part of the public library mission has become attempting to help bridge the digital divide. A study conducted in 2006 found that "72.5 per cent of library branches report that they are the only provider of free public computer and Internet access in their communities". A 2008 study found that "100 per cent of rural, high poverty outlets provide public Internet access, a significant increase from 85.7 per cent last year". The American Library Association (ALA), addresses this role of libraries as part of "access to information" and "equity of access"; part of the profession's ethical commitment that "no one should be denied information because he or she cannot afford the cost of a book or periodical, have access to the internet or information in any of its various formats." In addition to access, many public libraries offer training and support to computer users.

Once access has been achieved, there still remains a large gap in people's online abilities and skills. For many communities, the public library is the only agency offering free computer classes and information technology learning. As of 2008, 73.4 per cent of public libraries offered information technology training of some form, including information literacy skills and homework assignment help. A significant service provided by public libraries is assisting people with e-government access and use of federal, state and local government information, forms and services.

Internationally, public libraries offer information and communication technology (ICT) services, giving "access to information and knowledge" the "highest priority." While different countries and areas of the world have their own requirements, general services offered include free connection to the Internet, training in using the Internet, and relevant content in appropriate languages. In addition to typical public library financing, non-governmental organizations (NGOs) and business fund services that assist public libraries in combating the digital divide.

ORIGINS AS A SOCIAL INSTITUTION

The culmination of centuries of advances in the printing press, moveable type, paper, ink, publishing, and distribution, combined with an ever growing middle class, increased commercial activity and consumption, new radical ideas, massive population growth and higher literacy rates forged the public library into the form that it is today. Public libraries are not a new idea; Romans made scrolls in dry rooms available to patrons of the baths, and tried with some success to establish libraries within the empire. Naturally, only those few that could afford an education would be able to use the library, where those less than rich or without control of money; women, children and slaves could not.

In the middle of the 19th century, the push for truly public libraries, paid for by taxes and run by the state gained force after numerous depressions, droughts, wars and revolutions in Europe, felt mostly by the working class.

Matthew Battles states that:

"It was in these years of class conflict and economic terror that the public library movement swept through Britain, as the nation's progressive elite recognized that the light of cultural and intellectual energy was lacking in the lives of commoners."

Libraries had often been started with a donation, an endowment or were bequeathed to various, parishes, churches, schools or towns, and these social and institutional libraries formed the base of many academic and public library collections of today. Andrew Carnegie had the biggest influence in financing libraries in the United States of America, from the east to west coast. From just 1900 to 1917, almost 1,700 libraries were constructed by Carnegie's foundation, insisting that local communities first guarantee tax support of each library built.

The establishment of circulating libraries by booksellers and publishers provided a means of gaining profit and creating social centers within the community. The circulating libraries not only provided a place to sell books, but also a place to lend books for a price. These circulating libraries provided a variety of materials including the increasingly popular novels. Although the circulating libraries filled an important role in society, members of the middle and upper classes often looked down upon these libraries that regularly sold material from their collections and provided materials that were less sophisticated. Circulating libraries also charged a subscription fee, however the fees were set to entice their patrons, providing subscriptions on a yearly, quarterly or monthly basis, without expecting the subscribers to purchase a share in the circulating library. Circulating libraries were not exclusively lending institutions and often provided a place for other forms of commercial activity, which may or may not be related to print.

This was necessary because the circulating libraries did not generate enough funds through subscription fees collected from its borrowers. As a commerce venture, it was important to consider the contributing factors such as other goods or services available to the subscribers. Many claims have been made for the title of "first public library" for various libraries in various countries, with at least some of the confusion arising from differing interpretations of what should be considered a true "public library". Difficulties in establishing what policies were in effect at different times in the history of particular libraries also add to the confusion.

The first libraries open to the public were the collections of Greek and Latin scrolls which were available in the dry sections of the many buildings that made up the huge Roman baths of the Roman empire. However, they were not lending libraries. The "halls of science" run by different Islamic sects in many cities of North Africa and the Middle East in the 9th century were open to the public. Some of them had written lending policies, but they were very restrictive. Most patrons were expected to consult the books on site. The later European university libraries were not open to the general public, but accessible by scholars.

HISTORY

A public library is a library funded by public money, such as taxpayer money. The purpose of a public library is to provide books, Internet access and many other resources to the public for free. Even DVDs and movies are available for free rentals. Public libraries are not new, in fact the first organization that was considered to be a public library was created in the late 1500s.

- The first public library was created in England. At that time, the only people who were able to use libraries were individuals who joined a cathedral or were enrolled in college. This public library was called Francis Trigge Chained Library. This public library actually still exists and is famous for its long standing history of giving the people free access to all library resources. Although this library was the first, it stood nearly alone in its existence until the mid 1800s. That was the time period in which public libraries began to become popular.
- In England, Parliament decided to make a committee dedicated to considering the creation of multiple public libraries. The committee was supposed to decide if a public library was something that would benefit the public. The committee reported back that public libraries would be beneficial, since so many people were poor. The recommendation was to open multiple public libraries throughout the country. This decision led to the Public Libraries Act of 1850. The act allowed all cities to collect taxes for public library support, providing that the population of the city had at least 10,000 people.
- This was quickly followed by the Public School Law, created in 1870. The point of this law was to raise the literacy rate of the public, since it was very low at the time. The only people who really knew how to read were rich people and scholars. Obviously, this literacy need increased the need for public libraries. By the 1870s, over 50 cities had created public libraries of their own. Only 30 years later, the number of public libraries hit 300. This was the time when public libraries began opening everywhere, and the United States began funding them as well. A public library was funded by public money, but it was also common for the people to help out these public libraries grow and flourish. Womens' clubs and the wealthy donated books to these public libraries to improve their selections.

Today, there are hundreds of thousands of public libraries in the world. The larger the city, the more public libraries will be found there. Unfortunately, despite the great need and desire for public libraries, funding for them are cut consistently by the state legislature. Large amounts of money to fund public libraries are made by private donors who have the wealth and desire to see a public library being used.

17th Century

In the early years of the 17th century, many famous collegiate and town libraries were founded throughout the country. Francis Trigge Chained Library of St. Wulfram's Church, Grantham, Lincolnshire was founded in 1598 by the rector of nearby Welbourne. Norwich City Library was established in

1608, and Chetham's Library in Manchester, which claims to be the oldest public library in the English-speaking world, opened in 1653.

Other early town libraries of the UK include those of:

- Ipswich (1612),
- Bristol (founded in 1613 and opened in 1615), and
- Leicester (1632).

Shrewsbury School also opened its library to townsfolk. In Bristol, an early library that allowed access to the public was that of the Kalendars or Kalendaries, a brotherhood of clergy and laity who were attached to the Church of All-Hallowen or All Saints. Records show that in 1464, provision was made for a library to be erected in the house of the Kalendars, and reference is made to a deed of that date by which it was "appointed that all who wish to enter for the sake of instruction shall have 'free access and recess' at certain times".

Early 18th Century

At the turn of the 18th century, libraries were becoming increasingly public and were more frequently lending libraries. The 18th century saw the switch from closed parochial libraries to lending libraries. Before this time, public libraries were parochial in nature and libraries frequently chained their books to desks.

Libraries also were not uniformly open to the public. In 1790, The Public Library Act would not be passed for another sixty-seven years. Even though the British Museum existed at this time and contained over 50,000 books, the national library was not open to the public, or even to a majority of the population. Access to the Museum depended on passes, of which there was sometimes a waiting period of three to four weeks. Moreover, the library was not open to browsing.

Once a pass to the library had been issued, the reader was taken on a tour of the library. Many readers complained that the tour was much too short. At the turn of the century, there were virtually no public libraries in the sense in which we now understand the term *i.e.* libraries provided from public funds and freely accessible to all. Only one important library in Great Britain, namely Chetham's Library in Manchester, was fully and freely accessible to the public.

However, there had come into being a whole network of library provision on a private or institutional basis. Subscription libraries, both private and commercial, provided the middle and middle to upper class with a variety of books for moderate fees. The increase in secular literature at this time encouraged the spread of lending libraries, especially the commercial subscription libraries. Commercial subscription libraries began when booksellers began renting out extra copies of books in the mid-18th century. Steven Fischer estimates that in 1790, there were 'about six hundred rental and lending libraries, with a clientele of some fifty thousand. The mid to late 18th century saw a virtual epidemic of feminine reading as novels became more and more popular. Novels, while frowned upon in society, were extremely popular.

In England there were many who lamented at the 'villanous profane and obscene books' and the opposition to the circulating library, on moral grounds, persisted well into the 19th century. Still, many establishments must have circulated many times the number of novels as of any other genre. In 1797, Thomas Wilson wrote in The Use of Circulating Libraries: "Consider, that for a successful circulating library, the collection must contain 70% fiction". However, the overall percentage of novels mainly depended on the proprietor of the circulating library. While some circulating libraries were almost completely novels, others had less than 10% of their overall collection in the form of novels.

The national average at the turn of the century hovered around novels comprising about 20% of the total collection. Novels varied from other types of books in many ways. They were read primarily for enjoyment instead of for study. They did not provide academic knowledge or spiritual guidance; thus they were read quickly and far fewer times than other books. These were the perfect books for commercial subscription libraries to lend. Since books were read for pure enjoyment rather than for scholarly work, books needed to become both cheaper and smaller. Small duodecimo editions of books were preferred to the large folio editions. Folio editions were read at a desk, while the small duodecimo editions could be easily read like the paperbacks of today. Much like paperbacks of today, many of the novels in circulating libraries were unbound.

At this period of time, many people chose to bind their books in leather. Many circulating libraries skipped this process. Circulating libraries were not in the business of preserving books; their owners wanted to lend books as many times as they possibly could. Circulating libraries had ushered in a completely new way of reading. Reading was no longer simply an academic pursuit or an attempt to gain spiritual guidance. Reading became a social activity. Many circulating libraries were attached to the shops of milliners or drapers. They served as much for social gossip and the meeting of friends as coffee shops do today. Another factor in the growth of subscription libraries was the increasing cost of books.

In the last two decades of the century, especially, prices were practically doubled, so that a quarto work cost a guinea, an octavo 10 shillings or 12 shillings, and a duodecimo cost 4 shillings per volume. Price apart, moreover, books were difficult to procure outside London, since local booksellers could not afford to carry large stocks. Commercial libraries, since they were usually associated with booksellers, and also since they had a greater number of patrons, were able to accumulate greater numbers of books. The United Public Library was said to have a collection of some 52,000 volumes--twice as many as any private subscription library in the country at that period. These libraries, since they functioned as a business, also lent books to non-subscribers on a per-book system.

Private Subscription Libraries

Private subscription libraries functioned in much the same manner as commercial subscription libraries, though they varied in many important ways. One of the most popular versions of the private subscription library was a gentleman's only library. The gentlemen's subscription libraries, sometimes known as proprietary libraries, were nearly all organized on a common pattern. Membership was restricted to the proprietors or shareholders, and ranged from a dozen or two to between four and five hundred.

The entrance fee, *i.e.* the purchase price of a share, was in early days usually a guinea, but rose sharply as the century advanced, often reaching four or five guineas during the French wars; the annual subscription, during the same period, rose from about six shillings to ten shillings or more. The book-stock was, by modern standards, small and was accommodated, at the outset, in makeshift premises--very often over a bookshop, with the bookseller acting as librarian and receiving an honourarium for his pains.

The Liverpool Subscription library was a gentlemen only library. In 1798, it was renamed the Athenaeum when it was rebuilt with a newsroom and coffeehouse. It had an entrance fee of one guinea and annual subscription of five shillings. While no records survive of the commercial library lendings, we have the Bristol Library's continuous record of borrowings from 1773 to 1857. An analysis of the registers for the first twelve years provides some fascinating glimpses of middle-class reading habits in a mercantile community at this period.

The largest and most popular sections of the library were History, Antiquities, and Geography, with 283 titles and 6,121 borrowings, and Belles Lettres, with 238 titles and 3,313 borrowings. Far below came Theology and Ecclesiastical History, Natural History and Chemistry, Philosophy, Jurisprudence, Miscellanies, Mathematics, etc., and Medicine and Anatomy, all with fewer than 100 titles.

The most popular single work was John Hawkesworth's Account of Voyages in the Southern Hemisphere which was borrowed on 201 occasions. The records also show that in 1796, membership had risen by 1/3 to 198 subscribers and the titles increased five-fold to 4987. This mirrors the increase in reading interests. A patron list from the Bath Municipal Library shows that from 1793 to 1799, the library held a stable 30% of their patrons as female. It was also uncommon for these libraries to have buildings designated solely as the library building during the 1790s, though in the 19th century, many libraries would begin building elaborate permanent residences. Bristol, Birmingham, and Liverpool were the few libraries with their own building. The accommodations varied from the shelf for a few dozen volumes in the country stationer's or draper's shop, to the expansion to a back room, to the spacious elegant areas of Hookham's or those at the resorts like Scarborough, and four in a row at Margate.

Private subscription libraries held a greater amount of control over both membership and the types of books in the library. There was almost a complete elimination of cheap fiction in the private societies. Subscription libraries prided themselves on respectability. The highest percentage of subscribers were often landed proprietors, gentry, and old professions.

Towards the end of the 18th century and in the first decades of the nineteenth the need for books and general education made itself felt among social classes created by the beginnings of the Industrial Revolution. The late 18th century saw a rise in subscription libraries intended for the use of tradesmen. In 1797, there was established at Kendal what was known as the Economical Library, "designed principally for the use and instruction of the working classes".

There was also the Artizans' library established at Birmingham in 1799. The entrance fee was 3 shillings. The subscription was 1 shilling 6 pence per quarter. This was a library of general literature. Novels, at first excluded, were afterwards admitted on condition that they did not account for more than one-tenth of the annual income.

Rate-supported Libraries

Although by the mid-19th century, England could claim 274 subscription libraries and Scotland, 266, the foundation of the modern public library system in the U.K. is the Public Libraries Act 1850. Prior to this, the municipalities of Warrington and Salford established libraries in their museums, under the terms of the Museums Act of 1845. Warrington Municipal Library opened in 1848. Salford Museum and Art Gallery first opened in November 1850 as "The Royal Museum and Public Library", as the first unconditionally free public library in England. The library in Campfield, Manchester was the first library to operate a free lending library without subscription in 1852.

Norwich lays claims to being the first municipality to adopt the Public Libraries Act 1850 but theirs was the eleventh library to open, in 1857, being the eleventh in the country after:

- Winchester,
- Manchester,
- Liverpool,
- Bolton,
- Kidderminster,

- Cambridge,
- Birkenhead and
- Sheffield.

The Scottish-American philanthropist and businessman, Andrew Carnegie, helped to increase the number of public libraries from the late 19th century. County libraries are a later development which were made possible by the establishment of County Councils in 1888. They normally have a large central library in a major town with smaller branch libraries in other towns and a mobile library service covering rural areas.

NORTH AMERICA

Canada

In 1779 Frederick Haldimand, the Governor of Québec City, founded the first subscription library in Canada. Until then, Canada's libraries were mostly religious institutions, and the general public was not admitted. However, even though "Haldimand's library, like other subscription libraries, appealed primarily to an urban elite", it was the nation's first step towards the public library as it is known today. Haldimand's library later merged with the Literary and Historical Society of Quebec, which displays the original Québec Library collection within its library. This and similar association/social libraries were examples of early prototypes of public libraries.

They were public in that membership was allowed regardless of class or religion, and many in Canada eventually evolved into free public libraries. Subsequently legislative collections were established in 1791 in Upper and in 1792 in Lower Canada; and in 1796 the first public library was founded in Montreal. In 1800, libraries were established in King's College, Nova Scotia, and at Niagara, where the first public library in Upper Canada operated for twenty years, in spite of losses during the War of 1812. In Saint John, New Brunswick in 1883, following the efforts of Colonel James Domville in procuring a collection of materials to replace the many private collections lost in the Great Fire of Saint John, New Brunswick the first free, tax-supported public library was established. Guelph, Ontario and Toronto, Ontario opened public libraries that same year as well. Due to Canada's size and diversity, the development of the modern Canadian public library was more of a slow evolution than a quick transition as each of the provinces' specific conditions had first to be addressed.

The public library therefore took on many forms in Canada's earlier years; the three most prevalent of these forms were school-district libraries, Mechanics Institutes, and association/social libraries. In 1850, school-district libraries were initiated in Canada. Public servant Joseph Howe started one in Nova Scotia, and politician Egerton Ryerson started one in Ontario. New Brunswick and Prince Edward Island followed suit in 1858 and 1877, respectively. The hope was that both children and adults could benefit from the local school authorities, where financial assistance was provided from colonial legislatures, but the departments of education proved to be too centralizing for locals and this practiced was phased out. Mechanics Institutes also contained libraries that the working class could access inexpensively. The first Canadian library of its kind was established in 1828 in Montréal, Québec. Other communities took up this idea as well – notably those in Halifax, Nova Scotia, Hamilton, Ontario, Toronto, Ontario and Victoria, British Columbia. Like the school-district libraries, these institutes eventually ceased or were replaced by public libraries.

The public library that opened in Toronto, Ontario, was mostly due to a campaign by city alderman John Hallam. James Bain became the first chief librarian, and built a comprehensive collection of Canadian literature and history. The Toronto Public Library was one of the first libraries to choose free status, and it was the largest of them all. Its development flourished after 1900 when Carnegie grants began to aid in building construction and the expansion of collections and services. During this time, open access and children's departments were introduced, and standard cataloguing and classification systems were adopted. Many of the original branches, funded by a Carnegie grant, still stand and continue to be operated by the Toronto Public Library. Other provinces were affected by Carnegie as well and followed Ontario's lead in legislating tax support for library services. British Columbia acted in 1891, Manitoba in 1899, Saskatchewan in 1906, and in Alberta, the first legislation officially passed by the legislative assembly was the Library Act.

The act was passed March 15, 1907. The next provinces to follow were New Brunswick in 1929, Newfoundland in 1935, Prince Edward Island in 1936, Nova Scotia in 1937, Québec in1959, and then the Northwest Territories in 1966. As they stand today, public libraries in Canada are "governed by provincial statues and are primarily financed by municipal tax revenues and other local income, with provincial grants supplementing local funding. [They are also] the responsibility of a local or regional library board with authority to appoint or dismiss employees, control library property, establish policies, and budget for library operations."

Though the services offered vary from local branch to local branch, public libraries in Canada are not only places to read and borrow books; they are also hubs of community services, such as early reading programmes, computer access, and tutoring and literacy help for children and adults. Throughout the years, Canadian libraries have been subject to the political and economic influence of the nation. During World War II, public libraries experienced development setbacks, but expansion resumed in 1945. Then, in the 1960s, Canadian public libraries felt the benefits of the era's emphasis on education – service expanded, buildings were remodeled or constructed from scratch, and Centennial Grants were provided in order to improve the system. This period of growth ended in due to the inflationary period in the 1970s and the two recessions during the 1980s.

However, in the late 1990s this trend reversed and the National Core Library Statistics Programme reported in 1999 that public libraries served 28.5 million municipal residents – a total of 93% of the Canadian population. Nevertheless, in 2011 the tides turned for public libraries in Canada once again, specifically in Toronto. The city is now undergoing a heated debate regarding Mayor Rob Ford's proposed budget cuts for the Toronto Public Library, which is currently one of the most efficient public library systems in all of North America.

Mexico

In 1646, Don Juan de Palafox y Mendoza, bishop of Puebla and Viceroy of New Spain, expelled the Jesuits from New Spain, and with the confiscated books founded the Biblioteca Palafoxiana—the first public library in New Spain. It was in Puebla and open to all readers. The Biblioteca Palafoxiana exists today and is listed on the UNESCO Memory of the World Programme.

United States

As the United States developed from the 18th century to today, growing more populous and wealthier, factors such as a push for education and desire to share knowledge led to broad public support for free libraries. In addition, money donations by private philanthropists provided the seed capital to get many libraries started.

In some instances, collectors donated vast book collections. William James Sidis in *The Tribes and the States* claimed the public library, as such, was an American invention. But exactly what constitutes a "free public library" is subject to dispute, and the term "invention" doesn't seem applicable to the many facets of an institution such as a library. Throughout history, knowledge in different forms has been shared in different ways.

Writing was recorded on papyrus and stored in scrolls and kept in vast libraries such as the Library of Alexandria in Egypt. In ancient Greece, knowledge was passed by one person reading aloud to a group of scribes from a text; this resulted in sometimes different and error-prone versions of the same text. Monks in the Middle Ages copied manuscripts by hand. After the invention of the printing press by Johann Gutenberg, books became prevalent, and different institutions such as universities and governments and churches found ways to keep and share them.

There are disputes about which was the first public library in the nation. Early American cities such as Boston and Philadelphia and New York had the first organized collections of books, but which library was truly "public" is subject to dispute. Sidis claims the first public library was Boston's in 1636, although the official Boston Public Library was organized later in 1852. In 1698, Charleston's St. Philip's Church Parsonage had a parish library. In 1731, Benjamin Franklin and his friends, sometimes called "the Junto", operated the Library Company of Philadelphia partly as a means to settle arguments and partly as a means to advance themselves through sharing information. Franklin's subscription library allowed members to buy "shares" and combined funds were used to buy more books; in return, members could borrow books and use the library. Today, the Library Company continues to exist as a nonprofit, independent research library.

A town in Massachusetts wanted to name itself Franklin in honour of the famous Pennsylvanian, and in return, Benjamin Franklin donated books for use by local residents; while Franklin had been asked to donate a church bell instead, he declined on the basis that "sense" was preferable to "sound". One source considers the Franklin library in Massachusetts to be the first public library in the United States.

Another source claims the library in Darby, Pennsylvania which opened in 1743 is the "oldest continuously operating free public library" in the United States. But other libraries claim to be the first public library, including the Scoville library in Salisbury, Connecticut, which was established in 1803. The library in the New Hampshire town of Peterborough claims to be the first publicly-funded library; it opened in 1833. And a library in Massachusetts in the town of Arlington claims to have had the first free children's library; it opened in 1835.

Finances

In the trend from private to public libraries, big city libraries had the largest book collections and the most funding. The forerunner of the New York Public Library in Manhattan was a library established by the Earl of Ballamont around 1700. A newspaper described the call for the "first public librarian" demanding that "he must not be too young, for this would render him liable to be despised by the youth" and "he must be of an even temper" with "great diligence" and "sufficient learning" and "have a genius peculiarly adapted to the calling." In 1849, the library was officially established, and consolidated in 1901.

Today, it is considered to be one of the most important public libraries in the nation. New York governor and book lover Samuel J. Tilden bequeathed millions to build the New York Public Library. He believed Americans should have access to books and a free education if desired. In 2005, the library offered the "NYPL Digital Gallery" which made a collection of 275,000 images viewable over the web; while most of the contents are in the public domain, some images are still subject to copyright rules. In 1902, one account suggested "the village library is growing more and more an indispensable adjunct to American village life." Around the turn from the 19th to the 20th century,

Scottish-American businessman Andrew Carnegie donated over $60 million, which was a vast fortune in 20th century dollars, to build over 2,811 free public library buildings in the United States. They were often known as Carnegie libraries.

Carnegie envisioned that libraries would "bring books and information to all people." Libraries have been started with wills from other benefactors; for example, the Bacon Free Library in South Natick, Massachusetts was founded in 1881 after a benefactor left $15,000 in a will; it has operated as a public library since then. Once the idea of the public library as an agency worthy of taxation was broadly established during the nineteenth and early twentieth centuries, librarians through actions of the American Library Association and its division devoted to public libraries, the Public Library Association, sought ways to identify standards and guidelines to ensure quality service.

In 2009, with the economic downturn, many public libraries have budget shortfalls. The library in Darby, Pennsylvania found expenses were greater than revenues from local property taxes, state funds, and investment income; it was on the risk of closing, according to a newspaper report. Many public libraries face budgetary problems; the report noted that "tax dollars that support them are dwindling as property tax revenue declines along with home values and sales taxes fall as consumers spend less. As local funding drops, libraries are turning to their endowments and draining the investments." Many libraries have foundations behind them to support them financially, and rely on the help of well-heeled donors as well as local corporations for funds.

Services

Most public libraries today are supported by tax monies from local and state governments, and some have foundations to support them with additional capital. Libraries lend books and materials freely, but charge fines if materials are returned late or damaged. Libraries often keep many historical documents relevant to their particular town, and serve as a resource for historians in some instances; for example, the Queens Public Library kept letters written by unrecognized Tiffany lamp designer Clara Driscoll, and the letters remained in the library until a curator discovered them. In 2009, big city libraries have multiple branches and offer numerous services.

For example, the Boston Public Library has 26 neighbourhood branches and offers free Internet service; it has two restaurants and an online store which features reproductions of photographs and artwork; and it promotes itself with a website. It answers more than one million reference questions annually. The library uses wireless technology software networks to offer more services and keep costs under control. The Boston library offers digitized content, video, a wider range of formats and, as a result, "research documents now have broader accessibility within the community and around the world," and help communities by offering public access computers, mobile Wi-fi access, and free job search tools. Libraries promote cultural awareness; in Newark, New Jersey, the public library celebrated black history with exhibits and programmes.

Libraries also partner with schools and community organizations to promote literacy and learning. One account suggested libraries were essential to "economic compet-itiveness" as well as "neighbourhood vitality" and help some people find jobs. Some library buildings are notable for their particular architectural styles; in the town of Beaver Dam, Wisconsin, architects designed the Williams Free Library in the style of Richardsonian Romanesque.

EUROPE

France

The National Library of France is one of the oldest libraries in the world still in service today as it traces its origin to the royal library founded at the Louvre by King Charles V in 1368, but at the time it was conceived as the private library of the French kings and it opened to the public only in 1692, during the reign of Louis XIV.

Claude Sallier, the philologist and churchman, had an idea that was advanced for its era—to make culture accessible to all. From 1737 to 1750 he made books available to the town of Saulieu, forming France's first public library. The pioneer of modern public libraries in France was Eugène Morel, a writer and one of the librarians at the Bibliothèque nationale. He put forward his ideas in the 1910 book La Librairie publique.

Italy

The Malatestiana Library also known as the Malatesta Novello Library, is a public library dating from 1452 in Cesena, Emilia-Romagna. It was the first European civic library, *i.e.* belonging to the Commune and open to everybody. It was commissioned by the Lord of Cesena, Malatesta Novello. The works were directed by Matteo Nuti of Fano and lasted from 1447 to 1452.

Poland

The Zaluski Library was built in Warsaw 1747– 1795 by Józef Andrzej Zaluski and his brother, Andrzej Stanis³aw Zaluski, both Roman Catholic bishops. The library was open to the public and indeed was the first Polish public library, the biggest in Poland and one of the earliest public libraries in Europe.

In 1794, the library was looted on orders from Catherine II of Russia. Much of the material was returned in the period of 1842-1920, but once again the library was decimated during World War II during the period following the Warsaw Uprising. The Zaluski Library was succeeded by the creation of the

National Library of Poland in 1928.

Australia

Library services in Australia developed along different paths in the different States. In 1809 the Reverend Samuel Marsden advertised in England for donations to help found a 'Lending Library for the general benefit of the inhabitants of New South Wales'. The library would cover 'Divinity and Morals, History, Voyages and Travels, Agriculture in all its branches, Mineralogy and Practical Mechanics'. No Public Library came to fruition from this although some of the books brought to the colony after this call survive in the library of Moore Theological College.

The place of Public Libraries was filled by Mechanics' Institutes, schools of arts, athenaeums and literary institutes. Some of these provided free library services to visitors. However lending rights were available only to members who were required to pay a subscription. In 1856, the Victorian colonial government opened the Melbourne Public Library. This was however purely a reference library. In September 1869, the New South Wales (NSW) government opened as the Free Public Library, Sydney by purchasing a bankrupt subscription library. In 1896, the Brisbane Public Library was established. The Library's collection, purchased by the Queensland Government from the private collection of Mr. Justice Harding. In 1932, the Carnegie Corporation of New York, funded a survey into Australian libraries. It found 'wretched little institutes' which were 'cemeteries of old and forgotten books'.

There was also criticism of the limited public access, poor staff training, unsatisfactory collections, lack of non-fiction, absence of catalogues and poor levels of service for children. Lending libraries in Sydney and Prahran were praised as examples of services which were doing well, but these were seen as exceptions. In NSW, The Free Library Movement was established in response to the Munn-Pitt Report. This collection of concerned citizens, progress associations, returned servicemen and trade unions advocated a system of public libraries to serve the needs of all people. The birth of the movement took place at a public meeting in the Chatswood-Willoughby School of Arts, Sydney, in 1935. George Brain, President of the Middle Harbour Progress Association, ran the meeting.

George Brain initiated the resolution which brought the Free Library Movement into existence in NSW as well as the election of provisional office bearers, including himself as Honourary Secretary. This movement was stalled by the onset of World War II in 1939. In 1943, the Queensland Parliament passed the Libraries Act, establishing the Library Board of Queensland to manage the operations of the Public Library of Queensland, and coordinate and improve library facilities throughout the State of Queensland. In November 1943, at the official opening of the new Public Library of New South

Wales building, William McKell, the New South Wales Premier, announced that the Library Act would be fully proclaimed from 1 January 1944. After the war, and with George Brain now in NSW parliament as a principle advocate for the Free Library Movement, the passing of Library Acts in NSW and the other states at the end of the war marked the beginning of modern public libraries in Australia.

Even after the war, the development of free lending libraries in Australia had been agonizingly slow: it was not until the 1960s that local governments began to establish public libraries in suburban areas. Currently there are 1402 Australian public libraries plus 78 mobile libraries. Australians generate more than 110 million library visits per year. There are more than 9.9 million library members more than 41.5 million items to use and borrow, plus more than 11,600 computers for public use. It costs $882.3 million to run Australian public libraries. They return at least $2.6 billion-worth of community benefits. All this costs Australians $830 million - just over 10c a day each with a benchmark for best practice funding being 20c per day.

The 2007 Americans for Libraries Council (ALC) report on library valuation stated, 'A benefit-to-cost ratio of 3:1 or better is common among the library valuation studies ALC reviewed. Because this type of economic analysis is commonly used across industries and businesses, it puts libraries into an evaluative framework that permits comparisons with other types of organizations. When this occurs, public libraries consistently outpace other sectors, such as transportation, health, and education, on the efficient use of tax dollars'.

FUNDING PROBLEMS

Most public libraries rely heavily on local government funding. Some proactive librarians have devised alliances with patron and civic groups to supplement their financial situations. Library "friends" groups, activist boards, and well organized book sales supplement government funding. With the cost of running local government increasing at a rate far above inflation, libraries are compelled to look beyond the tax base of the communities they serve. In the United States, among other countries, libraries in financially strapped communities compete financially with other public institutions, such as police, firefighters, and schools.

Many communities are closing down or reducing the capability of their library systems, at the same time balancing their budgets. Jackson County, Oregon, closed its entire 15-branch public library system for six months in 2007, reopening with a private-public 'partnership' and a reduced schedule. This example of a funding problem followed the failure to pass of a bond measure and cessation of federal funding for counties with dwindling timber revenue, in a state with no sales tax. In December 2004, Salinas, California almost became the first city in the United States to completely close down its entire library system. A tax increase passed by the voters in November 2005 allowed the libraries to open, but hours remain limited. The American Library Association says media reports it has compiled in 2004 showed some $162 million in funding cuts to libraries nationwide. Survey data suggests the public values free public libraries.

A Public Agenda survey in 2006 reported 84 per cent of the public said maintaining free library services should be a top priority for their local library. Public libraries received higher ratings for effectiveness than other local services such as parks and police. But the survey also found the public was mostly unaware of financial difficulties facing their libraries. Recently, many US cities, including Philadelphia, New York, Trenton and San Diego, have been facing the issue of making job cuts and service reductions in order to save money.

Most of these cities have decided to cut library funding by closing down several branches and cutting hours and staff members in the branches that will remain open. Philadelphia, however, has decided to keep their 54 branches open. In order to save money during this financial crisis, Mayor Michael Nutter has proposed to cut funding for recreational parks and decrease the budget for police and fire services.

Nutter has announced that the Philadelphia public library branches will not be affected by the budget cuts at this time. In various cost-benefit studies libraries continue to provide an exceptional return on the dollar. A 2008 survey discusses comprehensively the prospects for increased funding in the United States, saying in conclusion "There is sufficient, but latent, support for increased library funding among the voting population." Public libraries, long supported by various government entities, have seen a decline in monetary support for several decades, due to various influences.

The American Library Association states that 41% of states saw a decline in state budgets for public library funding in 2009 Cases in point are the libraries in Salinas, California, Rochester, New York, and Buffalo, New York, but there are many other long-standing public libraries now having to find new sources of income to keep them operating.

- In California, the passage of Proposition 13 in 1978 removed the property tax as a source of funding for libraries, school programmes, and other public services. This action provided tax relief for homeowners on one hand, but forced severe budget cuts to the services they enjoyed.
- The cost of creating, maintaining, and upgrading electronic hardware, networks, and resources has put a strain on many library budgets.
- The cost of printed matter such as books and magazines has risen over time, while funding has remained static or declined.

DEVELOPMENT OF PUBLIC LIBRARIES IN INDIA

Public libraries arose worldwide along with growth in education, literacy, and publications. Every country has its own public library history with influential leaders. Monarchs, wealthy people, and philanthropists have all made a contribution to society in the form of public library development. India is no exception.

Libraries were established in ancient India mainly by the patronage extended by emperors, major capitalists, and scholars. Indian emperors and kings were supported scholars and scholarship. There is evidence of well-developed libraries even in the sixth century A.D. The famous Nalanda University in Bihar had its own magnificent library with a massive collection of manuscripts covering the universe of knowledge. Admission to library was restricted to scholars.

Other ancient universities, such as Taxila and Vikramashila, also had valuable libraries. Muslim influence in India during the 13th century A.D. marked the dawn of another era of learning and scholarship. The Mughal period gave a further stimulus to the growth of libraries. Mughal rulers attached considerable importance to libraries and appointed scholars as librarians. The Mughal emperors were patrons of art and literature. In the period of Emperor Babur, Humayun, and Akbar many new libraries were established and existing ones further developed. Mughal libraries featured magnificent buildings, rare manuscripts, and scholar librarians.

The names of Maharaja Sawai Man Singh of Jaipur and Maharaja Ranjit Singh of Punjab will be remembered with appreciation in the history of library services in India. The Maharaja of Tanjuar started the famous Saraswati Mahal Library in 17th century A.D. It remains a unique institution in its nature of collection and services Libraries established by the kings and capitalists functioned like private institutions and the admission was limited. Service to the general public had to wait for the British. Unfortunately, the arrival of the British and resulting political disorder also brought chaos to the Indian way of life.

This was a severe blow to the cultural heritage of India, which had arisen from the Indus valley civilization. When libraries began developing in India during the early nineteenth century, they were a western product. In 1808, the Government of Bombay proposed to register libraries, which were to be given copies of books published from the "funds for the encouragement of literature".

The "Sinha Committee", this was the beginning of the first phase of public library development in India. During the first half of the 19th century, the three presidency towns of Bombay, Calcutta, and Madras had public libraries. These libraries were mostly financed by Europeans residing in these towns. Of these, the establishment of the public library at Calcutta in 1835 was the most significant. This was the library which later developed into the National

Library of India. Almost simultaneous, subscription libraries were started in many Indian cities. These were, of course, not public libraries in the true sense of the term, and did not provide free books for all. Founded in imitation of their western counterparts, the use of these libraries was confined to small, affluent portion of society.

The first three decades of the 20th century can be looked on as the golden age of the Indian library system. On January 31, 1902, the Imperial Library Act was passed and Lord Curzon transformed the Calcutta Public Library into the Imperial Library in 1906. Developments in Baroda were also notable. The development of public libraries in Baroda was unique. Baroda developed a network of public libraries to serve the entire Princely State.

Maharaja Sayaji Rao Gaekwad III of Baroda who traveled all over the world was deeply impressed by the role played by public libraries in the promotion of education in the United States and thought of extending such benefits to his own subjects. In 1910 he invited an American expert, William Alson Borden to organize the public library system for his state. The public library movement that flourished in Baroda was a glorious one. But that was not a general trend of that period because in no other part of India, a parallel development occurred.

Yet another development during the period was the organisation of a host of conferences such as:

- The first conference of library workers and persons interested in the library movement was held at Beswada, Andhra in 1914.
- The first All India Library Conference of Librarians was held in 1918 at Lahore.
- The first All India Library Conference was held at Calcutta in 1933.
- The first All India Public Library Conference was held at Madras in 1934.

With the existence of democratic governments in several provinces beginning in 1937, another phase of the library movement began. Between 1937 and 1942, a number of village libraries and travelling libraries sprang up in Assam, Bihar, Punjab, and Travancore. It was estimated that there were about 13,000 village libraries in India in 1942.

Another remarkable development was the appointment of the 'Library Development Committee' by the Government of Bombay, with A.A.A. Fyzee as its chairman. The Committee ambitiously recommended a comprehensive library system to be implemented in three successive stages. Because of financial constraints, the government could only implement part of the recommendations.

After Independence

After independence, the growth of libraries in general has been remarkable, although not as remarkable as that of academic and special libraries. At the time of independence, India was facing a host of challenges. Those in the rural population, 88 per cent of the total, were nearly all illiterate. Transportation was poor and mass media merely nominal. Nevertheless, the public library scene in India improved considerably during the post independence period, though it is still lacking on several fronts.

Verma and Agrawal argue that to compare our public libraries with those of the developed nations on equal footing, we have to go a long way. The 1951 census, the first conducted after independence, found 2,843 local governments in the urban and rural areas in India, of which 320 were rural district boards.

Only about one third of local governments maintained public libraries, about 950. In addition, there were about 1,500 subscription libraries. So-called public libraries were primarily reading rooms with a few hundred books for reading on the premises. The Delhi public library deserves special mention. It was founded in 1951 as the first UNESCO Public Library Pilot Project under the joint auspices of UNESCO and Government of India. The purpose of the library was to adapt "modern techniques to Indian conditions" and to serve as a model public library for Asia.

The establishment of Delhi Public Library, the involvement of union government in the public library movement, and the enactment of public library legislation in some states are the main factors which contributed to the improvement of public libraries after independence. Although the government of India allotted funds for public library development in its five-year plans, this funding was not connected to effective planning.

Advisory Committee for Libraries

The Government of India appointed a committee in 1957 to report on the status of public library development in the country. It is also called the Sinha Committee, after its chair, the late Dr. A.P. Sinha, who was at that time Director of Public Instruction in Bihar.

The Sinha Committee's charge included:

- Determining present reading needs, how they are met, and what part existing library systems play in meeting the needs;
- Determining reading tastes, what agencies provide suitable literature, and how reading taste can be improved;
- Recommending future library structure in India;
- Recommending areas of cooperation between libraries and education systems;
- Considering the training of librarians and the conditions of their service;
- Recommending the administrative and financial measures necessary to support public libraries in India.

The committee submitted its report to Dr. K.L. Shrimali, who was Minister for Education, on the 12th of November, 1958. The Committee described the situation as dismal and called libraries in most cases, "a stagnant pool of books," because new books were not added regularly. The committee at the same time observed that wherever large collections did exist, they were not fully used because of rigid rules. Library users were not trusted and were required to deposit large sums of money as a kind of insurance, which lower income people could not afford. As of March 1954 there were 32,000 libraries in India, with a little more than 7,100,000 books and a total circulation of about 37,700,000. The report observed that genuine public library service was rarity, and that public library service throughout the country was unsatisfactory. The committee recommended creating state library networks based on uniform library legislation.

The chief recommendations of the report were:

- Library service should be made free to every citizen of India;
- The hierarchy of public library service in the country should begin with National Library, and proceed to State Central Library, District Library, Block Library, and Panchayat Library;
- An independent Director of Social Education and Libraries should be set up in every state, with a fulltime senior class-1 officer of the rank of Deputy Director of Education to plan, organize, and administer library services;
- An All India Library Advisory Council should be constituted as a central agency to review and assess the work done at the state level;
- Library Associations should actively assist the development of libraries in the country;
- University libraries should cooperate with public library systems by allowing selected public readers to use their collection;
- State governments should accept responsibility for public library services in their states;
- Librarians and social education workers should cooperate to promote literacy;
- A library cess of six paisa for each rupee of property tax should be levied with the permission of local bodies.
- The Government of India should match the amount collected in the states. State governments should also give matching grants to local bodies over the succeeding 25 years, their contribution should be raised to three times the cess collected.
- State and national governments should enact comprehensive state library laws incorporating the right of every citizen to have free access to libraries. The Government of India should provide necessary financial assistance to the state governments for this purpose.

RAJA RAM MOHAN ROY LIBRARY FOUNDATION

Another positive step taken by the Central Government was the establishment of the Raja Ram Mohan Roy Library Foundation (RRRLF) at Calcutta on May 22, 1972, as a part of the bicentenary celebrations of the birth of Raja Ram Mohan Roy, a social reformer of the early 19th century. Its objectives are library development in general and rural library development in particular. It provides financial assistance to public libraries in the form of matching grants. It assists State Central Libraries and District Central Libraries, which has helped many states and Union Territories develop rural public library services.

Main Objectives of RRRLF

The main objectives of RRRLF are:

- Promotion of the library movement in India;
- The adoption of a national library policy by the central and state governments;
- Development of a National Library System by integrating the services of National Libraries, State Central Libraries, District Libraries, and other types of libraries through an interlibrary lending system;
- Propagation and adoption of library legislation in the country;
- Provision of financial and technical assistance to libraries;
- Provision of financial assistance to voluntary organizations and library associations for the promotion of library development;
- Periodic publication of reports on library development;
- To act as a clearing house for ideas and information on library development in India and abroad;
- To advise the Government of India library development;
- Promotion of research in problems of library development

The primary objective of RRRLF is the promotion of the library movement. The rest are subsidiary objectives. RRRLF is the first government-sponsored body specifically created for this purpose.

The foundation also has a programme of assistance to libraries for workshops, conferences, and exhibits. The foundation has taken the major initiative for the formulation of a national policy on library and information systems by the Government of India.

The current programmes of assistance are:

- Collection building;
- Rural libraries and mobile library service for rural areas;
- Seminars, workshops, conferences, training courses, and exhibits;
- Facilities and equipment for storage and display of materials;
- Public library buildings;

- Television and VCR equipment for educational purposes;
- Assistance to voluntary organisations providing public library services;
- Assistance to children's libraries or children's sections of general public libraries

During the last three decades, the foundation has assisted more than 500 libraries, including many in rural areas

NATIONAL POLICY ON LIBRARY AND INFORMATION SYSTEM (NAPLIS)

In 1985, a committee was set up under the chairmanship of Prof. D.P. Chattopadhyay to formulate a National Policy on Library and Information System (NAPLIS). The Committee submitted its report in May 1986. Following that, another committee looked at implications of the report and created an action plan for its implementation.

The Empowerment Committee submitted its report in April 1988 and an Implementation Cell was formed to implement its recommendations within a period of six months. Yet another Working Group, under the Joint Secretary to the Government of India in the Department of Culture, was constituted to examine its recommendations for implementation. The Working Group submitted its report in July 1993 and suggested implementing only 29 of 60 recommendations made by the NAPLIS.

The following are some of the recommendations of NAPLIS related to public libraries:

- Proposals for maintenance and development of public libraries should preferably come from State Legislative Enactment. The Central Government may revise the Model Public Library Bill. Funds for library development should come from each state, either from general revenue or from local taxation. Central Government agencies may provide funds under Plan Expenditure.
- Efforts should emphasize rural public libraries. A village or a cluster of villages with an adequate population should have a community library/rural community centre, which will also serve as an information centre. Resources from various agencies engaged in the public health, adult education, State and central government, etc., should be used to build up and maintain this centre.
- The central government increase its assistance to state governments in the development of public libraries. The RRRLF, as the national agency for coordinating and assisting the development of public libraries, should be suitably strengthened in order to do this.
- Standards and guidelines for library service should be created.
- There should be a system of national libraries consisting of National Library, Calcutta as the National Library of India, National

Depository libraries in Delhi, Bombay, Madras, National Subject Libraries, and others. These national libraries should form part of one integrated system.

- A National Commission on Libraries and Information System or National Commission on Informatics and Documentation may be constituted by an Act of Parliament to serve under the Ministry of Human Resource Development. The Commission will have representation from appropriate central and state agencies and could provide guidance and coordinate library development programmes in all sectors. This body will have the primary responsibility for the implementation of NAPLIS programmes.
- National Depository libraries; Connemara Public library, Chennai; Central Library, Bombay; and Delhi Public Library, Delhi should concentrate on development of collections and preservation of Indian culture produced in the languages of their regions, supplementing and complementing the efforts of the Indian National Library.
- The Indian National Bibliography should have a comprehensive coverage of the national output of documents and should be updated regularly. This responsibility should be vested in the National Library.
- Government should create a national awareness of the need to preserve the nation's cultural heritage. National libraries should be responsible, with preservation facilities created there. Links between libraries, archives, and museums should be established for the purpose of national preservation.
- The Ministry of Rural Development has a plan for one community centre in every Panchayat Centre. The Department of Culture and the Ministry of Rural Development have agreed to provide library services at each of these Rural Community Centres.
- An important link should be established between community centre library and primary schools. If the schools do not have libraries of their own, the community centre library should provide children with adequate services.
- A community centre library should have an important role in adult education programmes.
- A district library should provide facilities and recreation for the disabled and low-income people, *e.g.*, literature in Braille.
- Libraries should be built in areas of tribal concentration and in minority communities to help in developing and sustaining their distinctive cultures.
- Libraries should be equipped with relevant resources, such as

publications covering Open University and vocational educational courses, for their role in support of distance education.

- All public libraries within a state should form a part of a network extending from village library through community centre library, district library, and state network, and should be linked to the national information grid.

1951-1956

- The first five-year plan for educational development included a proposal for "Improvement of Library Service." This proposal envisioned a network of libraries throughout the country, coordinated by National Central Library at New Delhi
- During the first five-year plan, nine state governments, *i.e.* Assam, Madhya Pradesh, West Bengal, Punjab, PEPSU, Rajasthan, Savarashtra, Bhopal, and Vindhya Pradesh, decided to set up State Central Libraries.

1956-1961

- At this time, the government allocated funds to set up a national network of libraries in its 320 districts. As a result, most states established State Central Libraries and District Libraries as the main distributing centres

1961-1966

- During this period, the system of central government assistance to the states was changed, and funding for libraries was kept to a minimum. It was up to the individual states to take initiative and develop their public libraries. The programme to assist state governments in establishing state central libraries, district central libraries, and block development libraries was abandoned.
- The decision was a major setback to the development of public libraries. During this period four national libraries were established at Delhi, Calcutta, Bombay, and Madras. A Working Group on libraries was appointed by the Planning Commission in 1964 to take a stock of library development.

The working group submitted its report on 7th September 1965 with following recommendations:

- The central and state governments should share responsibility for providing adequate public library service. New government agencies in the central government under the Minister of Education, a directorate of libraries and a state library advisory council in each state should be set up to execute the programmes effectively.

- State central libraries should be established in four states: Madhya Pradesh, Mysore, Nagaland, and Orissa.
- States which do not possess adequate functional buildings for their state central libraries should be provided with library buildings.
- The state central library must have a children's section.
- There should be 335 District Libraries for the 327 districts in the country, *i.e.,* in large and populous districts, two district libraries may be provided.
- New buildings should be constructed for the existing 100 district libraries.
- Block libraries are the chief feeding centre for the rural reading public, and therefore, 2,500 new block libraries, covering 75% of blocks in the country should be constructed.
- A sum of 10 million rupees shall be provided for distribution of grant in aid to such libraries of urban and rural areas which depend on subscription and donations.
- Three public libraries on model of Delhi Public Library should be set up
- The Institute of Library Science established by the Ministry of Education at Delhi University in 1958-59, and then closed in 1962, should be reopened. Such institutes should be established at the state levels also to train graduate and undergraduate librarians to meet future requirements.
- A sum of Rs.10,000 shall be allocated as financial assistance to all national level and state level library associations to create library consciousness in the country by organizing seminars, conducting surveys, and producing library literature.
- A programme of book production should be undertaken.
- A draft of the Library Act should be produced

1969-1974

This plan proposed a substantial sum for the social education programme. A much lower sum was allocated. Of this, only a very small amount was available for the development of libraries in the country.

1974-1979

This plan included measures to strengthen the buildings, collections, and staff of the central and state libraries, as well as strengthening the district, block, and village libraries. During this period, attempts were made to develop a district-level library system, so that district library could act as a leader for the smaller libraries in the district. The adult education programme was the hallmark of this plan. The programme was to be supported by a network of libraries at the village and block levels and various community centres. Thus steps were taken to strengthen not only the village and block libraries, but also the central, state libraries and the district libraries

1980-85

This plan emphasized establishing a network of rural public libraries to sustain literacy and disseminate information to rural areas. It discussed the necessity of integrating school and college libraries with the system of public libraries. During this period, 26 states or union territories out of 31 had established state central libraries and 291 district libraries.

1985-90

During this period, the Commission's objective was to address the needs of 90 million people in the Adult Education Programme. The network of libraries was to play a role in the development of literature for neo-literates. Library systems were to be strengthened, with specific attention given to improvement of facilities at national level institutions.

An important development was the 1986 adoption of National Literacy Mission, which emphasised the education of women and the establishment of rural libraries. In addition, the RRRLF set up an Integrated Research Cell-cum-Computer Unit for promoting research in librarianship and database of public libraries in the country There were two annual plans for the years 1990-91 and 1991-92.

1992-97

During this period it was proposed to reorganize the Central Reference Library into the National Bibliographical and Documentation Centre, which would also have a computer centre. The Delhi Public Library set up two new libraries in its service area. RRRLF created programmes to help state central libraries purchase reprographic equipment, to help libraries process rare books, and to give special assistance to networks of public libraries that were at least 100 years old.

1997-2002

During the 9th five year plan, the National Library, Kolkatta, undertook several major initiatives to upgrade and modernize its collection building programme, reader services, and conservation of library material. The major activities completed during the period were automation of the circulation system in the lending section, setting up of a local area network, improved reader services, and more efficient collection management.

The conservation activities in the library got a major advance with the purchase of modern equipment to preserve rare books and other materials. The Central Reference Library, Kolkatta computerised various functions during the Ninth Plan. As a result, the publication of the Indian National Bibliography is now up to date, with records available online. Funds were provided to the Delhi Public Library and Central Secretariat Library, Delhi, for acquisition of new material in different languages and media as well as for modernizing their infrastructure. The benefits of these efforts can be seen in improved reader services, networking, and resource sharing.

The Central Secretariat Library organized a number of computer training programmes for resource sharing, standardization of cataloguing formats, and co-operative acquisition. Funds for modernizing and computerization were also provided from central grants to the Connemara Library, Chennai, Thanjavur Maharaja Serovji Sarasvati Mahal Library, Thanjavur and the State Central Library, Mumbai. Besides these, the RRRLF provided assistance to public libraries across the country for collections and storage, construction, and seminars and workshops.

Tenth Five-year Plan (Action Plan)

The Planning Commission proposed further modernization of central and public libraries during the Tenth Plan. A national bibliographic database would be developed to encourage resource sharing, networking, and to improve reader services. The Commission resolved to strengthen public library infrastructure through the RRRLF. The Tenth Plan focused on upgrading existing libraries, including private collections, and widening the programme for bibliographic control and documentation. To make readers services more comprehensive and effective, the National Library is expected to act as the ultimate referral centre for various subjects. To keep pace with the latest developments in information technology in public libraries, the upgrading and networking of central and state libraries was also planned.

5

Agencies in the Promotion and Development Library Management

STATE LIBRARY AGENCIES

Continuing education for professional and support staff in all the professions has been receiving increasing emphasis in recent years. The need to update current practice through new knowledge and insight of societal conditions and client needs has had its impact in the library and information science fields.

The advances in automation and technology, the proliferation of knowledge, and the growing recognition of the need to provide access to the rapid delivery of information in many formats have given priority emphasis to continuing library education as a means of responding to the changes taking place in our society. State library agencies have a continuing responsibility for a planned approach to the development of library and information services in each state. This planned approach includes the need for the continuing education of library personnel to meet changing service demands. This object reviews the background for the continuing education role of the state library agency, the development of continuing education for libraries, the implications of these developments, current programmes in progress, and trends which may indicate future change.

Historically, state library agencies have had the responsibility for statewide library development, particularly public library development. The provision of advice, assistance and consultant services has been one of the primary means employed. Included in the advisory activities were the conducting of workshops and other educational and staff development programmes. State library agencies having responsibility for school library development as units of state departments of education carried on similar programmes and activities to improve school libraries. Following the enactment of the federal Library Services Act (LSA), state library agencies moved into a new era of growth and influence. The requirement to develop state plans and the attendant emphasis on establishing libraries, creating library systems and extending library services created the need for staff development and continuing education activities as a major component in the achievement of desired objectives.

A U.S. Office of Education study of state library extension resources and services compares the data from 1955-56 prior to LSA with the re- sources and services of state library agencies in 1960-61. For the purposes of this chapter, the report of consultant activity and training programmes during this period is of interest. Forty-eight States reported 16,466 field visits compared to 6544 in 1955-56; 44 states held or sponsored some 1600 training programmes for over 56,000 persons from 1956 to 1961. These pro- grams served professional (36 %) and nonprofessional (22 %) personnel and public library trustees (26 %).

The responsibility of state library agencies for the planning and administration of federal funds under the Library Services Act of 1956 and the Library Services and Construction Act (LSCA) of 1964 gave added impetus to national documents and conferences concerned with improving the capabilities of state library agencies. These reports emphasize a stronger focus on goals, purposes and long-range plans with the attendant need for highly skilled consultants and related staff development activities in the field in order to implement the statewide programme.

All state library agencies view continuing education and consultant services as a major responsibility of the agency. In a recent survey, about one-half of the state library agencies considered the continuing education responsibility to be a shared responsibility and not solely the responsibility or of the state library agency. In recent years national activities of major importance have contributed to an increased awareness of continuing education responsibility and to an increase in planned activities of state library agencies.

In the regional hearing conducted in 1972 by the National Commission on Libraries and Information Science (NCLIS), one of the identified priorities was the availability of continuing education for the development and maintenance of competencies which are needed to deliver the library and information services required by the nation. Subsequently, NCLIS funded a study in 1973 to recommend a nationwide programme of continuing education which culminated in Continuing Library and Information Science Education. This report made recommendations which eventually led to the formation of the Continuing Library Education Network Exchange (CLENE). The NCLIS report outlines the develop-ment of library continuing education and comments on the necessity for continuing life- long learning.'

Based on responses from the field, an operational definition of continuing education was developed which includes the following:

- The implication that lifelong learning is necessary to keep the individual up to date,

- Assurance that the individual carries the basic responsibility for his/her own development,
- Diversification to new areas of interest, and
- Involvement in educational activities beyond those considered necessary for entrance into the field.

In comparison with other professions, the librarians felt that continuing education should be pro- vided for all levels of personnel, not solely professional, and that it not be limited to improved competence for the job held now or aspired to in the future. In its plan for continuing education, the report suggests roles and responsibilities of the individual agencies and organizations in order to coordinate efforts, including those of the individual employee, the employing library, the state library agency, the library schools, and state, regional and national associations.

Major responsibilities outlined for the state library agencies include coordination of continuing education programmes on a statewide basis, identification of continuing education needs of the state, provision of a link between librarians in the state and national and regional plans, and the appointment of a continuing education coordinator on the state library agency staff. The other major responsibility is three- fold: the planning, implementation and evaluation of statewide continuing education programmes based on identified needs.

These initial efforts to provide a suggested outline of responsibilities continued to receive attention through CLENE as a newly formed national organization. State library agencies which joined CLENE as sustaining members, as well as the state library agency directors and continuing education staff members, influenced some of the priorities of CLENE. In 1976 CLENE received a USOE, Title II-B grant to provide an "Extended Institute to Train State Library Agency.Personnel to Implement and/or Strengthen Statewide Systems of Continuing Education for Library/Information/Media Personnel." The workshop phase of the institute was held November 7-13, 1976, at the Illinois State Library. Continuing education personnel from twenty-five state library agencies met to develop planning and implementation skills in continuing education. For participating states the institute spurred development of statewide coordinated planning among providers of continuing education in the state.

During this period several regional consortia of states were formed with a primary concern for continuing education. CELS grew out of a survey of members of six state library associations where the need for Continuing education was strongly expressed. State library agencies are major financial contributors to this programme. The Western Interstate Commission on Higher Education (WICHE) had a major continuing education component funded in large part by five state library agencies. The Western Council of State Libraries has succeeded WICHE in this regional effort.

State library agencies were asked to report on activities in needs assessment, programmes in continuing education, the extent of cooperation of other agencies in planning and implementing continuing education programmes, recent changes and improvements in state library agency continuing education programmes, and trends and new developments in continuing education. Forty responses to the questionnaire were received. State library replies indicate that all state library agencies have a responsibility for continuing education. Several have stated that the agency statutes define this responsibility but most suggest that agency planning documents cover these functions.

Cooperation with other continuing education agencies is extensive; 63 per cent of the respondents work closely with state library associations, and 34 per cent with library schools. State universities, higher education commissions, state departments of education, and other agencies were also listed. State staff are active participants on the continuing education committees of other agencies, and either library associations or the state library agency has formed a continuing education committee for coordinated planning and programmes. The formation of continuing education planning committees representing all types of libraries is a recent development in many states.

These committees are in various stages of the development of guidelines, policy statements or state plans for coordinated continuing education programmes. Examples of plans underway can be found in Illinois, Michigan, Ohio and Louisiana. Oklahoma reported the formation of a state committee in 1978, Maryland in 1977. Pennsylvania is planning a special project in 1978 with a director and task force to develop continuing education coordination. States participating in the Western Council of State Libraries and CELS are the primary planners for the continuing education programme of the regional consortia. Coordinated planning appears to be one of the more significant activities now underway.

Continuing education needs were identified by the majority through surveys and questionnaires at state, regional or local levels;consultations with local staffs and "perceived changes in the library climate," evaluation of current programmes and of new national library trends and programmes were also cited. The responses did not indicate the types of libraries involved in the needs assessment process. The influence of continuing education committees and recently formed task forces has not yet been felt to any great degree in the development of continuing education programmes as reported.

The continuing education programmes sponsored by state library agencies are directed primarily to public library staffs, although programme offerings to reach a broader group were listed. All respondents listed public library directors and public library professional staff as participants; twenty-six listed nonprofessional public library staffs. However, twenty- one listed academic librarians;twelve, school librarians;twelve, multi-type participants; and two listed institutional and special library staffs. Principal topics in continuing education programmes covered a wide range including copyright, networking, automation, planning, management, public relations and audiovisual materials. However, over one-third of the respondents offered basic or refresher courses to public library staffs in such areas as reference, children's services, storytelling, and young adult services. A few states mentioned law materials, oral history, censorship, and government documents. Workshops on community needs and development of special services to disadvantaged, senior citizens and other groups reflect the outreach programme priorities of some states.

Wisconsin reported a continuing education programme for public library and staff through the University of Wisconsin using the Education Telephone Network (ETN). Once a month for about two hours, several topics are discussed by a group or panel. Local libraries may purchase sets of materials related to the programme.

Topics covered in the last two years include:

- Networks,
- Censorship,
- School-public library cooperation,
- The independent adult learner,
- Deaf awareness, and
- Service to special groups.

Alaska and Hawaii reported the use of video cassettes to bring continuing education programmes to remote areas, and West Virginia reported that the capability now exists there to provide this form of continuing education programming. Frequently, continuing education programmes sponsored by the state library agency are executed by contract with a university or other educational organization. Some states do this extensively; others use this method for institutes in such areas as management.

Recent changes and improvements in the continuing education activities of state library agencies reflected the increased emphasis and direction given a planned and coordinated programme. The establishment of a new position of continuing education coordinator was listed by five states; assignment of this responsibility to an established position was listed by many states.

Several states were engaged in "train the trainer" programmes with the shift to local library systems of responsibility for staff development and training in their own institutions, particularly for nonprofessional staff. State programmes will provide for more advanced and intensive training and attempt to ensure continuity in programme offerings. At least two states - North Carolina and Maryland -provide reimbursement to public library staffs for attending out-of-state institutes.

The responsibility of the continuing education coordinator for developing and disseminating information on continuing education offerings in-state and nationally; for maintaining a master calendar; for providing continuing liaison with library schools, library associations and other educational agencies; and for assuring a programme of needs identification and developing plans to meet needs were mentioned. These activities reflect to a marked degree the influence of the CLENE report and subsequent programmes and activities of CLENE. It should be noted that state library agency personnel active in CLENE are frequently those most active in continuing education development in their respective states.

Several states commented that NCLIS and CLENE had provided the impetus for renewed continuing education activity at the state level; one saw CLENE as the key to noteworthy, effective state library agency work in continuing education. The continuing education programmes of CLENE itself provide state library agency personnel the opportunity to gain knowledge, exchange information, and encourage the further coordinated development of continuing education activities of state library agencies. Changes and trends seen as important and needed for further development of continuing education include the development of more non- traditional methods for the delivery of continuing education programmes, as well as education techniques more suitable to adult learners.

States ex- pressed the need for improved needs assessment and evaluation skills and techniques. At least one-half the states were interested in a recognition system for continuing education. This seemed to be the national trend of greatest interest. Some states are currently using the continuing education unit (CEU) in institutions of higher education for library programmes. CEUs are directly related to certification in several states. South Dakota State Library provides voluntary certification for public libraries based on CEUs. Michigan and North Carolina have proposals for recertification of public librarians through approved programmes in continuing education and the CEU. The "college without walls" programme in New Hampshire and Vermont has prompted library staff to indicate that continuing education programmes should provide some academic credit.

A nationally recognized CEU programme for librarians was specifically cited by several respondents. The study recently completed by CLENE, Model Continuing Education Recognition System in Library and Information Science, was first discussed in January at a CLENE meeting and is to be further examined and discussed at a national convention sponsored by NCLIS in June 1978. State library agencies will need to give the proposal and comments from the field serious study, since it has implications for an increased state library agency role. This object has attempted to provide a summary of the development of continuing education responsibilities in state library agencies as viewed in the literature and reported from the agencies themselves. A few other points and issues need to be raised. State library agencies have a continuing responsibility for the improvement of the quality of library services in the state. In that respect they are in a unique position to assess the impact of continuing education programmes on library services in the state, and have a responsibility to do so.

There is no documentation to determine whether this is being done, but the need to develop the evaluation and performance criteria for this purpose is evident. In the author's opinion this would lead to fewer programmes of longer duration, involving participants in more appropriate learning situations and plans for implementation in their libraries. Another issue is the responsibility of the individual for his own continuing education and for the pursuit of programmes that satisfy individual needs and interests.

State library agency programmes are geared primarily to the perceived needs of the institution and to the priorities of the state library plans and objectives. To the extent that these coincide with individual needs and interests and that participation is voluntary and encouraged, the interests of both can be served. By publicizing continuing education programmes at state, regional or national levels, state library agencies are helping individuals to become aware of other opportunities.

Each state library agency needs to define its own role in continuing library education in relation to those of library schools, library associations and other providers of continuing education programmes. State library agencies should continue efforts to make possible situations in which innovators and practitioners can reach each other, invent ways to be mutually instructive and supportive, define steps by which to strengthen the drive towards improved continuing education programmes, and undertake cooperative endeavours that ultimately may matter greatly in the capacity of library personnel to deliver the library and information services needed in today's society.

EMERGING ROLE OF PUBLIC LIBRARIANS AS E-GOVERNMENT PROVIDERS

In an effort to become more efficient, governments are moving more information and services to the Internet. As part of this transition, some agencies have begun to use technology and EGovernment to justify the elimination of staff, many of whom provide face-to-face programme support. The result is fewer agency staff able to assist government programme applicants and beneficiaries.

This increase in E-Government at the expense of agency staffing raises a number of issues regarding government service delivery and support. In particular, as fewer government agency staff are able to assist existing and potential beneficiaries, citizens seek a range of assistance elsewhere. One such institution is the public library. As local agency offices close, more citizens use the public library to: use free access to computers and the Internet; receive computer and Internet skills training; search for government servicerelated information and forms; seek government programme assistance; and receive assistance in accessing government websites, navigating programme requirements, and completing online forms. In short, the need for government agency programme and service support has not diminished, but rather, it is possible that some agencies shifted the burden of support to other entities. Although E-Government offers the potential to increase the efficiency and effectiveness of government services, E-Government as a means to reduce staff and service support may limit this potential.

This is particularly the case if local agencies such as public libraries – where staff members are neither programme experts nor case workers – are expected to compensate for the reduction in government agency staff and services. This chapter presents findings from an exploratory study that assesses the impact of E-Government on public libraries, the E-Government support roles of public libraries, and citizen expectations from public libraries regarding E-Government services. For the purposes of this chapter, the term "citizen" will be used to represent all residents of the state of Florida, regardless of nationality or country of citizenship.

Role of Public Libraries in E-Government

The E-Government Act of 2002 states the goal of E-Government as enhancing "governmental functions and service," achieving "more efficient performance," and increasing "access to Government information, and...citizen participation in Government". Since the passage of the E-Government Act, E-Government has quickly become an increasingly popular element of service delivery at the federal, state and local levels. If E-Government services are planned and executed well, they allow government agencies to increase effectiveness and efficiency, and can increase citizen trust in government.

The challenges that libraries encounter in providing E-Government vary geographically, as planning and execution of E-Government service varies between states, municipalities, and counties. Even different agencies within county governments approach E-Government in a number of different ways, and with varying levels of success. In addition to increasing effectiveness and efficiency of services, governments have increased their use of E-Government in an effort to cut operating costs.

The Florida Department of Children and Families' (DCF) eliminated almost ten thousand staff positions between 1999 and 2007 with the introduction of its ACCESS Florida E-Government programme, three thousand of which are attributable directly to the ACCESS Florida initiative. The DCF ACESS programme is a "modernized public assistance service delivery system... based on streamlined workflows, policy simplification, technology innovations and partnership with local community organizations".

This programme largely eliminates DCF offices, instead, funneling applicants and programme participants to a network of Community Partners for assistance with applications and administration of accounts. DCF now counts public libraries among its Community Partners – agencies and organizations willing to provide Internet access and service assistance applicants. A close examination of the DCF Community partners list reveals that, in most counties, libraries are the only partners charged with providing free Internet access to any citizen who enters requesting service. Other partners are limited to specific constituencies.

Since 1994, the Information Use Management and Policy Institute at Florida State University has conducted a national survey of public library internet connectivity. Between 1994 and 2007, Internet availability in libraries grew from approximately 21% to over 99%. Bertot, Jaeger, Langa and McClure write, "...by meeting user information needs through public access computing and Internet services, public libraries were able to serve a larger community need for access to e–government services and resources".

The 2008 national survey found that approximately 95% of public libraries provide asneeded assistance to patrons with understanding and using E-Government resources, while 69% help with E-Government applications and services. Sixty three per cent of respondents indicated that the public library was the only free public internet access point in the surrounding community. Thus, public libraries provide substantial E-Government service and resource support. One can view Government to Citizen EGovernment as a three-part system comprised of the public, the government agency involved and the networks and points of access that allow citizens to participate in EGovernment with that agency. By seeking EGovernment information at the library and requesting assistance from librarians, citizens have added a fourth component to the system: the local librarian as a surrogate agency service provider. In this capacity, the librarian facilitates what ideally develops into discourse around the design of the E-Government implementation in question. As library activities write:

"To develop citizen-oriented EGovernment services that achieve cost savings implies that governments...actively seek to discover what citizens want from E-Government"

Some provides a useful framework for understanding the implications of this "fourth party" service provider. The object outlines a four-part chain of interaction in E-Government development that includes developers (agencies), local designers (developers), service providers (libraries) and citizens. The framework proposed by the library activities it is in the best interest of all parties to collaboratively develop effective ways to collect and channel patron feedback for successful, iterative development of the E-Government system. Citizens in need of government services do not bear sole responsibility for involving librarians in EGovernment service. Some agencies refer citizens to public libraries to access web-based forms or applications that are not available in their offices. The DCF ACCESS website encourages applicants to "apply for public assistance (food stamps, temporary cash assistance, and Medicaid) using the internet wherever it is available including home, a library, or a school".

Because they are, in many cases, the only organizations offering free Internet access in their communities, the public library plays an instrumental role in leveling out differences in citizen access to personal computers and the Internet, moving the E-Government system away from exclusion of segments of the population, and towards "design for all".

In this role, many libraries have begun to evolve into "one-stop shops" that now include assistance with government service programmes, access, and delivery. This is a substantive departure from a longstanding role of public libraries that serve as access points to government information and forms (*i.e.*, tax forms during tax season). For example, though librarians provided tax forms in the past, they did not serve as tax accountants who assisted patrons complete and file their taxes. Now, citizens come to the library seeking government programme and services assistance, not simply access to information. This shift seems to occur in direct relation to government agencies cutting back in their provision of programme support services due to the adoption of E-Government technologies.

PURPOSE AND OBJECTIVES

The purpose of this exploratory study was to identify the E-Government related needs of citizens who access government related information at the library, and to identify current library E-Government practices in order to provide practical guidance to public libraries in meeting the needs of local community members they serve.

Specifically, the study addresses the following questions:

- What E-Government services and resources do public libraries typically provide?
- What types of E-Government assistance and/or resources do members of libraries' community members request?
- Why do citizens seek E-Government services and resources at the public library?
- What barriers and issues do librarians face in providing E-Government services and resources?

Answers to these questions can help ascertain EGovernment needs from a user perspective, but also foster understanding the impacts of E-Government on community-based support organizations such as public libraries.

The study was exploratory and used an iterative multi-method approach. Limited to public libraries in the state of Florida, the study used:

- Interviews with public librarians. The interviews explored and identified the E-Government services public librarians provided, and the issues encountered by public librarians in providing EGovernment services and resources.

- E-Government workshops. The study team conducted five E-Government workshops in key geographic regions to explore E-Government service provision by libraries in the regions.
- Survey of workshop attendees. The survey asked librarians to identify the most frequently provided E-Government services, and to identify issues encountered by patrons seeking E-Government assistance in local libraries.
- Librarian-maintained reference log files. The log files captured specific E-Government service and resource transactions provided to users in libraries.
- User survey. The survey explored the reasons why users came to the public library for E-Government services and resources, library services requested and used to engage in E-Government services, and issues encountered while engaging in E-Government services. The survey was available in English, Spanish, and French Creole. The survey was primarily in print format, though a web-based Survey Monkey version of the survey was available in English.

The interviews and workshops informed the development of the log file and user surveys. User surveys and log files were pre-tested to ensure their usability and ability to capture valid and reliable data.

Key Issues

The study found a number of issues raised due to local, state and federal E-Government implementations.

Access and the Digital Divide

The transfer of some services from face-to-face to Internet-only highlights the gap between those who have and do not have access to the Internet. The digital divide continues to exist, to the detriment of citizens without access. In many communities, public libraries provide the only free access to the Internet, and thus the only link to E-Government. In some cases, E-Government is a matter of convenience. Some patrons seek websites and forms that make application for a service simpler than walking into an agency office or calling a phone number. In other cases, E-Government is the only option. The Florida Department of Children and Families, which deals primarily with a low-income constituency, has moved its services and applications to an Internet-based application system. Since DCF closed many of its offices, applicants have begun seeking help at public libraries. In many locations in South Florida, the only way to make an appointment at the United States Citizenship and Immigration Service office, which processes immigrant visas, permanent residence and citizenship applications, is to use the web-based appointment system. ECitizenship and E-Participation rely on access to the Internet, making access an issue of democratic participation. But access is only part of the divide, and a basic one.

Users require computer and Internet use training, information resource selection, web site navigation, and a range of other types of assistance to engage in successful E-Government efforts. It is not the case that the library simply opens its doors and provides access to a computer and the Internet. Rather, that technology access leads to a number of other types of assistance requests and needs from government service applicants and beneficiaries that agencies are unable or unwilling to provide.

Resolving Life Events: The Evolving Role of the Librarian as Case Worker

The increased emphasis on E-Government in public libraries threatens to alter the role of the librarian from neutrally situated information provider to that of social worker. Instead of being asked to provide information, reference staff report being asked to help patrons resolve problems, advise patrons on which forms they need to use, and at times, assist patrons in completing applications. Patron requests ranged from help with enrolling children in childcare, to finding family members, to setting up businesses, to help going through the trademark process.

Increasingly, librarians are taking on the role of the social worker, referring patrons to one agency or another, and becoming more involved in patrons' personal lives. In addition, the needs of citizens change over the course of the year. Librarian surveys, conducted in late 2007, suggested that the greatest volume of EGovernment services were provided on behalf of the Department of Children and Families. In contrast, librarian log data collected in early 2008 suggested that most E-Government services were provided on behalf of the IRS. Together, the data demonstrate that E-Government related information needs change fluidly with external life events, such as tax season, and DCF application deadlines. This evolution of librarian as information provider to case worker has multiple and profound implications. Not only is this a substantial shift in librarian duties, but it also requires librarians to become facile with multiple agency programmes. And, given that user life events can cut across multiple agencies, programmes, and eligible benefits, the knowledge and skills librarians need are numerous. A number of librarians commented that they had no training in being a social case worker and felt uncomfortable serving in that role.

Skills and Training

Librarians expressed concern and anxiety that they are unprepared to provide the services requested by users. While some agencies have made significant efforts to reach out to libraries and community centers that serve their target populations, many have not made any efforts to provide training to nonagency staff. As a result, libraries that embrace the role of E-Government service provider must pour significant resources into training staff, most often without assistance from local agencies. In short, librarians that engage in the provision of EGovernment services and resources are self-taught and can often lack an essential programmatic perspective. There is a need for increased communication and cooperation between libraries and the government agencies on state and local levels. Local agency offices are often unaware of the level of service libraries are able to offer, and direct patrons to the library for services they may not provide. They also argued that state agencies often shut down local offices without consideration for the restrictions of the local library's funding, resources, or space.

To some degree, librarians do not have a choice whether to assist or not assist someone needing help in using E-Government resources or services. If the person is present and needs assistance then the librarian will likely try to assist them as best they can – regardless of the level of training the librarian has received regarding E-Government. Thus, an area for additional research is the quality of the EGovernment services that librarians can provide – especially in the current Florida context of severe budget cutbacks, reduced library hours of operations and increasing overall library use.

Liability

As library staff members are asked to assist patrons with forms and applications, and to handle more sensitive personal information, librarians and administrators grow more concerned over possible liability issues. This anxiety includes civil and criminal concerns. Fear over possible lawsuits against library staff, administrators, and city/county councils, and criminal consequences associated with entering false information on behalf of library patrons lead some libraries to avoid EGovernment altogether. A few local library administrators restrict librarians from providing assistance with E-Government forms. In some cases, library staff members are instructed to limit EGovernment help to locating forms as requested, and to provide no help in interpreting or completing applications. But overall, there are no clear guidelines as to "how much assistance" in filling out forms requiring a range of personal information and explanation is too much assistance on the part of the librarian.

Forcing Technology Management Changes

Library public access computer and Internet resources are not limitless. Libraries only have a certain number of public access computers available for use. Indeed, 82.5% of libraries report that they have insufficient public access computers some or all of the time and 93.4% have time limits on workstation use. Given this, libraries have had to purchase, install, and maintain public access management software that manages user workstation registration process, enforces time limits, and resets the computers after each session. Time limits, imposed to alleviate public access computer and Internet access demands on limited library resources, are often in direct conflict with E-Government services requirements, which can often take considerable time and effort. Librarians either have to try and remove the time limit features, set up E-Government workstations, or risk the loss of E-Government application and other information by users. Thus, EGovernment service provision can impose a substantial management and infrastructure burden on libraries.

An Unfunded Mandate: Resources and Burden Shifting

When state and federal agencies send citizens to county-funded public libraries to access EGovernment forms, schedule appointments and seek information instead of providing that information in the traditional office setting, they add to an overall increase in the number of patrons requesting EGovernment services. Library services are provided by local tax revenue and libraries' budgets are significantly stressed. The increase in EGovernment users taxes the human and financial resources of already strained local libraries, increasing costs associated with staff time, computer equipment, and Internet bandwidth.

Although Florida's budget reductions represent an extreme case, reduced library funding is a national issue, made worse by downturns in the economy Agencies that choose to exchange face-to-face services for Internet based services are, in many cases, actually shifting personnel and operating costs to locally funded organizations that provide "free" public Internet access and assistance. Local agency offices are often unaware of what level of service libraries are prepared to offer, and direct patrons to the library for services they may not be in a position to provide.

State agencies often shut down local offices without consideration for the restrictions of the local library's funding, resources, or space. While some local libraries are able to absorb the costs associated with a spike in use, others cannot, and risk closure when local agency offices close their doors. This burden shift amounts to an unfunded mandate from state agencies to local, city and county governments that fund local library systems. Libraries are put in the position of providing services that they may not have the staff, expertise, equipment, or funding to deliver, or risk the ire of a patron base that provides the library's funding. Because public libraries are not legally mandated, community support is sometimes the only protection a library has at its disposal to maintain its operations. The extent to which reductions in state staffing at DCF, for example, have resulted in increased costs for public libraries in Florida, reductions in other library services, and staff time to meet E-Government service demands is an area for future investigation.

6

Policy of National Library and Library Legislation

NATIONAL POLICY ON PUBLIC LIBRARIES IN INDIA

Pre–Five-Year Plan Period

The programmes executed by provincial and central governments since 1910 for the social and adult education of the populace have paved the way for the enactment of library laws and rules for grants-in-aid in the country. Hence, public library finance is part of the education budget. The level of literacy in 1941 being as low as 16 per cent, universalization of elementary education and eradication of illiteracy in the nation were the aims of the education policy of the government. To fulfil this goal, a variety of programmes were undertaken such as extension services, continuing education, social education, part-time education, refresher courses, non-formal education, and adult education.

In order to accelerate the pace of socio–economic development, the government considered public libraries to be an integral part of development projects. In 1948, the first public library bill was passed in the state of Madras, mainly due to the efforts of the eminent librarian S.R. Ranganathan. One of the earliest Advisory Committees-the Sinha Committee, appointed in 1957-recommended that public libraries be developed on the basis of a hierarchical network. The hierarchy should have the national central library at the apex, followed by state central libraries, district libraries, block libraries and panchayat libraries. This is the foundation upon which the public library system has been built.

First Five-Year Plan (1951–1956)

The first plan provision was ₹ 140 million for social education, physical education, and youth welfare, out of the total budget for education of ₹ 1.33 billion. Libraries were considered to be part of social education. ₹ 5 million was set aside for establishment of the national central library, but this sum was not used.Improvement of library services was mentioned in this plan for educational development. The essence of the scheme was to establish district libraries in each state, which were to be supplemented by a state central library. The government of India also initiated a scheme, "Integrated Library Service," with the support of the state government. The scheme targeted units in every area selected by the governments for intensive educational development.

The experimental project was meant to monitor the impact of a number of educational institutions in areas covering 100 villages. Each area was to have five model community centers, plus a main library with branches to distribute books to 20 villages. This pilot project was implemented in 29 areas in the country. Nine states made plans to open state central libraries, and some others were in the process of setting up district libraries in about 100 districts. This cost approximately ₹ 10 million, of which nearly two–thirds was contributed by the government of India. Thus, libraries were considered to be an essential part of the Community Development Programme that was launched during the first plan period.

Other important developments included establishment of the Delhi Public Library in 1951. The Central Reference Library in Calcutta was established in 1955. Connemara Public Library, in Madras became the State Central Library in 1950 under the provisions of the Madras Public Libraries Act of 1948; in 1955, it became one of the three depository libraries. At the end of March 1954, the country had 32,000 libraries with a book stock of about 7.1 million volumes; an amount of ₹ 9 million was spent on library services. By 1951, the level of literacy had risen to 18.33 per cent.

In 1954, the Delivery of Books Act was passed to include newspapers. The act obligated every publisher in India to deposit a copy of its publication with the National Library in Calcutta; the Asiatic Society Library, Bombay; Connemara Public Library, Madras; and the Delhi Public Library. On the basis of books received under this act, India has a national bibliography which is published by the Central Reference Library, Calcutta. The bibliography, however, does not include textbooks, musical scores, maps, and atlases.

Second Five-Year Plan, (1956–1961)

Of the ₹ 2.040 billion budgeted for education, ₹ 100 million was proposed for social education, physical education, and youth welfare. This plan contained the same provisions as the first plan, plus additional provisions for establishing integrated library service. There were three objectives. First, state and district libraries were to be set up in each state. Second, the library services were to be organized on the basis of legislation. Finally, district libraries were to form the link between the state central library and village libraries. As a result, nine states in India established state central libraries and 254 district libraries. But the national central library was still not established. In 1960, the state of Andhra Pradesh enacted library legislation. During this plan period, a total of ₹ 2.040 billion was spent on educational development, of which ₹ 9 million was spent on library development. Even though ₹ 18.6 million was provided, the states only used 48.6 per cent of this amount.

Thus, the number of libraries nearly doubled in 1964 as compared to 1951, and the expenditure on public libraries in this period increased three–fold. A UNESCO report published on the occasion of the Public Library Seminar held at Delhi in 1955, India had 24,086 public library service points at the time. The level of literacy in 1961 increased to 28.31 per cent. The Advisory Committee for Libraries was appointed in 1957 by the Government of India, with K.P. Sinha as the chairman. The committee drafted a Model Library Bill and drew up a 25-year plan.

In 1959, the committee submitted a report with recommendations, some of which follow:

- Enact library legislation, in all constituent states, to establish public libraries;
- Build nationwide library service with detailed suggestions for financing through the state and central governments;
- Extend public library service to the blocks, panchayats, and villages; and,
- Create an independent Department of Social Education and Libraries.

Third Five-Year Plan, (1962–1967)

The amount of ₹ 5.6 billion was budgeted for education in this plan period, but the amount to be spent on libraries was not clearly indicated in the plan. Of this amount, ₹ 620 million was expected to be available for social education. During this plan period, the system of central government assistance to the states was changed, and funding for libraries was kept to a bare minimum. Thus, it was up to the individual states to take the initiative and develop their public libraries.

With the beginning of this plan period, the scheme to assist state governments in establishing state central libraries, district central libraries, and block development libraries was abandoned. The central government decided to let the states decide on the development; the decision was a major setback that hindered the development of public libraries. During this plan period, four national libraries were to be established at Delhi, Calcutta, Bombay, and Madras. District–level libraries were to be established in all the states. A sum of ₹ 32.3 million was made available to the states for this purpose. In 1962 the central government sent a model Public Libraries Bill to those state governments which had not adopted any library legislation, hoping to persuade these states to show an interest in passing the legislation.

A Working Group on Libraries was appointed by the Planning Commission in 1964. Group recommendations included:

- By the end of the Fifth Five Year Plan, set up libraries at block headquarters and in every village having a population of 5,000;
- Encourage the Programme of Adult Education to use the services of the public libraries to eradicate illiteracy.

As of January 1, 1965, according to the information received from the states by the Working Group:

- Twelve of 18 states/UT had state central libraries;
- 205 of 327 districts had district central libraries;
- 1,394 blocks of 5,223 had block development libraries;
- 28,317 villages out of 566,878 had village libraries.

Library legislation was passed in two states during this period: Karnataka in 1965, and Maharashtra in 1967.

Fourth Five-Year Plan, (1969–1974)

The education budget was estimated at ₹ 7.120 billion of which the social education component was ₹ 100 million. Thus, the tempo that had built for the development of library services slowed. However, ₹ 130 million was provided in this plan period for provision of information services, which included information centers, radio transmitters, film production, mobile cine vans, and other media. The literacy level rose to 34.45 per cent in 1971.In 1972, the Working Group on Development of Public Libraries was constituted by the Government of India Planning Commission to make recommendations for library development. These recommendations were to be included in the Fifth Five Year Plan.

The group submitted detailed proposals for:

- Allotment of ₹ 310 million for the development of public libraries; but the amount actually provided was a meager ₹ 20 million;
- A network of libraries to cover the whole country, and other recommendations similar to those made earlier by the Advisory Committee.

Figures provided in 1973 concerned the number of public libraries, and read as follows:

- Fifteen of 21 states/UT had state central libraries;
- 235 of 376 districts had district central libraries;
- 1,500 of 3,100 sub–districts had sub–district central libraries;
- 50,000 villages of 566,878 had village libraries;
- 1,800 of 2,641 towns had town libraries.

In 1972, during this plan period, the central government established the Raja Rammohun Roy Library Foundation. The foundation was created as an autonomous body under the Department of Culture, controlled by the

Ministry of Education, for the development of public libraries in India. This foundation matches the funds of the states for purchasing furniture and books, organizing conferences and seminars, and providing mobile library service to the rural areas. It also advises the central government on all matters relating to library development in the country.

Fifth Five-Year Plan, (1974–1979)

An adult education programme was the emphasis of this plan. The programme was to be supported by a network of libraries at the village and block levels, and various community centers. Thus, steps were taken to strengthen not only the village and block libraries, but also the central and state libraries, and the district libraries. The states were assisted by the Raja Rammohun Roy Library Foundation, which was established in 1972. During this plan period, the amount of ₹ 15.620 billion was allocated for general education, and ₹ 350 million was budgeted for social education.

The only state that enacted a public library law during this plan period was West Bengal, in 1979. In 1978, the government adopted the National Adult Education Programme, but it did not recognize the public library as an agency that could be assigned a role in solving the literacy problem. Rather, the public library was relegated to the role of post–literacy work. This view was also promulgated by the Draft National Policy on Education (NPE), 1979. However, the need for the rural public library system to play a role in continuing education in the villages and rural areas was recognized.

In 1979, the Ministry of Education in the Department of Culture established a library section under the charge of an under secretary. The goal: to promote development of public libraries in India. Since then, libraries have not been part of the social education budget. Instead, they have been included in the art and culture component of the budget.

Sub–Sixth Five-Year Plan, (1980–1985)

This plan emphasized minimum essential education of all adults, to be achieved by inter-sectoral cooperation and interand150; agency coordination. These efforts were to be supported by post–literacy, continuing education through a network of rural libraries as well as instructional programmes conducted through mass communication media. The amount allocated for general education was ₹ 21.622 billion. The art and culture component was ₹ 839 million.

During this period:

- Twenty–six states/UT out of 31 existing in 1982 had established/ designated state central libraries;
- Out of 401 districts, 291 had district central libraries;
- Out of 5,027 blocks, 1,798 development blocks had block libraries;
- Out of 575,936 villages, 41,828 had village libraries;
- Out of 2,643 towns, 1,280 had town libraries.

Of the 29 metropolitan cities with a population of 400,000 and above, only four — Madras, Hyderabad, Bangalore, and Delhi — have city public library systems with central libraries, branches, and deposit stations. Thus, it is estimated that approximately 20 per cent of the literate population has access to public library service. A Working Group on Modernization of Library Services and Informatics in the Seventh Plan was appointed by the Planning Commission in 1983. In its 1984 report, the group recommended formulation of a National Policy on Library Services and Informatics in support of similar recommendations made earlier by other committees. From its establishment in 1972, to 1982, the Raja Rammohun Roy Foundation provided funds of ₹ 250 million to assist 15,000 rural libraries. In 1982, the Delhi Public Library became a copyright library. The level of literacy increased to 43.56 per cent in 1981.

Seventh Five-Year Plan, (1985–1990)

During this Plan period, the Planning Commission's objective was to address the needs of 90 million people, ages 15–35, in the Adult Education Programme. The network of libraries was to play a role in the development of literature for neoliterates. Library systems were to be strengthened with specific attention given to improvement of facilities at the national-level institutions. The general education budget was ₹ 47,753 million; ₹ 4.821 billion constituted the art and culture component.

An important development during this period was the 1986 adoption of the National Literacy Mission, which emphasized the education of women and also the establishment of rural libraries. In 1989, there were 7,180 main libraries and 18,000 service points. The collections of the National Library of Calcutta were increased significantly. The Central Secretariat Library started creating a database on the epic "Mahabharata." The Raja Rammohun Roy Foundation set up an "Integrated Research Cell-cum-Computer Unit" for promoting research in librarianship, and also started a database of public libraries in the country.

A Committee on National Policy on Library and Information System was appointed in 1985 by the Government of India, Department of Culture. The resulting final report was submitted in 1986. This policy stressed the need to establish strong links between a village's community library and primary school. If the school lacked a library, the community library was to provide the children with adequate resources. Furthermore, a children's section was to be organized in every public library.

The National Policy on Education, 1986 barely mentions libraries. It states that a nationwide movement for improvement of existing libraries and the establishment of new ones will be taken up, provision will be made in all educational institutions for library facilities, and the status of librarians improved. The school library programme, "Operation Blackboard," was initiated with the provision of essential teaching and learning materials.

The National Book Policy–1986 also had an impact on libraries, as it recommended:

- Provision of reading material for children by all the agencies involved;
- That 10 per cent of the annual education budget of the governments be used to purchase books for libraries.

During this plan period, these states passed library acts: Manipur in 1988, Assam in 1989, Haryana in 1989, and Kerala in 1989.

Eighth Five-Year Plan, (1992–1997)

The money allocated for this period for general education is ₹ 168.133 billion; for art and culture, ₹ 7.276 billion has been allocated. Universalization of elementary education, eradication of illiteracy in the 15-35-year age group, and strengthening of vocational education in relation to emerging needs in urban and rural settings are the major thrusts of the plan. These goals are to be achieved by using formal, non-formal, and open channels of learning. The plan states that in those states with an advanced library system, rural libraries should become the focal points for post–literacy and continuing education programmes. Book promotion is also emphasized in this plan, to be promoted by the organization of a National Centre for Children's Literature, which should produce 3,000 titles annually. Important books are to be translated into the various Indian languages, and books for neoliterates published. Publishers and voluntary agencies will be given assistance, and the school library programme, undertaken as part of the "Operation Blackboard" scheme of the National Policy on Education-1986, will continue.

Public libraries of national importance are to be provided funds for improvements/innovations such as the following:

- The Khuda Baksh Public Library proposed establishment of an Institute of Oriental Studies and open regional units for research on Indo-Islamic and comparative religion;
- The Rampur Raza Library would acquire sophisticated equipment for preservation of its collections;
- The Asiatic Society, Calcutta, is to open an art gallery, introduce a desktop publishing system, and construct a new building;
- The National Library proposed making microfilms available, producing a national union catalogue, and providing book production statistics;
- The Central Reference Library is to be reorganized into a National Bibliographical and Documentation Center with a computer center; and,
- The Delhi Public Library is to open two new libraries within its service area.

The Raja Rammohun Roy Foundation proposes assisting state central libraries in their quest to obtain reprographic equipment. The Foundation also hopes to assist certain libraries in the processing of rare books, and to provide assistance to rural libraries, and to those public libraries that have completed 100 years of service. The Model Public Libraries Act is based on the national seminar on this subject, which was held February 14, 1990, in New Delhi.

The seminar was organized by the Indian Library Association in collaboration with the Raja Rammohun Roy Library Foundation. This excellent document encompasses all aspects of legislation important to the establishment of public libraries. The National Cultural Policy, 1993 is the new policy designed by the Government of India. It was created by merging the National Policy of Library and Information Science, the National Book Policy, and other related policies dealt with by the Department of Culture of the Ministry of Human Resource Development.

LIBRARY LEGISLATION

The Nature of the Problem

It would appear at first sight that provision and public maintenance of a system of public libraries would be an obvious step in any country where education and the promotion of literacy were considered important. Education, after all, is not an end in itself; the individual must not only have access to the printed word during his period of formal education, he must have the means of enlarging his experience after school and university, and this necessarily implies organized collections of printed materials. If a library is an essential adjunct to school or college, it is an essential adjunct in the world outside.

One would also think that the legislative base for such a system of public libraries would be a comparatively simple matter, and that those libraries would automatically be free for all to use. It is almost universally recognized that education should be compulsory, and that it should be free up to a certain level. True, cost can be a limiting factor but few countries today do not devote a large proportion of their resources to educational provision. Neither of these assumptions is in fact correct.

Systems of public libraries, as against individual public libraries, have only recently been recognized as essential, even in advanced countries, and many countries, some with a secure basis of culture and education, do not have generally applicable public library legislation. Examples are France, Belgium, the Netherlands and Italy. Even where public library legislation has been long established, it can be seen from the examples studied here that, in the framework of the modern State, public library law is noticeably defective. The development of public libraries has probably been hampered by the paradox that they were in fact recognized as instruments of popular education and social welfare long before the conception of compulsory education and before the legal framework of the modern State was established. The concept of the public library has been essentially that of a local community project. All countries have public libraries, buildings where books are provided for general reading, either free of charge or for a small subscription. They have been provided in thousands all over the world by charitable bodies, educational, social and religious organizations, by philanthropic individuals, as memorials to a person or to commemorate an occasion.

The public libraries in England and the United States in the early nineteenth century were typical, but they are not always a passing phase of development. The traveller interested in the phenomenon will come across examples almost anywhere: in Asia, for example, the Hardinge Library in Delhi, the Connemara Library in Madras, the Raffles Library in Singapore; in Africa, the King George VI Memorial Library in Tanga, the Connaught Library in Nairobi. Some become moribund.

Some are being or have been incorporated by good fortune into a national or local public library system. Some operate even today with some success. But they are not public libraries in the modern accepted sense, nor were they, for that matter, in the nineteenth century. Edward Edwards, pioneer of the public library in Great Britain, summed up their built-in failure over a hundred years ago, in evidence to the Select Committee on Public Libraries of the House of Commons in 1849:

- Without some assured provision of the means of continued increase, as well as simple preservation-no man ever secured to posterity the true advantage of a public library. To those persons, therefore, who took thought of such matters, two principles to start with seemed plain. The one that new libraries should be formed in a catholic spirit. The other, that they should be freed from all dependence either in gifts or in current 'subscriptions', for their permanent support. The first principle involved the corollary that the new institutions and their management should stand entirely aloof from party influences in politics or religion. The second principle involved the corollary that the maintenance must be by rate, levied on the whole tax-paying community, and administered by its elective and responsible functionaries.

This statement quite obviously implied that a legal basis was necessary, if the public library was to be a permanent institution and on the implications of this statement most of the public library legislation of the nineteenth century and early twentieth century was founded. In 1949, Unesco issued the first international declaration on the need and the functions of the public library, and in it was contained the same principle:

- This manifesto, by describing the potentialities of the public library, proclaims Unesco's belief in the public library as a living force for popular education and for the growth of international understanding and thereby for the promotion of peace.

- The public library is a product of modern democracy and a practical demonstration of democracy's faith in universal education as a lifelong process.
- Though primarily intended to serve the educational needs of adults, the public library should also supplement the work of schools in developing the reading tastes of children and young people, helping them to become adults who can use books with appreciation and profit.
- As a democratic institution operated by the people for the people, the public library should be: established and maintained under clear authority of law: supported wholly or mainly from public funds: open for free use on equal terms to all members of the community, regardless of occupa-tion, creed, class, or race.

The manifesto goes on to define the purposes and list some of the services of the public library. It did not, however, attempt to deal with a problem that was already engaging the attention of public librarians and those concerned with the spread of education and literacy, that there must not only be a legal base, but that that base must give equal opportunity to all citizens to use the services of public libraries. In other words, the legislation must be mandatory and cover the whole of the area falling within the scope of the legislation. The legislation must also provide for something more than opportunities for voluntary co-operation between libraries-it must provide for a nation-wide service, even though the public library remains a locally rooted institution. In 1953, Unesco organized its first seminar on public libraries in developing countries, at Ibadan, in Nigeria. Eighteen countries were represented, mostly in West Africa. Legislation was one of the primary subjects discussed, and in the general report of the seminar, the following statement of principles was included:

- Only legislation can empower the appropriate authorities to provide the service and ensure adequate financial support and efficient administration according to a national standard. Only legislation can define the functions of the providing authority, create the conditions in which it may fulfil those functions, and ensure development.

Library law for national schemes should include the following elements:

- General authorization of expenditure without fixing a maximum.
- Compulsory implementation whenever conditions become favourable. The basis of favourable conditions, it is suggested, is the possession of necessary finance and all requisite material by the providing authority, the existence of a tested organization and

the presence of trained and experienced personnel. Compulsory provision is never likely to precede compulsory primary education.

- The obligation to employ only qualified and trained personnel as librarians, and to authorize development only when professional librarians are available to administer the service.
- Service for the entire population in some form or other.
- The inter-lending of books between libraries so that the book resources of the whole territory shall be available to all.
- The book stock shall embrace every shade of opinion, without prejudice to anyone.
- The national scheme in all its parts shall aim at free service.

An addendum to this statement pointed out that there was great difficulty in arriving at a conclusion regarding compulsory legislation, since it was recognized that permissive legislation might well allow for a high standard to be set by enthusiastic authorities, which would act as an inspiration to others. This, and other proposals of the Ibadan seminar, were an act of faith at the time they were published, in view of the conditions of West Africa at the time, just beginning to emerge from colonial rule, with very few African librarians.

But the statement was the beginning from which can be traced the rapid development of public library services in Ghana, Eastern Nigeria and Sierra Leone, based on simple but mandatory legislation. In 1955, the Public Libraries Section of the International Federation of Library Associations published a memorandum on the development of public library services, of which one section was devoted to legislation:

Each State should adopt library laws which will include the following provisions:

- Appropriate local authorities must be empowered to expend public funds for public library purposes.
- The amount of local expenditure should not be limited: local authorities should be able to expend as much as they are willing and able.
- The public library purposes for which funds may be expended shall be so defined as not to restrict development.
- Local authorities should be empowered to enter into arrangements with other local authorities for joint schemes for providing the whole or any part of the service, and to contribute to the cost of schemes for cooperation and mutual assistance.
- Each local authority should appoint a library committee directly responsible to the local council.
- Each local authority should have power to appoint staff who shall be employed in accordance with the conditions and regulations applicable to other local government officers.

- The use of all the services provided must be available to all inhabitants free of any charge whatsoever.
- Though each local authority provides services primarily for the use of its own inhabitants and those who work or study in its area, other persons living outside that area should be able to use those services if they wish... when adequate library services are provided generally in a country or region, however, they should be available to all, regardless of place of residence, without payment.

As soon as practicable, all appropriate local authorities should be legally obliged to maintain adequate public library services. The document was adopted as a statement of policy, with the recommendation that it be sent for study to all governments and appropriate agencies concerned. One further example may be given of the continuing concern with the importance of library legislation. In October 1955, Unesco organized a further seminar on public libraries, this time at Delhi, India, where a successful demonstration project had been founded.

The seminar was held in the Delhi Public Library and twelve Asian countries were represented by forty-six librarians and educators. Again, public library legislation and its nature were under discussion, and the following proposals were accepted: Over-all control and co-operation of development, to provide for a permanent and progressive national public library service, can be obtained only by legislation, which should provide for the following:

- Opportunity for the development of public library service which will be available to all people on the basis of free and equal access.
- An independent service, and not one attached to another department.
- The constitution of a governing body, to be referred to in this report as the central library board, or in a federal state a number of such bodies, subject to a national body with advisory functions.
- Provision for adequate public finance.
- The constitution of district library boards responsible for administration of units of public library service.

Other parts of the report pay tribute to the work done by private bodies in founding and maintaining public library services, but affirm that planned direction and control are now required, and that these cannot be achieved by subsidy to private organizations. On finance the report states: It is of fundamental importance that finance should be by public funds, whether national, state or local, or a combination of these... differences in the structure, powers and financial resources of government at local, state, and national level are such that a simple statement of general applicability cannot be made. It can be said however that sources of finance must be adequate for the support of the service established. The proportion of local funds to national or state funds is a matter for decision by individual governments.

On the unit of service:

- At an early stage in the establishment of a national public library service, the question arises of the convenient administrative unit. This may be defined as the smallest autonomous unit of public library service... the selection of this unit as the real basis for the development of public library service, is a matter of some importance. It should be a viable area as regards finance and administration, and should conform as for as possible to existing local government boundaries... for ideal development, the area chosen should contain both rural and urban districts.

It is illustrative of the complexity of the problem that these four authoritative statements on public library development, issued over a short period of time, should vary so greatly in their emphasis. The Unesco Manifesto concentrated on the value and use of the public library, but said nothing about its financial or legislative base. The Ibadan seminar defined as a first principle that only legislation could provide the necessary secure and permanent foundations. It said nothing about the administrative unit on which implementation must depend, or financial problems, but it did prescribe mandatory legislation under favourable conditions.

The IFLA statement, though it defined the nature of public library service, proposed what was in fact permissive legislation, and it did not make any proposals about central control, the size of the administrative area, or financial viability of local authority areas. Although it said there should be no upper limit on expenditure, it did not mention the vital problem of minimum expenditure. The Delhi seminar proposals, with the previous statements before it, went much further, and proposed legislation which would provide for overall control, viable areas and financial support at national and local level. But it found itself in difficulties when it attempted to define the nature of the viable area. Any acceptable general statement must be vitiated by the enormous differences between countries in national administrative and executive structure, local government and its relationship to central government, the powers existing at different levels of government, and above all, the financial capacity of these different levels.

The stage of educational and technical development of a country must also be taken into account, but this is possibly not quite as important as it may appear. While literacy is obviously a primary requirement of public library use, most countries now have an extensive programme of primary and secondary education, and in many countries, too, advanced technology exists side by side with primitive standards of living in some areas. It should also be remembered that in the last century, in some countries, notably the United Kingdom, public library legislation actually preceded general legislation on education. It would be a mistake, also, to assume that the problems of public library legislation are confined to the developing countries. If there is one thing that emerges quite clearly from this study of public library law, it is that the problems of an adequate and effective library law are just as great in the more advanced countries as in the developing ones, apart from the fact that some advanced countries do not yet have a general public library law.

In some countries, such as the United Kingdom, the United States and Canada, the problem is primarily one of reshaping law which is defective and inadequate to meet the need of the user of the public library in the twentieth century, who requires access to the enormous and increasing flood of printed material, numbered in books by the hundred thousand, and periodicals by the thousand.

These requirements create in their turn a need for more and more specialized and trained personnel. The search is for a legislative base for viable units which can meet the readers' needs, and provide not only the material, but the technical services, equipment and staff required. In other advanced countries, such as Norway and Denmark, the problem is not one of the viable unit, which in fact cannot be provided, but of compulsory co-operation to give the same results.

The problems facing the developing countries may be different, but not so very different. It has often been stated that in social legislation, some African and Asian countries are at the stage others had reached in the nineteenth century. This is only superficially true. We are all living in the twentieth century. If the legislation of the nineteenth century is to be repeated, there is a long road to travel. Not only long, but unnecessary. The example of the past is to be learned from, not repeated.

Basic Principles and Practical Considerations in the Framing of Legislation

Assuming for the purpose of this chapter that new legislation is being considered, the first consideration in the framing of legislation is, of course, the nature of the State itself and the place that legislation takes in its structure. Particularly in social legislation such as the establishment of public libraries, which has primarily a local impact, account must be taken of the nature of the authority by which national government passes on its responsibilities, the basis of taxation at local and national level and in a federal State, the constitutional rights of established organisms within the State.

Even where there is no general legislation, in countries where the doctrine of ultra quires does not apply and organs of local government may establish any service they are not specifically forbidden to do, public libraries may exist perfectly legally by local legislation, and this in turn will cause difficulties in framing a general law. This is the case in the Federal Republic of Germany, and to some extent in the Netherlands and Belgium. Apart from this, there are patterns in the relationship of local government to national government which must be taken into account. H. F. Alderferl in his study of local government in developing countries, identifies four basic patterns, which are established in developing countries either through adoption or by passing on of previous colonial development. The French pattern, which exists in a large part of Africa, carries the doctrine of ultra vires much further than in England or the United States. Local government has no powers not granted to it by constituted authority.

Local government also is subject to executive jurisdiction which is independent of the administrative and legislative branch to a great extent. Generally, he states, French local government is characterized by centralization, chain of command, hierarchical structure, executive domination and legislative subordination. The English pattern, as defined by Alderfer, is characterized by decentralization, with local decision-making bodies with more or less independent powers, as against concentration, in the French pattern, where all power lies with the central government with local units acting as agents.

The English pattern generally implies also legislative dominance, the committee system and voluntary citizen participation. The Soviet system is one of 'democratic centralism', with all organs as links in one continuous chain of governmental power. Communist Party direction and leadership exist at all levels, and local agencies are not law-making or executive bodies in their own right, but subject to correction not only at the next higher level but at other levels. The 'traditional' form of local government is non-Western, though in Western forms there are traditional residues. The pattern is one of a chief or local leader, or a group of people, having jurisdiction over a village or group of villages. Essentially the form is non-urban, but it has deep roots and cannot be ignored as a working unity.

The Indian panchayat system of local government is an example of a traditional form being incorporated into the local government system of a modern State, organized generally on the English system. The clash between two systems, and the different types of law that may be produced, was illustrated in Africa when, at a UNESCO seminar at Enugu in I961, the question of a model Act for African countries was discussed. The Act proposed was on the English model. This was simple and mandatory, giving almost unlimited authority to an independent board, subject to central government control. It was this type of legislation which has been successful in practice in Ghana, Eastern Nigeria and Tanzania.

The delegates from the French-speaking countries could not accept this since it was not an acceptable type of legislation for their countries, and they proposed a different model Act for their purposes. Without quoting this in full, it can be said that it was at once more detailed and less specific. Though it set up a directorate attached to the Ministry of Education, and advisory bodies, it could be said to be rather a statement of intention than a legislative instrument. Subsequent decrees in the various territories have similar structure.

Thus, the decree for the Ivory Coast goes into some detail on expenditures and staff required, but does not provide for means of raising the necessary funds or an organization charged with continuous development. The differences may be more apparent than real, given a determination to create a public library service, but it does seem that in Europe, the Scandinavian countries, the United Kingdom and Ireland have been more successful, through planned co-operation between local and national government, than for instance, in France. A recent survey in Le Monde of the public libraries of Paris showed enormous variations in expenditure on libraries in the various communes, with seemingly no co-operation or standards imposed centrally. A generous system of subsidies for building is offered by the central government, but there does not appear to be any way of forcing local authorities to take advantage of them if they do not wish to provide their share.

There are other, important factors to consider in pre-consideration of legislation. Some investigation must be made of the practical problems, and a body of facts built up. While the survey is important, it must be a practical move towards action, and not an end in itself or a means of delaying action. One of the most successful librarians in charge of a library service in a developing country has said that until a service is provided it is impossible to say what sort of service is needed.

A careful analysis at grass roots level involves a detailed statistical examination of a community-its growth rate, its educational levels, its literacy rates; it involves the testing of different types of reading materials and a survey of existing places for reading and studying. Such an approach overlooks the complete lack of basic statistics on which to base the survey. And above all, it ignores the sense of urgency which permeates any developing country trying to pull itself into the twentieth century by its bootstraps. I am sure that these critics would produce a magnificent report. . . and that report would probably conclude that the contemplation of any form of library service was premature.

By the time it appeared it would have been overtaken by events, such is the speed of development of Africa today. This may be overstating the case against survey, but it is true that a survey should be made after decision-to discover specific problems and how they might be overcome.

These problems can be summarized as follows:

- *Educational Situation:* The provision of libraries depends on adult literacy, and is also concerned with the provision of primary education. Literacy rates based on averages are deceptive-for instance, the adult literacy rate in India is less than 20 per cent, but in Delhi in 1954 it was nearly 40 per cent and is now over 50 per cent. The Government of India report of 1959 did not consider that a literacy rate of 20 per cent was any barrier to a nationally organized public library service, but of course one would assume that a low average literacy rate would suggest concentration on urban areas. In terms of cost relative to use, there would be no point in providing for an elaborate system of mobile libraries to serve rural areas.

- *Language and Book Production:* The number of languages in use and their relative importance is a factor in pre-consideration. Allied to this is the matter of book production. Lack of book production in the national language is an extreme limiting factor, though the establishment of public libraries may well stimulate production and in fact has done so in some countries. But it must be observed that the success of public library development in some African countries has been due largely to the fact that English is the established language of communication, thus giving immediate access to an abundant source of material.
- *Population Density and Concentration:* It goes without saying that a rural and scattered population is more difficult to provide for than an urban one. The problem therefore is not one so much of over-all density as of concentration, and this can well affect the unit of administration
- *Communications:* This also affects the matter of the unit, and administrative arrangements. Decentrali-zation may well be necessary. This may be a problem of organization rather than legislation, but it must be considered.
- *Income and tax structure:* This affects the time factor during which legislation can be expected to come into effect, and also the proportion of cost to be met from various sources.
- *Existing Legislation:* This may exist nationally or locally, and consideration must be given to its possible incorporation in new legislation. In some countries, Ceylon is an example, effective public libraries exist in some areas through local legislation, and a new library law must take into account their existence and their legislative base.
- *'Trained Librarians and Training Facilities:* While most countries will have trained librarians, though not in public libraries, pre-consideration must take into account the availability of trained librarians to implement legislation. Opportunities for training abroad must also be considered. While it is an important consideration, the availability of trained librarians is no more than a temporary limiting factor, since there is little point in training

unless there are opportunities for employment. In India and Pakistan, facilities for training and qualification are in advance of employment possibilities in the public sector-not only bad planning but wasteful public policy.

These are some of the major items For pre-consideration and survey. The objective is to determine what a country can afford, how great is the need, what structure is required, and how legislation can assist rapid development, without placing too great a burden on financial ability or the administrative structure. None of them should be over-emphasized. The objective remains the same; the limiting factors affect how it is to be attained and at what speed. In this connation, the object by E. M. Broome repays careful study. Nearly all these limiting factors were present, but none of them deterred the Government of Tanzania from passing legislation and implementing it with determination and success.

As was reported at the Delhi seminar:

- In all countries represented at the seminar, public library service is already being provided in some degree, and the time is ripe for further development. In no country do the material difficulties appear to be unsurmountable, nor is a low literacy rate a decisive adverse factor. The rate of development may vary with the speed of overcoming these problems, but the basis for public library services should be laid now. The major deficiencies in present provisions are: lack of over-all control, and the existence of small unco-ordinated units; lack of, or deficiencies in, existing legislation; lack of sufficient funds and government interest; and lack of trained and experienced librarians.

Practical Considerations in Framing Legislation

It has been said that it is easier to pass a law than it is to change it, and this is a lesson to be learned from existing legislation. In the United Kingdom, for nearly seventy years only minor amendments were made to the enabling legislation, despite the fact that under the existing law there was no means by which county councils could set up public library services for rural populations.

Legislation should therefore be flexible and allow for changes in social conditions, in local-government structure and in the tax base. It should be capable of immediate application, but with progressive application. Study is made of the comparative merits and defects of existing legislation, but certain basic problems can be enumerated for primary consideration.

The Public Library as an Independent Service or Part of a National Library Service

In any country which can even consider the foundation of a public library service, there will already be in existence many libraries of high standard: university libraries, libraries of institutions, government departmental libraries, technical libraries and almost certainly a national and probably state libraries. It is tempting to think that there is an advantage in creating an integrated library service of which such libraries are a part. But it must be remembered that public libraries are for the whole community, whereas all other libraries are designed to serve a section of the community for a special purpose, and that purpose must be their prime consideration.

Techniques are similar, but basic purposes are different. Uniting all libraries in one piece of legislation at an early stage is hardly practical, since not only would it tend to stifle the growth of the public library, but it would also entail bringing independent libraries under the legislation, and this would undoubtedly be resisted. At the same time, there is an obvious need for provision for cooperation and some co-ordination, probably best organized around the national library. Bibliographical and interloan functions should be of value to all libraries. The national library could therefore be usefully linked to the central public library authority.

The Central Authority

The need for a central authority charged with carrying out the provisions of legislation is clear. Should it be an independent body or one linked to, or subordinate to, a government department? This is a matter for decision at governmental level. There are advantages in making the central authority part of the department of education, with a department for libraries and controlling body, which should have more than advisory functions.

The central board or authority is a modern device of government much used in developing countries, and experience of its past success in other circumstances will affect legislation for public libraries. But the implementation of legislation should not be left to any other body but education, and if education is chosen as the implementing and organizing department, then a section including trained librarians is essential, with advisory and inspecting functions.

Permissive or Mandatory Legislation

It has been shown that permissive legislation is of limited effectiveness, even when accompanied by financial inducements. Legislation should therefore require action to be taken, wherever the ultimate source of action. But provision should be made for progressive implementation at a rate to be determined by resources.

Relationship Between Local and Central Authority

It is generally accepted that the public library is a local community service. In fact, this becomes less and less true with the explosive growth in production of information material and technical developments in library organization. The answer must be sought in the local government structure of the country concerned. In some countries, a nationally controlled public library service has been created, with provision for some devolution to local government at later stages. The existence of federally organized states also presents some problems. But it must be stated that local interest is desirable and must be stimulated. This implies the passing over of some authority, or the creation of local advisory bodies.

The Size of' the Unit

Assuming that local authority interest is essential, the question then arises: what unit, what size and with what authority? The lbadan seminar, speaking for the situation in Africa, concluded that since recognition of local authority was only beginning, the sole public authority should be the national or state agency. At the same time, the appropriate local authority must eventually be given a responsible place in any national scheme of book service. The roots of the service must be in the local community rather than in the state, regional or national headquarters.

The size and authority of the local unit are important questions, even when there is a suitable urban authority. An urban authority should never be the sole local unit, since its economic and social catchment area is equally important for public library purposes. The requirements for a viable unit, as we have seen, were well stated in the report of the Delhi seminar, but it is already clear, fifteen years later, that they are expanding. In developed countries for example, much larger units than previously thought necessary are now postulated, and the basing of a service on too small a unit can be disastrously hampering in later development. Apart from size, there are other considerations. Whatever the attachment at national level, it is generally conceded that at local level the public library service should be executively independent of other agencies, whether education or other departments such as cultural affairs or social education.

The public library serves all, but is not solely a part of any, SO it should remain independently governed and administered. The question of policy control is a matter of the form local government takes. There is much to be said for the board system, independent but responsible to the local-government system, but this is not always legally possible. But it should be possible at all times to bring into consultation persons of knowledge and goodwill.

Finance

It is generally now accepted that financial support for public libraries should come from public funds, that is, taxation. It is also generally recognized that the service should be free to the user, though this is not always the case in practice. In most developing countries, this means major support at national level, with assistance at local level so far as practicable, having regard to the limitations of local taxation in most developing countries. The acceptance of this principle has been a major limiting factor in public library progress, even in advanced countries, as will be demonstrated in study of existing legislation. It follows, therefore, that any unit at local level must be a tax-raising body, and provision for funds from taxation at a national level must be written in to any legislation. In a federal system, of course, another stage of financial support will be introduced.

Various calculations of the cost of a public library service have been made, but they are of little value in view of changing needs, and could not sensibly be included in basic legislation. No one would expect a public library service to spring armed and ready from the ground, like Jason's dragons' teeth, and financial provision must depend on the rate of implementation of legislation. The Government of India report of 1959 postulated a period of twenty-five years for the creation of a full service, but its calculations as to cost are already completely out of date.

Given progressive implementation, standards of service required are also a matter for progressive regulation, and not a suitable one for inclusion in legislation. The power to make regulations on standards and other matters should, however, be given.

Other Considerations

There are several other considerations which may have to be taken into account in framing legislation, but their importance will vary according to country. In some countries, there will be a problem of fitting in private or subscription libraries to the system. There must also be some provision for co-operation between libraries, but this again will vary with the primary decisions already taken.

If a linkage with the national library, for instance, is envisaged, or if the unit of service is the whole country, then these provisions can be taken care of automatically under regulation. But if existing resources, as provided by various agencies, are to be fully utilized, then some provision for co-operation and inter-lending must be made. Although university and institutional libraries may not be fully integrated, their resources, after their first priorities are met, should be circulated generally. Whether library education, or the encouragement of library associations, should be incorporated in legislation is a moot point.

It could be fairly argued that if opportunity for employment of qualified people is given by the provision of a public library service, then educational institutions will provide the necessary further education facilities for training librarians and technicians, without any legal requirement to do so. Library associations, also, should not be too dependent on legislative assistance. Again, the provision of a service will itself exert the necessary stimulus for the creation of an active body of professional librarians. And if such associations are to encourage further progress and technical improvement, they should be independent. All these problems and others applying to particular countries will need to be closely considered before framing suitable legislation in terms which will create a permanent, expanding public library service available to all people, whatever their age, status or geographical situation.

The way in which the problems have already been approached and the answers embodied in legislation is the subject of the next stage. There are many lessons to be learned, and the gap between intentions and results is often a depressing commentary on how the goodwill of legislators can be frustrated by circumstances unforeseen or unsuspected. Government and legislation are, alas, by no means an exact science.

But in the framework of the modern State, legislation as an instrument of authority is necessary. In the case of public libraries it can truthfully be said that no successful public library system can exist without legal authority, but that many devices have been necessary to get round defective legislation. Public libraries happen to be the subject of this study, but no doubt authorities on law and government could produce better examples of problems caused by legislation rather than solved by it.

The Pattern of Legislation Comparative Solutions

The main body of this study consists of summaries of the existing legislation in fourteen countries, and taking into account the federal countries, twenty Acts are considered, with others mentioned in passing. More could have been chosen, but in fact, not more than thirty countries have effective general library legislation, less than a quarter of the independent nations of the world. Of the countries chosen, four are developing countries, two are countries with centrally planned economies and three are federally organized.

This, therefore can be considered a reasonably representative sample, ranging from the most advanced countries, where coverage is complete and basic standards established, to a country which has only just become independent, Botswana. They all have one thing in common; in none of them is legislation, even now, entirely satisfactory and effective, in that it encourages development to the point of greatest efficiency and maximum results. All have problems to some degree, despite the fact that in most of the countries considered there has been revision of law in the last ten years.

The advanced countries, most of which have had public library legislation in some form for many years, but with varying effectiveness, have no great problem of financial ability to provide a nationwide system of public libraries, if that ability can be brought to bear. The problem is rather one of an inadequate and unsuitable local-government structure, and the supplementation of local resources, or in some examples, replacement of local initiative, by central-government intervention. A pattern clearly emerges in nearly all recent legislation, first of a search for a larger and more viable unit of service, which must be both geographically and financially able to deploy larger resources for public library service, and second of the creation of a central advisory body to encourage improvement of public library service. One can see similarities in the solutions adopted, but there are also wide variations.

It is proposed in this chapter to show by comparison the major similarities and variations of the law as it stands in advanced countries. There are important lessons to be learned by the developing countries in framing their own legislation, and it appears that the advanced countries could also learn from their neighbours. In making these comparisons, it must of course be borne in mind that though public library law is evolutionary in character, it cannot be separated from the general body of law of a country, and it must be set in the executive, social and geopolitical structure of the country concerned.The fact that some countries with a high educational and cultural standard have not so far been able to enact general mandatory legislation on public libraries proves this to be the case.

Permissive legislation has been replaced by mandatory legislation in most countries. The appropriate local authorities are now required rather than permitted to provide a public library service. In some countries, notably the United Kingdom, Finland and Sweden, mandatory provision is not necessary, since coverage is already complete. In Norway, obligatory provision is laid down in the Act, and in Denmark a date is set for all communes to provide public libraries.

In Canada and the United States, though provision is not mandatory, the problem is no longer one of provision but of viability, and this could be said generally of all the countries considered, except the countries having centrally planned economies, where the law has nothing to say on this. But it would appear that in Hungary, at any rate, there is complete coverage.

Central Government and Advisory Bodies

In all countries, the intervention of the central government, either at state or federal level, or both, has led to the setting up of a central body to guide future progress, and this is the most common feature in all recent legislation. These central bodies may take many forms, either advisory or executive.

They may be independent, or responsible to a department of State. Their membership may be drawn from organizations or individuals. Their constitution and powers can be summarized as follows:

Czechoslovakia

The Central Library Council is an advisory body in the Ministry of Education and Culture. There are two bodies, one for Bohemia-Moravia and one for Slovakia. Membership consists of representatives of authorities and expert librarians. All proposals concerning libraries are submitted to them, and they have the right to initiate proposals themselves.

Denmark

The Library Council consists of sixteen members representing all sections of the Danish Library Service. They are appointed by the Minister of Cultural Affairs, are consulted in all matters of importance to the working of the Libraries Act, and have the right to initiate representations. The chairman is the Library Director, head of the State inspectorate.

Finland

The library delegation is an advisory body responsible to the Central Board of Schools. There are twelve delegates, representing the Department of Education, local authorities, library training and other organizations working for libraries and adult education. The delegation can take the initiative in submitting proposals to the Central Board of Schools.

Hungary

The National Council for Library Activity, responsible to the Ministry of Culture, has a section for public libraries. It has also a working organization, the State Institute of Libraries, similar in some respects to the State inspectorates of Scandinavian library systems. The functions of the National Council are advisory and technical, but being a direct organ of central government, it obviously has great prestige.

Ireland

The Library Council has as its main purpose the operation and supervision of the Irish Central library, and a secondary purpose of assisting local library authorities to improve their services. Its membership is by nomination, and a majority of the members are nominated by universities or the National Library. The powers of the Library Council are considerable, since it considers applications for grants from local authorities and its functions are much more than advisory. In view of the form of local government in Ireland, it can be said to be an executive body with potentially great powers. In fact, the original secondary function has become the primary one.

Qntario

The Provincial Library Council is an advisory body responsible to the Minister for Education, and it consists of nine members appointed by the minister, and one for each regional system. It has certain functions under the Act and may also make recommendations regarding development and co-ordination of library service.

Quebec

The Quebec Public Libraries Commission is responsible to the Minister for Cultural Affairs. Its membership is six persons nominated by the minister, whose qualifications shall be their interest in the development of public libraries, and the Director of Public Libraries of the Province.

The powers and duties of the commission are wide, in that it is generally charged with the study of the best means of developing public library services, and it must report every three months on its findings regarding the working of the Public Libraries Act.

United Kingdom

The Library Advisory Councils, set up by the Minister of Education under the 1964 Act, one for England and one for Wales, have no set number of members, nor any stated qualifications for membership. They are nominated directly by the minister, and actually the representatives are drawn from local authority members, university and public librarians representing all the major interests of local government and various sizes and types of library.

The function of the councils is purely advisory, and their main work is in connexion with the achievement of standards and the general working of the Act. But by their existence, they have become the advisory bodies for libraries in general, and on such matters as librarianship training.

Washington State

The State Library Commission is an executive commission appointed by the Governor, and responsible for administration of federal and state funds for improvement of public library services. It operates through the state library and appoints the state librarian, who acts as secretary to the commission. Though its main functions are executive, it also has advisory responsibilities. The functions of these bodies are mainly advisory, and as will be seen generally from their constitutions, are intended as a source of expert opinion on public library development.

They are useful bodies, but equally important, their existence creates a secretariat, and that secretariat, whether clearly laid down in legislation as in Quebec, or not, as in England and Wales, inevitably assumes supervisory functions. Those functions can be of inspection and control, as in Finland and Denmark, or they can be limited to advice to the appropriate minister and the right to ask for regular reports and give advice to individual library authorities. Even where there is no central coordinating body, there is invariably a central coordinating government department.

In Norway, the State inspectorate is recognized by the Act, and the State Inspector is a direct appointment of the Crown, though responsible to the Ministry of Church and Education. In Sweden, there is a Library Section of the Central Board of Education, and its functions include supervision of State grants, approval of building plans, and supervision of the School of Librarianship. With the change in local government law, its functions are now more limited, being more advisory than supervisory.

In the United States, in addition to the state departments concerned with public libraries, now established in most states, there is an office in the Department of Education in Washington charged with supervision of the very substantial grants under the Library Services and Construction Act. Except in Scandinavia, where they have been in existence for many years, the emergence of these bodies and the departments attached to them is comparatively recent, and their influence on public library development is bound to increase. It will be noted that the usual attachment of the library councils and their civil-service bureaux is to the Ministry of Education, in some cases to the Minister of Culture. But this attachment at central-government levels does not necessarily imply any attachment of public libraries at lower levels of government to any particular department.

Provision for Co-Operation

In most countries, legislation shows a marked preference for the provision of public library services within the existing local-government framework, and an equal reluctance to interfere with those existing agencies, even when they are clearly not viable. The only exception to this in recent legislation, where smaller authorities are required to give up their powers, is in England and Wales, where there is provision for the compulsory surrender of library powers by authorities of less than 40,000 population.

Even here, the clauses have not so far been used, since a major local-government reform is expected to make them unnecessary. Local-government reform in Sweden and Denmark is also making the problem less urgent, though it will still exist. Failing the forcible creation of larger public library authorities, the search for the larger unit must take the form of co-operation, and recent legislation is characterized by the creation of a superstructure of co-ordination, often at two or three levels, either mandatory or permissive.

Library authorities are either to be persuaded to join with others in a library system, or a superstructure of co-operation is created above them, in which they have the opportunity, or are compelled, to take part. Financial assistance is usually given. Some examples of this kind of provision are as follows:

Denmark

A number of suitable libraries are designated as county libraries, serving a district. Their functions are to assist the local libraries in the district by lending or obtaining for them books and other suitable materials they cannot provide themselves, and by giving advice and technical assistance. In the present legislation, the Library Director recommends which libraries shall be recognized as county libraries, and the minister shall ensure that the district served is of a suitable size and that the county library is able to carry out its functions. In the past, it is thought, too many county libraries were designated, and the districts were too small.

The provision is mandatory, that is to say, all libraries must join a district, and an advisory committee is formed to direct the work. National grants are made to the county libraries, and the county or counties must also contribute at rates laid down. The communes themselves do not contribute directly.

Norway

The system of regional central libraries is similar, except that the designated libraries have wider functions in super-vision of their local libraries.

The problems of establishment, and suitable areas, are very great in Norway, and though nineteen regional libraries have now been established, they vary greatly in resources. Again the inclusion in an area is mandatory, and grants are made to meet the cost, with supplementary grants from the areas covered.

Sweden

In addition to the establishment of county libraries on similar lines to Denmark and Norway, a further superstructure has been added of three inter-library loan centres, which lend to the county libraries and receive grants for their services from the State.

It must be emphasized that in the Scandinavian countries, the aid-giving libraries are the larger libraries in their area, and though they may establish special departments for their additional functions, in no sense, except in a limited way in Norway, do they administer or supervise the other libraries in their area.

Quebec

The regional libraries in Quebec are quite different from others, and serve a different purpose. They are intended, not to superimpose an additional system, but to encourage the provision of public library service in those sparsely populated areas which cannot provide for themselves, even with grant aid.

The system is fully described in the appropriate section, but briefly, when a minimum area containing 25,000 inhabitants can be defined, an ad hoc committee is formed. The kind of service depends on the size of the area and other factors, but generally, grant is 85 per cent of the total cost. Such a system is only required under extreme adverse conditions, but the similarity to the Norwegian system in its northern area is obvious.

Ontario

The Ontario method of creating larger areas is in effect a three-tier system. In a county, a combined library system can be formed at the request of 75 per cent of the authorities in the county, then a county library service is formed, and a separate public library board set up. But it is only responsible for that part of the county which has asked for inclusion. The system has obvious defects, but it does have the effect of helping some at least of the smaller authorities to combine.

Superimposed on this system of county libraries and independent libraries is provision for regional library systems, working roughly on the Scandinavian pattern, and having similar responsibilities. Substantial grants are available from state funds, but regions are not necessarily inclusive of all the libraries in their area since, throughout the legislation of Ontario, there are no mandatory powers.

United States of America

There are no mandatory powers in the United States, and most recent legislation, both federal and state, has written into it an injunction that the independence of the community library is to be respected and preserved. The creation of the larger unit therefore is by the voluntary amalgamation of independent libraries into 'systems', in which service is often provided by contract between one library and another. It is interesting to note that current thinking puts the minimum viability of a system at 150,000 population.

United Kingdom

A voluntary system of co-operation has existed for many years, with member libraries paying subscriptions usually on a per capita basis. The country is divided into fourteen regions for this purpose.

The 1964 Act legally recognizes this system, and provides for compulsory membership by all library authorities, and for amalgamation of the regions where necessary. Two of the largest regions, comprising London and the south-east of England, have already amalgamated, with the authority of the Ministry of Education. The purpose of the regions is principally inter-library co-operation, and for this purpose provision is made in legislation for bringing into the system other than public libraries.

LIBRARY LEGISLATION IN INDIA

India became an independent republic in January 1950. It is a federal union of states, there being seventeen states and ten union territories. The form of government is democratic, with a president and two Houses of Parliament. The Upper House, or Council of States, is indirectly elected, the members being elected by the legislative assembly of each state. The Lower House, or House of the People, consists of 500 members directly elected by adult suffrage. Each state has its own legislature, directly elected. Certain legislative powers are retained by the central government, but education, the most important function so far as libraries are concerned, is reserved to the states, though there is a central Ministry of Education with co-ordinating powers, including that of making grants for specific purposes.

These powers have been increased by the very large sums made available under successive Five-year Plans. The area of India is 1,262,275 square miles, and its population approxi-mately 5II million.

Local Government

Local government is in the hands of some 2700 municipal authorities which have primary functions relating to their own areas and frame their own budgets, though usually, however, these require approval at state level. For rural areas there is a three-tier system of panchayats, or local councils-at village, block and district levels.

Generally speaking, the block panchayats consist of groupings of village panchayats, but this does not apply to the whole of India, There are nearly 4000 block panchayats, and some 212,000 village panchayats. The district is the taxing authority below the state. The system is virtually complete and one can therefore say that local administration proceeds from state to city, district or municipality, and right down to its roots in the villages.

Education

The literacy percentage is approximately 24 - men 34.5, women 13. Despite this very low rate of literacy, very great progress has been made in education, and the rate has been improved by 8 per cent since 1951. Over ₹5,000 million were spent on education in 1964 and over 750,000 primary and secondary schools were in operation.

The official national language under the Constitution is Hindi, but under the Official Language Act of 1963, English will continue to be used as an official language for an indefinite period alongside Hindi. The regional language of the state is also taught at various levels. There are fourteen officially recognized regional languages.

Library Provision

In the light of the facts the problems of public library provision are very great. India is a very large country with a predominantly rural population, a small per capita income and a number of recognized languages. There are other problems, arising from the local-government system and the relations of the central government to the states.

India is a federal State and, as in Canada and the United States, provision of public libraries is reserved to the states and is their sole responsibility. Even grants under the Five-year Plans, given specifically in the past for public library development, were changed under the third plan to block grants to be spent at the discretion of the states. The central government has therefore no coercive powers to enforce legislation by the states, or to dictate the form of such legislation.

The legal powers to take over the many private or association libraries are also limited. To bring them into the public sector would require separate legislation which is unlikely to be voted. In view of the numbers of such libraries, this is important. Given a government determined enough to create a nation-wide public library system, the position could, of course, be changed. There is a national Ministry of Education, and it could be given coordinating functions.

In fact, the Advisory Committee of I 959 proposed this in the form of an All-India Library Advisory Council, with an executive committee nominated by the Minister of Education, and a secretariat consisting of a division of libraries in the Ministry of Education. It also suggested that the Government of India should contribute to the library funds of the state an amount equal to funds raised by property tax. Presumably, these proposals would require legislation at national level.

Despite many obstacles, India has a strong and continuing literary tradition, and there is a thirst for knowledge which is evidenced by the fact that over 10,000 periodicals and newspapers are published in India. Book production, although its organization is chaotic, flourishes and there is not in fact, any shortage of libraries.

Very few Indian towns or even large villages are without a library of some sort, provided by a charitable foundation, by an educational organization or by executive action on the part of state, municipal or district authority. Very few of these institutions are well endowed, many are little more than reading-rooms. In this connexion, the statement by the Advisory Committee on Libraries, which reported in 1959, is of value in estimating the true position:

- In India the phrase 'public libraries' is used in a very loose sense. It is used to denote any library which permits members of the public to use its material for reference or borrowing on payment of fees or rent. In this sense, all kinds of libraries, national, university, schools and subscription libraries, etc., would be public libraries. Because of the loose connotation of the term, it would appear from the statistics published by Unesco in 1956 that India leads the world in the number of public libraries, which is given as 24,086. The statistics are flattering; they express the aspiration rather than the achievement of the country. The internationally accepted definition of a public library is that it is a library which is:
  - Is financed out of public funds;
  - Charges no fees from readers and yet is open for full use by the public without distinction of caste, creed or sex;

- Is intended as an auxiliary educational institution providing a means of self education which is endless;
- Houses learning materials giving reliable information freely and without partiality or prejudice on as wide a variety of subjects as will satisfy the interests of readers. Were such a definition adopted, the number of public libraries in India could not be counted by tens, let alone by hundreds or thousands.

A framework of library provision does, however, exist, and it has been expanded by grants under successive five-year plans, at national level. In the first five-year plan, 1951-56, a scheme of improvement of library service was included calling for a network of libraries to be spread over the whole country. The kernel of the scheme was the establishment of district libraries, which would circulate books throughout the district. These were to be supplemented and supported by a central library for the whole state, or for a whole linguistic region.

A supplementary scheme to set up integrated library units was also commended to state governments in connexion with the areas selected for intensive educational development. Under successive Five-year Plans, the schemes have been developed but have not so far been backed up generally by a legislative base, despite strong recommendations by the Advisory Committee in 1959. These recommendations were for a comprehensive state library law, which would provide for free library service for all. Funds would be provided by a library rate on property tax, the income to be covered by a matching State grant.

The unit of library service would be the district. Proposals were also made for legislative action by the Government of India to collate the various Copyright and Book Deposit Acts and to make them viable for a national library service. The Act should also provide for assistance to state governments for public library service. Since provision of public libraries by executive action is an important feature in public library provision in developing countries, a typical example in India, that of West Bengal, is worthy of brief examination.

West Bengal Library System

West Bengal not only contains the largest city in India, Calcutta, but also India's National Library. Its population is over 65 million, and the principal language is Bengali. The literacy rate is 30 per cent. The first public library was opened in Calcutta in 1836 and it was followed during the nineteenth century by the founding of many other libraries on a subscription basis.

After independence, small grants were made by local authorities and from state funds, and in 1950, about 1,000 subscription libraries were receiving small grants. In 1956, a coordinated scheme was sponsored by the state government, with financial assistance on a 50 per cent basis from the Government of India.

In 1969-70 a sum of ₹4,313,000 was given in annual grants. All the districts of West Bengal now have a district library and much progress has been made in the provision of buildings, furniture and equipment. A reasonably coherent library system has now been established, with a state central library in Calcutta, over 68 district and area libraries and 579 rural libraries, with total staffs of over 1500.

Many of the libraries are still subscription libraries, and grants in fact are still given to many subscription libraries outside the system. While it is a source of satisfaction that public library service has been created, it cannot be denied that it is far from ideal. Since the entire service is under the Department of Social Education, district librarians have no real executive powers, and there appears to be little co-ordination of book stocks. Above all, the lack of a legislative and tax base necessarily makes for uncertainty in future planning.

The Delhi Public Library

Another example of executive action is the Delhi Public Library. This was founded by joint action of the Government of India and Unesco as a demonstration project applying Western concepts of book provision, furniture and equipment in a developing country.

In the final terms of agreement between Unesco and the Indian Government, the terms of reference for the project were set out: "It shall provide a public library service for the people of the City of Delhi and shall be a model for all public library development in India, and in all other countries where similar development of public libraries can be undertaken. The library shall be designed to carry out the policy of the Unesco Public Libraries Manifesto and to serve the needs of popular education."

The organizers of the library had, therefore, to plan for a library which would have complete open access to the shelves, which would make no direct charge to readers, and would be organized not for preservation, but for use by readers of all ages and all levels of education. These concepts were not new to India. They had been propagated by the devoted work of Dr. Ranganathan and his disciples. But between concept and execution there was still a wide gap, and the Delhi Public Library was the first in India, and probably the first in Asia, to apply these principles. The library was opened in 1951 by the Prime Minister, Mr. Nehru, and the present author was consultant to the project during the first year of its life. The government of the library is by the Delhi Library Board, an autonomous body acting on behalf of the Ministry of Education.

It is a well-balanced body, now with fifteen members. The Ministry of Education, the Finance Ministry, the Delhi Municipal Corporation, the Delhi Administration and the New Delhi Municipal Committee are all represented and four experts with technical qualifications or library experience are co-opted. The director of the library is secretary of the board and ex oficio member of it. Finance was jointly from the two sponsoring bodies in the first two years, but is now the sole responsibility of the Indian Government, with small grants from the municipal bodies.

The story of the Delhi Public Library has been told many times, and it is not proposed to repeat it here. From its inception it was an enormous success, enrolling over 10,000 members in the first few months and lending over 70,000 books. In 1966-67, membership had increased to 136,000 and annual issue of books to nearly 2 million volumes. Book stocks have increased from 14,000 to 350,000. It is still, in the words of a recent Indian writer, 'the only public library in India worth the name.'

In 1955, the author was invited by Unesco to make a detailed evaluation of the project. This was published by Unesco in 1957. In 1956, the Government of India notified its acceptance of this evaluation, the preamble of which began with the statement: 'During this period of five years the library has made gratifying progress and it has, therefore, been decided to place it on a permanent basis. ' After twenty years of existence, this statement is still the only basis on which the library operates.

Its functions have never been more clearly defined than in the original terms of reference as a pilot project, and it is still not a statutory body. More curious still, though it spends over I million rupees a year, by far the greatest expenditure of a single Indian public library unit, it still has not been given over-all responsibility for providing public library service in Delhi. In 1964, a further evaluation of the library was made by the board itself, which has this to say about the area of the library's responsibility: "A rather peculiar feature of the situation regarding public library service in Delhi is that in addition to the Delhi Library Board, three other bodies, *viz.*, the Delhi Administration, the Delhi Municipal Corporation and the New Delhi Municipal Committee operate a few libraries and reading rooms, and the New Delhi Municipal Committee proposes to open small lending libraries in the area within its jurisdiction.

There is no co-operation at all between the several authorities administering these libraries. The fact is stated here because of a possible wasteful duplication of effort and money." The fact that Delhi is the seat of government and has no state administration possibly accounts for the perpetuation of this rather odd situation. But one would have thought that a short enabling Act would have been possible giving the Delhi Public Library responsibility for providing all public reference and lending services in the Delhi area. Nevertheless, the Delhi Public Library has shown and continues to show that a modern public library can exist and can flourish in India.

Model Libraries Bill

In 1960, following the recommendations of the Advisory Committee on

Libraries, the Government of India appointed a committee for drafting a library bill. This was submitted to the Ministry of Education in 1963 and in 1964 the ministry circulated the bill for comments to the various state governments and professional organizations. No further action has yet been taken.

The bill is intended for adoption on a nation-wide basis. It would therefore need to be adopted by each state and presumably general legislation by the Government of India would be necessary to define the rights of the citizen to access to libraries, similar to those he has to education, to provide for some form of co-ordination of the various state library services and to provide for financial assistance for the state public library services as envisaged in the Model Bill.The exact form of such legislation, in view of the states' rights, is difficult to foresee, but a similar problem was solved in the United States with the Library Services Act.

A long process of legislation is therefore obviously involved, and an equally long process of organization. The integration of the present systems of public libraries provided by executive action will in itself present certain problems.

State Legislation

The Model Bill has been discussed at length because it is presumably the basis on which future legislation will be founded for all the states. But four Indian states have already passed legislation: two, Madras and Andhra Pradesh, before the publication of the Advisory Committee Report and the Model Bill, and two, Mysore and Maharashtra, after the publication of the Model Bill.

Madras Act

Madras State (capital: Madras) has a population of 37 million. The literacy rate is 30 per cent. Tamil is the principal language. Madras was the first state to pass legislation to create a public library system, in 1948. This was largely due to the unremitting efforts of Dr. Ranganathan, but the bill was watered down in its various stages to make it acceptable and it is generally agreed that in its present form not only is the Act defective but that its implementation has been unsound.

In the words of S. K. Mookerjee: "The Madras Act and its implementation in the sphere of library organization have taught us all a very good lesson. It has shown how completely the intentions of the legislature can be flouted and the public needs neglected when such implementation is entrusted to the wrong agency."

The main provisions of the Madras Act are as follows: A state library committee is formed for the purpose of advising the government. Its membership includes the Minister in Charge of Education, who is to be president of the board, representatives of universities and local library authorities and three persons nominated by library associations in the state. But the Director of Public Instruction is named as being ex officio Director of Public Libraries and a 'Special Officer' assisting the director in the administration of the Act is secretary of the committee.

It is quite clear that it is not intended that the special officer shall be a librarian and there is no place in fact in the Act for a state librarian with technical qualifications. It has been stated that the 'Special Officer', not a librarian, was in fact appointed with some haste. The Director of Public Libraries is charged with managing the State Central Library, superintending the work of local library authorities and superintending and directing all matters relating to public libraries in the state. The Act creates local library authorities, one for the City of Madras and one for each district, each district authority being given full powers of management of libraries within the district.

This is a much more sensible arrangement than the one in the Model Bill, in that it creates, in theory at any rate, more viable authorities. There are thirteen districts in Madras, so the average effective literate population of a district is around I million. The powers and duties of district library authorities do not, however, include provision for the appointment of a librarian, and there is no provision for a librarian on the committee. The power to make regulations also includes clauses: to 'provide for the admission of the public to public libraries in its area on such conditions and on payment of such fees as it may specify'; and 'requiring from persons desiring to use such libraries any guarantee or security against injury to, misuse, destruction or loss of the property of such libraries'.

These sections of the Act do, of course, nullify the whole function of public libraries if acted on, although they are permissive. Each local library authority is empowered to levy a library cess in its area, of six paise per rupee. This can be increased by an authority with sanction. The principal defects of the Act, apart from the omission of a requirement for trained staff with some status and the out-of-date provisions for access to the libraries, are that the Act does not in any way create a system of libraries. The State Central Library has no duties in relation to the district libraries and the district libraries have no duties in relation to each other. A parallel system of libraries is also created under the Act, since one of the duties of the director is to declare what libraries are eligible for government aid.

In the rules made under the Act, the director is to maintain a register of such libraries and conditions are laid down for eligibility for grant. There appear to be no provisions, as in the Model Bill, for eventual merging of these libraries within the public libraries administered by district authorities. Despite the defects of the Act, and its slow implementation, in recent years the public library service has obviously made some impression.

In 1965, total expenditure reached over 7 million rupees as against I,685,000 in 1957, and of this sum I,897,000 was raised in library cess. Over half the total expenditure in 1965, however, was by special grant, under the five-year plan, and it is not known whether this has been maintained since. Book stocks are reported as being nearly 2,500,000, visitors to the libraries nearly 18 million.

But one notes with surprise that there are in the whole state only 15,000 registered borrowers and only 143 trained library staff, of whom only I have full library qualifications. But however suspect some of the statistics, and it must be noted that criticism of the Madras library service by Indian librarians has been very severe, it is undoubtedly true that some progress has been made which would not have been made without a legislative base. It is to be hoped that the efforts of Dr. Ranganathan and others to improve the Act will eventually bear fruit and that Madras may then emerge as not only the first, but also the foremost, Indian state with a tax-based, legally founded, public library service.

Andhra Pradesh

Andhra Pradesh was a linguistic state formed from Hyderabad and parts of Madras State. A Telugu-speaking area, it has always had a strong library and literary tradition. In the words of an Indian librarian, 'the library movement has had a vast influence on the social and political life in Telugu land'. The population is over 40 million. When the new state was formed, there was already an Act in force for Hyderabad, while the parts of Madras taken over were covered by the Madras Act.

In 1960 an integrated Act was passed for the entire state. In many ways the Act is similar to the Madras Act, in the provision of a state library committee, the constitution of local library authorities, the levying of library cess and the matching of the funds raised in this way by grants from the state government. But generally the Act is a great improvement on the Madras Act, and corrects many of its defects. The Act creates a separate department of public libraries, although the Director of Public Instruction may be the director in charge of the department. But the librarian of the State Central Library has a place on the State Library Committee.

In the provisions for the district authorities and the city authority it is laid down that the District Librarian and the City Central Librarian shall each be secretary of the respective committee. The amount of library cess is fixed at four paise, which may be increased to eight paise at the discretion of the district authority. It is prescribed in the Act that no fees for admission to any public library shall be charged, but it is not clear whether a fee can be charged for borrowing of books. Again, a parallel system of libraries is formed, since under the definitions, a public library can be 'a library established or maintained by any local body or co-operative society and declared open to the public', or 'a library declared to be eligible for aid and receiving aid from the Government or from the Library Fund'. The duties of the Director of Public Libraries also include a declaration of what libraries are eligible for aid and under the rules of the Act conditions for such aid are laid down. It is clear that these are libraries outside those provided directly by the library authority, but there are no provisions, as in the Model Bill, for taking them over. The Act has been rapidly implemented, and appears to be working fairly satisfactorily.

Mysore Act, 1965

This Act has taken features from the Madras Act, the Andhra Pradesh Act, and the Model Bill and is a great improvement on all of them. Mysore is a Kannada-speaking State formed under the States Reorganization Act. The capital is Bangalore and the population is approximately 27 million. The literacy rate is 25 per cent (36 % males). The preamble of the Act states that it is: 'To provide for the establishment and maintenance of public libraries and the organization of a comprehensive rural and urban library service for the State of Mysore.'

The State Library Authority includes a member representing the State Library Association, but the State Librarian, though *ex officion* secretary of the authority, is not a member. A department of public libraries is formed under the Act, with the State Librarian at its head. This clause takes the administration of the public library out of the province of the Department of Education. The State Librarian is also specifically stated to be a whole-time officer with qualifications to practise as a librarian. All posts in the Department of Public Libraries are to be filled by appointment of persons employed by the state library service.

This may seem supererogatory, but is obviously intended to prevent appointment of persons already in other departments of the civil service. It is one of the grievances of Indian librarians that posts are often filled by people without library qualifications, coming by promotion from such departments as social education and community development. Local library authorities are specified for cities and urban areas with populations of more than 100,000, and for each district authority.

The chief librarian of the city or district is *ex officion* secretary of the local library authority. Development plans are to be prepared for each district and advisory committees formed by branch libraries and mobile libraries under the plan. The library cess is not confined to a levy on property, but is also levied on other taxes in city areas. It is limited to three paise in the rupee, subject to increase at discretion, with an upper limit of six paise. It will, of course, raise much more money, though the rate is the same, than property tax. The grant from the state to districts is met from land revenue tax, at the rate of three per cent. In addition the whole of staff salaries in the library authority is met by the state. The State Central Library has, among other functions, the task of providing facilities for the blind. This is not mentioned in any other Act. The Act also specifies a number of public libraries owned by societies which are to be taken over under the Act. Whether this is by prior agreement or not, it is an immense step forward.

The Mysore Act, it will be seen, is in many respects an improvement of the Model Bill, particularly in its creation of an independent library service and the widening of the tax base for urban libraries. The provision that all staff are employees of the state library service and paid by the state creates, for the first time in any of the Indian legislation, an integrated library system with the State Central Library at its head.

Maharashtra, 1967

Maharashtra, a Marathi-speaking State has a population of 46 million. Literacy is 30 per cent (males 42%). The Maharashtra Act, passed in 1967, has some of the features of the Mysore Act in that it creates a state library council, with a director of libraries who is a member of the council, acts as its secretary and must be a qualified librarian. A department of libraries is established and a state library service with staff salaries to be paid from state funds. There the resemblance to the Mysore Act stops.

A state library is to be established and a divisional library for every division. But provision for library service in a local area can only be made if the director is not satisfied that a local authority, society or trust is willing or competent to provide a public library service. No such library however shall be established without an opportunity being given to the local authority, society or trust to show because why the state authority should not establish a library.

The Act gives no powers of taxation; the Library Fund is made up solely from general and special grants, and central government grants. The general state grant is to be not less than 2,500,000 rupees, not a large sum. It is difficult to see from this how the Act can work satisfactorily, even though a functioning department and qualified staff are provided for.

SUMMARY

The Indian position has been dealt with at some length because of the variety of existing legislation and the fact that for the greater part of India there still is no legislation. This is not for want of trying. There must be few countries where there has been so much effort, so many reports, such unremitting lobbying of politicians.

Dr. Ranganathan has devoted a lifetime to the problem, as well as gaining an international reputation for his contributions to librarianship, and nearly every Indian state has been in consultation with him at one time or another over legislation. All states have active and persistent library associations, hampered by lack of funds it is true, but making up for it in publications and conferences. The will is there, the sympathy is there, but results have been more than disappointing. The main problem is, of course, one of taxation. The states' governments are reluctant to pass mandatory legislation that will increase the tax burden; the rural and urban areas have not sufficient potential revenue to provide library services; and the states themselves have a limited amount of revenue to disburse.

Finally, the central government, although it has distributed large sums for libraries under successive five-year plans, is reluctant to make permanent commitments. But eventually the problem must be solved by central government contributions to make up the deficiency in the states. It has been suggested that 5 per cent of the amount spent on education should be aimed at as the total. This would not provide expensive buildings and equipment, but it would provide a basic public library service. The difficulty is that the longer the central government hesitates to insist on mandatory state legislation, the more difficult it will be to provide this basic service.

A start must sometime be made on bringing the many semi-public libraries into a system and possibly channeling and consolidating the small sums they spend. Grant-in-aid to them altogether must amount to a respectable sum and a large part of it is wasted so long as these libraries are independent, using untrained staff and decrepit premises. The attitude is that they are better than nothing, but this is not true if they give the impression that they are a library service. There is also a danger that more states will pass defective legislation, and the more that do, the longer it will take to bring them into line.

The only Act which is reasonably acceptable so far is the Mysore Act and it is the only one to create a state-wide service. It is now nearly ten years since the Advisory Committee reported and gave a comprehensive view of the situation. It is surely time for the Government of India to make a definite move, if only because otherwise they may be faced with a series of defective and conflicting Acts by the states.

7

Principles for Public Library

USING THE YOUNG ADULT STANDARDS

These standards have been developed for use by:

- Young Adult Librarians to support requests to Library Directors and Boards for increased resources.
- Library Administration to advance young adult services with local and state governments and Boards of Trustees.
- Trustees to increase awareness of and support for young adult services.
- Regional Administrators and Regional Youth Services Consultants and Coordinators to strengthen existing services and create new ones.
- The Massachusetts Board of Library Commissioners to develop an action plan for implementation on a state level and to consider when formulating funding policy for Massachusetts libraries.
- The Massachusetts Library Association to advocate for young adult services in the professional community at large.
- Library School Faculty to strengthen the professional education of young adult librarians.
- Citizens to increase awareness of young adult library needs in their communities.
- Government and Local Officials to increase knowledge of the importance of library services to teens and the need for funding these services.
- Teens and Teen Advisory Boards to help develop a vision for services in their libraries and communities.

YOUNG ADULTS AS LIBRARY USERS

The Young Adult Library Services Association (YALSA), the term "young adults" refers to young people ages 12 to 18 who no longer see themselves as children but are not recognized by society as adults. The terms "YA," "teens," "teenagers," "adolescents," "youth," and "students" also identify young adults and will be used interchangeably throughout this document. As teens struggle to find their place in the family and society, they must work out new relationships with parents, peers and others. They experience rapid physical, emotional and social changes while developing their intellectual capabilities and personal values, understanding and accepting their sexuality, and identifying their educational and occupational options. Young adult library users deserve to be taken seriously and to have their requests treated equitably and their confidentiality preserved. Direct, respectful communication with them is the most effective means of engaging their interest in library services.

A cornerstone of young adult library services is the principle that young adults must be actively involved in decisions regarding collections, services and programmes intended for them. Their active participation ensures that the needs and ever changing interests of teens are being addressed. Young adults become lifelong library users and supporters when they are enthusiastically engaged in planning and decision-making. They play a key role in attracting their peers to the library.

Public libraries must provide more than token services to young adults. Since adolescents are not generally advocates on their own behalf, it is important that the library director, staff, and trustees understand their responsibility to give equal consideration to the needs of young adults in planning and implementing library and information services. Youth advocacy begins with the policies, procedures, space, collections and services within the library.

It also extends to the networks and coalitions library staff develop with schools and other libraries and community agencies. These standards are constructed in the belief that "by fully supporting library service to young adults, the library community is much more likely to retain members of this age group as library users who will, as adults, become lifelong learners and library supporters."1 The standards are based on the philosophy and definitions of library services established in three basic documents of the Young Adult Library Services Association: Directions for Library Service to Young Adults, New Directions for Library Service to Young Adults, and Young Adults Deserve the Best: Competencies for Librarians Serving Youth.

The Search Institute's Forty Developmental Assets as well as the Intellectual Freedom documents of the American Library Association (ALA), particularly the Library Bill of Rights, are also fundamental to quality service to young adults.

SERVICE

Quality library service to young adults is provided by staff who understand and respect their unique informational, educational and recreational needs. In accordance with the principles expressed in the Library Bill of Rights and Free Access to Libraries for Minors teenagers must have access on an equal basis with adults to all the services and materials the library provides. Cooperation among public, school and other libraries in the community is essential to serving young adults well.

Principles

Services to young adults in each public library must be based on a written policy outlining philosophy, goals and objectives consistent with established roles as stated in the library's long-range plan. The Young Adult Services staff and the library director should review both this essential document and its corresponding action plan on a regular basis to determine its effectiveness in serving the needs and interests of young adults in the community.

The policy should be based on the following principles:

- Young adults need and are entitled to free and equal access to all library services and resources, including programmes, information services, technology, reserves and interlibrary loan, virtual and remote services.
- Young adult department service hours will be no less than those of adult services, and staff will be available to serve young adults all the hours that the library is open.
- Young adults have the right to privacy and confidentiality in accordance with the principles expressed in the American Library Association's Statement of Professional Ethics and Massachusetts State Laws regarding confidentiality.
- Public library services for young adults complement but do not take the place of school libraries in the community.
- Each public library has the responsibility to make access to electronic resources, such as online databases and unfiltered Internet access, equally available to people of all ages.

Practices

To ensure that young adults are provided with the materials and information they need for school assignments, personal pleasure, and responsible decision-making each library must:

- Develop procedures for involving young adults in planning space, collections, services and programmes.
- Establish a physical space for young adult collections, which creates an environment that invites teen use.
- Employ at least one qualified librarian who is responsible for planning and supervising services to young adults.
- Develop and maintain a collection of diverse and current materials in various formats.

- Develop and provide reference services, including homework assistance, personal, career and college information. This reference service also extends to telephone and electronic information and referral.
- Plan and implement a variety of programmes that promote library use.
- Provide reader's advisory assistance.
- Provide library orientation and skills instruction.
- Develop meaningful volunteer opportunities for young adults within the library.
- Publicize the resources and services offered to young adults.
- Collaborate and cooperate with schools and other community agencies serving teenagers.
- Create and maintain a web presence specifically geared towards the needs of youth.
- Participate in resource sharing among networks and regions.
- Allocate sufficient funding to accomplish a complete service package including programming, collections, staffing, and facilities.

STAFF

The library acknowledges the distinct needs and characteristics of young adults by designating a staff member who will have professional expertise and responsibility in planning and supervising services for them. The library director and young adult librarian will work together to provide leadership that assures good library service to young adults, seeking additional expertise from the Regional Youth Services Consultant as needed. It is also essential that all staff members convey a service commitment to young adults since they are expected to use the full range of public library services. The goal of each library will be to employ a young adult librarian who has earned a master's degree from an ALA accredited programme with course work related to young adult materials and services.

Competencies

In order to be an advocate for young adults and an effective provider of library services, the librarian serving this age group must possess a wide variety of competencies and personal qualities. As a person who is expected to attract young adults to the library, the librarian must have:

- Genuine respect for teenagers and an ability to establish rapport with them.
- Communication skills to involve young adults in planning and implementing services intended for their benefit.

- The ability to elicit the input of young adults on library programmes and services and to present their ideas to the library administration and staff.
- Interest in and ability to learn new technologies and adapt them for use in young adult services.
- Interest in seeking out new trends in services to young adults.

As a professional librarian who is expected to develop services appropriate to this age group, the librarian must have:

- A broad and current knowledge of young adult literature, audio and visual materials, electronic resources, and emerging technologies.
- A broad knowledge of the intellectual, emotional, psychological, and physical development of adolescents.

As part of the management team of the library in which young adult services are valued, the librarian must have:

- A knowledge and understanding of the library's mission, goals, objectives, and policies.
- The ability to plan and implement programmes and to participate in the overall management and evaluation of library activities.

As an effective advocate for young adults, the librarian must have:

- The ability to communicate the needs of teenagers to library staff and administration.
- An awareness of current issues affecting adolescents in that community and society.
- The ability to communicate and collaborate with school personnel and other community agencies serving young adults.

Responsibilities of the Young Adult Librarian

The young adult librarian must assume a wide variety of responsibilities in the areas of management, service, community outreach and professional development.

As a manager the young adult librarian will:

- Plan and implement activities to achieve short and long term goals and objectives for young adult services as part of the overall library planning process.
- Assess budgetary needs of the young adult department and work with other library personnel to plan and implement the budget.
- Advocate for young adults in library discussions of policy-making and implementation of budget priorities.
- Work with library administration to seek supplementary funding to enhance library services.

- Train, supervise, and evaluate staff and volunteers.
- Identify, collect and interpret statistics as needed.

As a service provider the young adult librarian will:

- Select, evaluate, maintain, and discard young adult materials based on the preferences of young adults and the use of a variety of review sources.
- Provide reference, reader's advisory, and library orientation services to young adults.
- Promote information literacy skills by providing instruction in and access to electronic databases, the Internet, and other emerging technologies, and using those technologies to communicate with teens virtually.
- Involve young adults in planning and implementing services and selecting materials for their age group.
- Recognize diverse groups of young adults and develop programmes and acquire materials appropriate to their needs.b

As coordinator of outreach services the young adult librarian will:

- Establish contacts and collaborate with schools and other agencies to serve young adults.
- Promote, publicize, and represent young adult services and the library to the community and local agencies in cooperation with other library departments.

As a professional, the young adult librarian will:

- Participate actively in professional associations, take advantage of continuing education opportunities, and read professional literature related to libraries, youth services, and adolescent development.
- Identify current trends and issues affecting young adults and incorporate these findings into overall services to this age group.

Responsibilities of the Administration

The library administration will ensure quality services to young adults by supporting the young adult librarian in the provision of these services and working with the young adult librarian in maintaining contacts with other community agencies serving youth.

In addition, the administration will:

- Provide written job descriptions, which are regularly reviewed, for all staff responsible for young adult services.
- Assure regular performance evaluations are conducted using the job descriptions along with the goals and objectives set by each staff member.

- Designate a professional position in the library that will include responsibility for young adult services in the event the young adult librarian's position cannot be full-time.
- Develop a specific budget for young adult materials, programmes and services, with the young adult librarian's input.
- Assure scheduled time in the designated librarian's workweek that allows the librarian to serve young adults effectively.
- Allocate time for community outreach to schools and other agencies, for development of appropriate networks for serving young adult information needs, and for job-related professional activities.
- Compensate the young adult librarian with a salary commensurate with the formal qualifications mandated by the library and equivalent to that of other staff within the library who have similar levels of responsibility. The Massachusetts Library Association provides minimum salary recommen-dations.

Responsibilities of the Regional Library Systems

Each regional library system, in its plan of service, must include:

- A consultant with expertise in young adult services who provides advisory services to staff in local public libraries.
- A programme of service to those working with young adults.
- Continuing education programmes on young adult services.
- Opportunities for regular meetings between local young adult services staff and regional consultants.

JOB DESCRIPTION

Definition

Professional, administrative and supervisory work in planning and managing the activities of young adult services in the library and all other related work as required.

Supervision

- Works under the general direction of the Library Director or Coordinator of Youth or Adult Services.
- Performs responsible functions requiring considerable judgment and initiative in planning and overseeing services to young adults both within the library and the community.
- Supervises two part-time employees and an active volunteer programme.

Job Environment

- Performs work under typical library conditions; library hours may require evening and weekend work.
- Makes frequent contacts with the public, schools, other libraries, social service agencies, civic organizations and other professional organizations.
- Uses computers, peripherals, current technologies and other standard office equipment.

Essential Functions

- Plans, organizes, implements, supervises and evaluates services to young adults.
- Participates as part of the management team in developing goals, policies and procedures as relating to young adults.
- Advocates for young adults and young adult services with other community agencies.
- Initiates, plans and conducts a variety of programmes and activities to encourage the use of the library by young adults between the ages of 12 to 18.
- Involves young adults in planning and implementing services for their age group.
- Selects, evaluates, maintains and discards young adult materials based on professional judgment, preferences of young adults and acknowledged review sources.
- Provides reference and readers' advisory services, and library orientation to young adults.
- Collaborates with schools and other agencies to serve young adults.
- Promotes, publicizes and represents young adult services and the library to the community and local agencies in cooperation with other library departments.
- Works with library administration to seek supplementary funding to enhance library services, including state and federal grants.
- Trains, supervises and evaluates staff and volunteers.
- Identifies, collects and interprets statistics as needed.

RECOMMENDED MINIMUM QUALIFICATIONS

Education and Experience

Master's Degree in Library Science from an ALA accredited school; two years of professional experience, including supervisory and administrative experience, experience with young adults is preferred.

Knowledge, Ability and Skills

- Broad and current knowledge of young adult literature, digital and multimedia materials, and electronic resources, including communication tools such as e mail and instant messaging.
- A broad knowledge of the intellectual, emotional, psychological and physical development of adolescents is essential.
- Genuine respect for young adults and an ability to establish rapport with them.
- Ability to administer and direct the work of staff and volunteers.
- Ability to express oneself orally and in writing.
- Flexibility, initiative, energy, patience and tact to deal effectively with the public.
- Excellent people and reference skills.
- Planning and organizational skills needed.
- Has access to a limited amount of confidential information.
- Errors could result in lower standards of library service, waste of public funds and poor public relations.
- Familiarity with online circulation systems and online searching is required.

Physical Requirements

- Light physical effort required in carrying and shelving books, and in performing other typical library functions.
- Frequent standing, walking, bending, reaching and climbing.
- Ability to operate a keyboard at an efficient speed.
- Frequently required to sit and talk or hear, use hands to operate objects, tools or controls, and reach with hands and arms.
- The employee must regularly lift and/or move materials weighing up to 40 pounds.
- Vision and hearing at or correctable to "normal ranges."

COLLECTIONS

The young adult collection represents the unique needs and interests of adolescents in the community. Resources selected for teenagers should contribute to their intellectual and emotional growth as well as appeal to their popular, current and recreational interests. Both the public library and the school library collections are necessary for meeting the educational needs of young adults. This collection is the bridge for adolescents making the transition from juvenile collections and services to adult collections and services. It should contain materials appropriate for a wide range of abilities and maturity levels. Therefore, the collection may include items commonly found in either the adult or children's collections. In accordance with the Library Bill of Rights and its interpretations, young adults must have access to all areas of the library's collections.

Policy

Every public library's collection development policy, endorsed by the library's governing board, must define the purpose of the young adult collection by stating the following:

- Responsibility and criteria for selection and evaluation.
- General and specific populations and interests to be served.
- Level of curriculum and homework support.
- Roles of young adults in collection development.
- Relationship between the young adult collection and other collections in the library.

Content

Personal interest materials reflecting the needs and interests of teenagers are the primary focus of the young adult collection. Materials should be available in a variety of formats and subject areas, and the collection should meet the needs of teens of various ages and levels of maturity as well as reading abilities. No limit should be made on the availability of any material to all patrons. Paperbacks, graphic novels, magazines and popular music recordings are included in any collection for this age group.

Other media such as DVD's, web sites, computer/video games and recorded books are also popular. The young adult collection must reflect the cultural and socio-economic diversity of the community and acknowledge the emotional and informational needs of teens of all sexual orientations.

It should serve the needs of the visually and hearing impaired, learning disabled, and non-English speaking populations. Collection development also encompasses the full range of electronic resources available through the library website.

Budget

A portion of the library budget must be designated for young adult materials. Evaluation of the usage patterns of the library's entire collection, as well as a variety of statistics and output measures supplied by the young adult librarian, should determine budget allocations.

The young adult librarian should have full responsibility for expending the young adult materials budget. When the public library also serves as the school library, arrangements must be made for reimburse-ments from the school department budget.

Selection

The young adult librarian will:

- Select materials intended primarily for young adults, consulting a variety of professional selection and evaluation aids.
- Involve young adults in the selection process.
- Communicate with other library departments selecting materials used by young adults to determine the best location for these materials.
- Ensure prompt processing and full cataloging of young adult materials.
- Evaluate the strengths and weaknesses of the collection on a regular basis.
- Discard worn and outdated materials.

Promotion

To promote the collection effectively, the young adult librarian will:

- Identify the needs of the community, its teens, and its young adult service providers.
- Be familiar with materials in the collection in order to provide expert guidance to young adult and adult users.
- Encourage the independent use of the collection by using marketing strategies and reader's advisory tools such as booklists, displays, signage, and an active web presence to help youth locate materials they will find enjoyable and suited to their developmental needs.
- Work with schools and community groups to keep teens and adults abreast of materials in the collection.
- Maintain and update a web page devoted to the library's young adult services which publicizes materials to teens both inside and outside the library and encourages use of online databases.

Responsibilities of the Regional Library Systems

The regional library systems are responsible for assisting member libraries in collection development by providing:

- Patron access to online databases that meet the informational needs of young adults.
- Access to a collection of professional resources.
- Continuing education programmes.
- On-site consultations.
- Supplementary collections/deposits of young adult materials for public libraries under 25,000 population may be available.

CORE COLLECTION CHECKLIST

Though school assignments motivate teenagers to visit the library, a dynamic young adult collection focusing on popular, high interest materials will keep them coming back. Teen input is essential in developing a collection that reflects the interests and needs of a community's young people, and affords young adults the opportunity to become involved in library decision-making.

Your YA collection should include:

- Series books.
- *Fiction:*
  - Horror.
  - Realistic teen novels.
  - Mystery/suspense.
  - Romance.
  - Science fiction.
  - Fantasy.
  - Sports.
  - Adventure/survival.
  - Historical fiction.
  - Short stories.
  - Classics in paperback editions.
  - Multicultural fiction.
- Comics and graphic novels.
- Media tie-ins.
- Magazines.
- *Non-fiction:*
  - Recreational, *e.g.* rock and rap music, skateboarding.
  - Informational, *e.g.* health and sex education.
  - Educational, *e.g.* careers and college.
  - Reference, *e.g.* encyclopedias, student dictionaries, atlases.
- *Non-print:*
  - Musical media.
  - DVD and video.
  - Computer/video games
  - Learning tools.
  - Audio books.
- Pathfinders, both print and web-based.
- Website/collection of links.

FACILITIES

Every public library must have a clearly defined, separate area designated for young adults. This young adult area should be accessible to all adolescents, easily visible, functional and flexible in design. An environment that is comfortable and arranged to accommodate noise and movement will make young adults feel welcome. The design and graphics should make it evident that the area is for teens. Young adult involvement is essential in establishing an effective, dynamic young adult area.

Space

The young adult space should be established in a location that is easily supervised without making young adults feel intimidated. Because young adults need access to reference materials and assistance, proximity to reference services is important.

The space should not be adjacent to the children's service area. If the young adult area is unable to house programmes and activities, teens should have equal access to other programme facilities within the library. The space itself should be in compliance with the Americans with Disabilities Act.

The area should accommodate:

- Leisure reading, socializing, and snacking.
- Individual and group study.
- A public service area and workspace for the young adult librarian.
- Sufficient shelving for a diverse collection.
- Displays and exhibits.
- Computer access proportional to teen population.

Furnishings

Furnishings should be flexible so that as needs and activities change the area can be adapted accordingly.

The young adult area will include:

- Shelving for materials in various formats.
- Comfortable and durable seating and tables.
- Directional and informational signs.

The young adult area should include or be in proximity to:

- A public service desk, clock and telephone.
- Listening and viewing equipment.
- Computers and peripherals.
- Display equipment such as bulletin boards, display cases and slat-wall shelving.

Infrastructure

Services for young adults must take advantage of new methods to deliver the most effective access to information, learning and leisure pursuits. The library's infrastructure should support changing technology and ensure adequate lighting, ventilation, temperature controls, and acoustics.

Items to consider in the young adult area include:

- Electrical outlets in a variety of locations.
- Adequate wiring, including wireless capability, with flexibility to reposition and upgrade.
- Connections for in-house and external telecommunication resources.
- Soundproofing as required.
- Telephone jacks with convenient access.
- Trash receptacles.

Web Presence

Just as libraries set aside physical spaces in their buildings for young adults, so should they set aside web spaces by creating and maintaining a page or pages specific to the interests and developmental needs of young adults. An attractive and functional page should be designed with young adult input, evaluated regularly by young adults, and have interactive features.

The page may include but is not limited to:

- General contact information for library and specific contact information for the young adult librarian.
- A collection development policy for website content and links that includes a procedure for addressing challenges to controversial websites.
- Library programmes and activities for young adults.
- Annotated booklists and book reviews, or links to young adult literature sites that provide reader's advisory services.
- Promotion of young adult collections and resources.
- Informational and recreational links.
- Opportunities for teens to post reviews of materials.
- Interactive content that helps teens learn how to use library resources.
- Opportunities for teens to connect with each other.
- Opportunities for teens to connect with librarians who can assist them with research needs.
- Opportunities for taking part in programmes virtually.

PROGRAMMES

Successful library programmes support teens by meeting their developmental needs. They foster a sense of ownership and provide a structure for meaningful participation. Programming should be as varied as the needs and interests of young adults themselves and encourage use of the library. It is crucial that programmes presented for this age group include teenagers in planning and implementation. Teens who are involved in the programming process are essential advocates and promoters of a library's young adult services.

Principles

Programmes can range from informal activities to formally planned events and are intended to connect teens and libraries. The following principles govern the development, organization and management of library programmes for young adults:

- The philosophy, goals and objectives for young adult programming should be included in the library's written programme policy and long-range plan, and should be revised as necessary.
- All programmes should be created and developed with youth input, since the most successful programmes are the ones in which the young adults themselves participate in planning and executing.
- A specific proportional budget should be designated for planning, publicizing, and presenting young adult programmes.
- The young adult librarian must be provided with time and opportunities to establish relationships with teen users and to plan, prepare for, and carry out young adult programming.
- Ongoing communication and collaboration with schools and other community agencies serving young adults is essential in developing successful programming.

Practices

The young adult librarian, with the support of the administration and other staff members, will assume the responsibility of implementing the library's young adult programmes.

To ensure success, the following practices are necessary:

- Scheduling informational, cultural and recreational programmes for young adults, parents, and community members who work with teens on a regular basis.
- Developing personal contacts with young adults and encouraging promotion among teens themselves in order to publicize programmes.
- Utilizing high-quality print media, e mail notification or "blasts", and website publicity to create visibility in the community.
- Evaluating programmes and maintaining statistics unique to the young adult department to ensure continued improvement of and support for programming.

- Providing refreshments is an essential part of programming for teens.

Programme Content

Programming for young adults can be a rewarding and stimulating part of library service to adolescents. Library programmes can attract new teen users to the library and increase awareness of resources and services provided by the library for young adults.

As teens strive for competence, programmes that allow them to showcase skills are important. Youth participation programmes give teens opportunities to become involved in library decision-making and should address a genuine need of both adolescents and the library. If the library discusses the creation of responsible roles and tasks for young adults and solicits their opinions, then the administration must be sincere in its efforts to implement reasonable recommendations.

Examples of youth participation programmes include young adult advisory councils, teen trustees, teen Friends groups, young adult book review groups and literary magazines. Teens should also be active participants in the creation and maintenance of the library's web pages for teens.

The following is a list of different types of youth participation programmes with examples of each:

- Educational programmes offer support for formal education and curriculum needs. Examples include SAT workshops, school booktalking programmes, college application workshops and library skills orientation/tours.
- Cultural programmes excite and involve teenagers in literature and the arts. Examples include art shows, photography exhibits, theater productions, poetry coffeehouses or "slams," book discussion groups and writers' workshops.
- Informational programmes provide needed knowledge on a variety of subjects and may fill a void in the community. They also provide opportunities to form partnerships with other youth agencies. Examples may include substance abuse programmes, career programmes, babysitting workshops, craft classes, modeling seminars and forums on minors' legal rights.
- Recreational programmes are purely entertainment-oriented. Examples include role-playing or computer/video game tournaments, "battle of the bands" concerts, talent shows or "open-mic" nights.
- Intergenerational programmes feature projects in which teenagers interact with and gain appreciation for younger and older members of the community. Examples include theater groups, a senior/teen book discussion group, community gardens and storytelling for young children.

- Volunteer programmes in libraries foster self-confidence, self-esteem and dignity in young adults. Opportunities for volunteerism should include work that matters, not simply "busywork. Examples include summer reading programme volunteers and computer instruction for younger and older patrons.

BUDGET

- Estmated Cost:
  - Speaker's cost
  - Supplies and equipment
  - Staff time
  - Public relations
  - Other costs
- Funding Source:
  - Budget line- general revenue
  - Grant funds
  - Friends of the Library
  - Corporate sponsorship
  - Outside donations
  - Other
- Programme Approved:
  - Preliminary planning should be approved at this point before proceeding any further.
  - Approved by supervisor
  - Approved by director
  - Off desk planning time approved
- Equipment Needed: (make arrangements to rent, if necessary)
- Speaker Confirmation:
  - Contract sent
  - Contract returned and executed
  - Follow-up call(s)
- Room Set-up: (preliminary plan)
- Publicity and Promotion:
  - All library staff informed
  - Programme information posted to library website
  - Fliers distributed to schools, community groups, businesses and other libraries
  - Media releases to local newspapers, school newspapers, radio, TV, Friends of the Library
  - Newsletter, etc.
  - Visits to schools planned and approved
  - Book displays

- E mail or direct mailings to YAs, school and community liaisons
- Programme Details:
  - Room set-up
  - Equipment and supplies
  - Refreshments
  - Speaker's introduction
  - Speaker's check
  - Evaluation form and pencils
  - Fliers for next programme
  - Room clean up
  - Other

SAMPLE VOLUNTEER POLICY

The library often has uses for volunteers. These volunteers can fulfill permanent or temporary needs. Volunteers and their supervisors must adhere to the following when performing duties:

- Anyone wishing to learn, have a direct impact on the library, and become more involved in the community is encouraged to volunteer at the library.
- Any teenager who is legally old enough to work may volunteer at the library. This includes anyone over the age of 14. Any volunteer under the age of 16 must comply with Massachusetts Child Labour Laws4. This includes, but is not limited to, not working after 7 pm on a school night5, more than three hours on a school day6, and more than eighteen hours a week during the school year7.
- Volunteers can be asked to perform a variety of duties at the discretion of the volunteer supervisor. Temporary duties include working at programmes, or helping with a planning process. Teenaged volunteers are especially encouraged to become involved in writing any policies related to their needs and services.
- Volunteers will not be asked to perform duties also performed by paid staff. This includes working at public service desks. Adolescent volunteers should not be required to do identical work as high school pages.
- Those who are volunteering on a temporary basis, such as during a programme, a Friends of the Library event, or on a planning committee are not expected to perform duties not related to that event.
- Volunteers who will be helping on a more permanent basis will set up a regular schedule with the volunteer supervisor. Volunteers are welcome to terminate the arrangement at any time. Volunteers are free to take vacations or days off, although they are asked to please give notice to the volunteer supervisor.

CONFIDENTIALITY LAW

G.L.c. 78, Section 7. Establishment by Cities and Towns; records

Section 7. A town may establish and maintain public libraries for its inhabitants under regulations prescribed by the city council or by the town, and may receive, hold and manage any gift, bequest or devise therefor.

The city council of a city or the selectmen of a town may place in such library the books, reports and laws which may be received from the commonwealth. That part of the records of a public library which reveals the identity and intellectual pursuits of a person using such library shall not be a public record as deemed by clause Twenty-six of section seven of chapter four.

Library authorities may disclose or exchange information relating to library users for the purposes of interlibrary cooperation and coordination, including but not limited to, the purposes of facilitating the sharing of resources among library jurisdictions as authorized by clause (1) of section nineteen E or enforcing the provisions of sections ninety-nine and one hundred of chapter two hundred and sixty-six.

Library Bill of Rights

The American Library Association affirms that all libraries are forums for information and ideas, and that the following basic policies should guide their services.

- Books and other library resources should be provided for the interest, information, and enlightenment of all people of the community the library serves. Materials should not be excluded because of the origin, background, or views of those contributing to their creation.
- Libraries should provide materials and information presenting all points of view on current and historical issues. Materials should not be proscribed or removed because of partisan or doctrinal disapproval.
- Libraries should challenge censorship in the fulfillment of their responsibility to provide information and enlightenment.
- Libraries should cooperate with all persons and groups concerned with resisting abridgment of free expression and free access to ideas.
- A person's right to use a library should not be denied or abridged because of origin, age, background, or views.
- Libraries which make exhibit spaces and meeting rooms available to the public they serve should make such facilities available on an equitable basis, regardless of the beliefs or affiliations of individuals or groups requesting their use.

Madras Public Libraries Act

The Madras Public Libraries Act, subsequently renamed as the Tamil Nadu Public Libraries Act, was enacted in Madras State, India, in 1948. The act was the first of its kind to be enacted in India after independence. The Connemara Public Library became the first library to come under the purview of this act, as a "State central library".

Subsequently, nine district libraries were added during the Five year plan from 1951. The act was enacted based on research and activity by S. R. Ranganathan and the Madras Library Association. Other states have enacted public library acts modelled on the Madras Public Libraries Act.

Background

R. K. Bhatt has highlighted how free-to-access public library systems are a necessary adjunct to a developing society, with growing industrialisation and improving rates of literacy, and argues that legislation "is an essential need in any country because it puts the structure, management and finance of library systems on proper legal footing". Ranganathan recognised this. He had spent time training as a librarian in London around 1923 and was impressed by the system of public library legislation which existed there. Upon returning to India he began to campaign for something similar to exist in his own country.

The situation was complicated by the existence of various types of government, including provinces which were administered by the British Raj and various States under the control of princes. The fruits of his research and consultations were presented at the First All India Educational Conference in 1930. This report included a proposed Model Library Act. Although some areas, such as Baroda, had established public library systems prior to 1945, it was then that the first Act was passed, being the Kolhapur Public Libraries Act. This was followed in 1948 by the Madras Public Libraries Act, which became the first such Act to be passed in the newly independent republic of India.

Acts for other areas, such as Kerala and Haryana, followed and generally improved on the earlier legislation. Prior to the Act, the principal library of Madras was the Connemara Public Library, which had opened in 1860 and became a public library in 1896. A small refundable deposit was required to use it but it was essentially free. It became the State Central Library in 1948 and, in 1981, a depository library.

Provisions

The Madras Public Libraries Act provides for overall governance by a State Library Committee, presided over by the incumbent Education Minister for the State. The committee comprises members from various walks of life, including representatives from universities and from the State Library

Association, as well as a Secretary whose primary function is as assistant to the Director of Public Libraries (DPL). The latter role is assumed by the incumbent Director of Public Instruction. Revenue is obtained via a cess, a tax which is collected by local administrative bodies such as the Nagar Palikas and Panchayats. Those bodies remit the tax to their Local Library Association (LLA), which operates as an umbrella organisation at the mid-tier District administrative level.

The rate of taxation is fixed in law but the LLA can request a higher rate if the State government agrees to it. The State government matches the funds generated by the cess. The LLA determines the conditions of entry to the libraries under its control. Cities with a population in excess of 50,000 must have a central library of their own and provisions exist for expansion to include branch libraries and other means of devolved access if demand should require such. In addition to libraries that are administered by the LLA, the Act provides for a register of other libraries.

This is maintained by the DPL, who has the power to issue grants from State resources to those institutions listed. With the exception of the city of Madras, these grants cannot be less than the cess collected elsewhere. Further resources are obtained by a modification caused by the Act. The Press and Registration of Books Act of 1857 is amended such that a situation somewhat akin to copyright libraries exists. All publishers within the State are required to provide five copies of their output to the State government, which in turn passes on four of those copies to the State Central Library. Until various reorganisations of States, the Act applied to parts of what are now Andhra Pradesh and Kerala.

Evolution

Several perceived failings in the Madras Public Libraries Act have been addressed in subsequent Acts elsewhere. For example, the Hyderabad legislation, which later became the Andhra Pradesh Public Libraries Act, states that there should be a completely separate department of government to administer the libraries; that the head of the State Library Committee should be elected rather than defaulting to the portfolio of the current Education Minister; and that all local administrative areas should have their own library authority. Furthermore, the amount and extent of the cess collected was improved by extending the range of taxes upon which the surcharge was levied; and the government, through the State Library Council, has a duty to train the librarians.

A key strategy which was embodied in the Act was the formulation of a hierarchical system whereby the local libraries were connected to the District libraries and they, in turn, were connected to the State Central Library and the National Library. Centralised acquisition and resource sharing was envisaged. This strategy had formed a part of the Second Five Year Plan but it appears not to have been enforced with any haste; Brahmanda Barua wrote in 1992 that throughout India "The network principle has nowhere been applied in organising the libraries." Bhatt believes that the Karnataka Public Libraries Act is the most adequate and best functioning in the evolution of such Acts, and notes that the lack of provision for a cess in the later Acts for Maharashtra and West Bengal are a significant failing. In the case of Karnataka, there is a State Library Authority which is presided over by the Minister for Education, and also a fully-fledged Department of Public Libraries and local administrative bodies.

The cess applies to a wide range of taxes, including those on property and vehicles, and there is further funding in non-city areas as a consequence of the stipulation that the State government must give to the local bodies 3% of all revenues received from land taxes in their area. The financing of the State Library Authority is determined by the lower authorities and private libraries can request grants but are not automatically entitled to them.

Recent Situation Nationally

By 2002 there had been a total of 12 public library acts in place, although two of those - for Hyderabad and Kolhapur - had been superseded due to changes in the administrative structure of those areas, and two others had not been enforced. Narasimha Raju considered that these Acts had proved to be "by and large ineffective", due to a combination of poor financing, poor administrative structure and, in some States, the "lethargy and negative attitude" of their governments. Raju also identified problems with the rapidly changing face of technology and noted that most of the libraries were unable to adapt to developments in television, radio and video recording. The Indian Library Association had taken on the campaign to improve matters, principally by promoting new legislation to replace that which already existed and Raju noted that many believed legislation should exist for the entire country rather than being a piecemeal system.

Despite only eight Acts being in force, all 25 States and seven Union Territories had a central library and 75% of the Districts, which are the next tier of administration, had a similar facility. While legislated areas such as Maharashtra relied on volunteers and development of free libraries from the core of an existing subscription library system, Tamil Nadu, Karnataka and Andhra Pradesh were thought by T. Malleshappa to be the most developed when quantified by density of libraries and percentage of the population who had free access.

D. B. Eswara Reddy, writing in the same publication, bemoaned the poor provision below District level, with 90% of the rural population not having access even to a reading room or circulating library, let alone modern multimedia and computing technology. Despite legislation and theoretical targets, library facilities remained the preserve of the urban elite and, for example, in Andhra Pradesh most children in rural areas were first-generation literates.

FREE ACCESS TO LIBRARIES FOR MINORS

An Interpretation of the Library Bill of Rights

Library policies and procedures that effectively deny minors equal and equitable access to all library resources available to other users violate the Library Bill of Rights. The American Library Association opposes all attempts to restrict access to library services, materials, and facilities based on the age of library users. Article V of the Library Bill of Rights states, "A person's right to use a library should not be denied or abridged because of origin, age, background, or views."

The "right to use a library" includes free access to, and unrestricted use of, all the services, materials, and facilities the library has to offer. Every restriction on access to, and use of, library resources, based solely on the chronological age, educational level, literacy skills, or legal emancipation of users violates Article V. Libraries are charged with the mission of developing resources to meet the diverse information needs and interests of the communities they serve. Services, materials, and facilities that fulfill the needs and interests of library users at different stages in their personal development are a necessary part of library resources.

The needs and interests of each library user, and resources appropriate to meet those needs and interests, must be determined on an individual basis. Librarians cannot predict what resources will best fulfill the needs and interests of any individual user based on a single criterion such as chronological age, educational level, literacy skills, or legal emancipation. Libraries should not limit the selection and development of library resources simply because minors will have access to them.

Institutional self-censorship diminishes the credibility of the library in the community, and restricts access for all library users. Children and young adults unquestionably possess First Amendment rights, including the right to receive information in the library. Constitutionally protected speech cannot be suppressed solely to protect children or young adults from ideas or images a legislative body believes to be unsuitable for them. Librarians and library governing bodies should not resort to age restrictions in an effort to avoid actual or anticipated objections, because only a court of law can determine whether material is not constitutionally protected.

The mission, goals, and objectives of libraries cannot authorize librarians or library governing bodies to assume, abrogate, or overrule the rights and responsibilities of parents. As "Libraries: An American Value" states, "We affirm the responsibility and the right of all parents and guardians to guide their own children's use of the library and its resources and services." Librarians and governing bodies should maintain that parents – and only parents – have the right and the responsibility to restrict the access of their children – and only their children – to library resources. Parents who do not want their children to have access to certain library services, materials, or facilities should so advise their children. Librarians and library governing bodies cannot assume the role of parents or the functions of parental authority in the private relationship between parent and child.

Lack of access to information can be harmful to minors. Librarians and library governing bodies have a public and professional obligation to ensure that all members of the community they serve have free, equal, and equitable access to the entire range of library resources regardless of content, approach, format, or amount of detail. This principle of library service applies equally to all users, minors as well as adults. Librarians and library governing bodies must uphold this principle in order to provide adequate and effective service to minors.

The Freedom to Read Statement

The freedom to read is essential to our democracy. It is continuously under attack. Private groups and public authorities in various parts of the country are working to remove or limit access to reading materials, to censor content in schools, to label "controversial" views, to distribute lists of "objectionable" books or authors, and to purge libraries. These actions apparently rise from a view that our national tradition of free expression is no longer valid; that censorship and suppression are needed to counter threats to safety or national security, as well as to avoid the subversion of politics and the corruption of morals.

We, as individuals devoted to reading and as librarians and publishers responsible for disseminating ideas, wish to assert the public interest in the preservation of the freedom to read. Most attempts at suppression rest on a denial of the fundamental premise of democracy: that the ordinary individual, by exercising critical judgment, will select the good and reject the bad. We trust Americans to recognize propaganda and misinformation, and to make their own decisions about what they read and believe. We do not believe they are prepared to sacrifice their heritage of a free press in order to be "protected" against what others think may be bad for them. We believe they still favour free enterprise in ideas and expression.

These efforts at suppression are related to a larger pattern of pressures being brought against education, the press, art and images, films, broadcast media, and the Internet. The problem is not only one of actual censorship. The shadow of fear cast by these pressures leads, we suspect, to an even larger voluntary curtailment of expression by those who seek to avoid controversy or unwelcome scrutiny by government officials. Such pressure towards conformity is perhaps natural to a time of accelerated change. And yet suppression is never more dangerous than in such a time of social tension.

Freedom has given the United States the elasticity to endure strain. Freedom keeps open the path of novel and creative solutions, and enables change to come by choice. Every silencing of a heresy, every enforcement of an orthodoxy, diminishes the toughness and resilience of our society and leaves it the less able to deal with controversy and difference. Now as always in our history, reading is among our greatest freedoms.

The freedom to read and write is almost the only means for making generally available ideas or manners of expression that can initially command only a small audience. The written word is the natural medium for the new idea and the untried voice from which come the original contributions to social growth. It is essential to the extended discussion that serious thought requires, and to the accumulation of knowledge and ideas into organized collections. We believe that free communication is essential to the preservation of a free society and a creative culture.We believe that these pressures towards conformity present the danger of limiting the range and variety of enquiry and expression on which our democracy and our culture depend.

We believe that every American community must jealously guard the freedom to publish and to circulate, in order to preserve its own freedom to read. We believe that publishers and librarians have a profound responsibility to give validity to that freedom to read by making it possible for the readers to choose freely from a variety of offerings. The freedom to read is guaranteed by the Constitution. Those with faith in free people will stand firm on these constitutional guarantees of essential rights and will exercise the responsibilities that accompany these rights.

We therefore affirm these propositions:

- It is in the public interest for publishers and librarians to make available the widest diversity of views and expressions, including those that are unorthodox, unpopular, or considered dangerous by the majority
  - Creative thought is by definition new, and what is new is different. The bearer of every new thought is a rebel until that idea is refined and tested. Totalitarian systems attempt to maintain themselves in power by the ruthless suppression of any concept that challenges the established orthodoxy. The power of a democratic system to adapt to change is vastly strengthened by the freedom of its citizens to choose widely from among conflicting opinions offered freely to them. To stifle every nonconformist idea at birth would mark the end of the democratic process. Furthermore, only through the constant activity of weighing and selecting can the democratic mind attain the strength demanded by times like these. We need to know not only what we believe but why we believe it.
- Publishers, librarians, and booksellers do not need to endorse every

idea or presentation they make available. It would conflict with the public interest for them to establish their own political, moral, or aesthetic views as a standard for determining what should be published or circulated.

- Publishers and librarians serve the educational process by helping to make available knowledge and ideas required for the growth of the mind and the increase of learning. They do not foster education by imposing as mentors the patterns of their own thought. The people should have the freedom to read and consider a broader range of ideas than those that may be held by any single librarian or publisher or government or church. It is wrong that what one can read should be.

- It is contrary to the public interest for publishers or librarians to bar access to writings on the basis of the personal history or political affiliations of the author.
  - No art or literature can flourish if it is to be measured by the political views or private lives of its creators. No society of free people can flourish that draws up lists of writers to whom it will not listen, whatever they may have to say.
- There is no place in our society for efforts to coerce the taste of others, to confine adults to the reading matter deemed suitable for adolescents, or to inhibit the efforts of writers to achieve artistic expression.
  - To some, much of modern expression is shocking. But is not much of life itself shocking? We cut off literature at the source if we prevent writers from dealing with the stuff of life. Parents and teachers have a responsibility to prepare the young to meet the diversity of experiences in life to which they will be exposed, as they have a responsibility to help them learn to think critically for themselves. These are affirmative responsibilities, not to be discharged simply by preventing them from reading works for which they are not yet prepared. In these matters values differ, and values cannot be legislated; nor can machinery be devised that will suit the demands of one group without limiting the freedom of others.
- It is not in the public interest to force a reader to accept the prejudgment of a label characterizing any expression or its author as subversive or dangerous.
  - The ideal of labeling presupposes the existence of individuals or groups with wisdom to determine by authority what is good or bad for others. It presupposes that individuals must be directed in making up their minds about the ideas they examine. But Americans do not need others to do their thinking for them.

- It is the responsibility of publishers and librarians, as guardians of the people's freedom to read, to contest encroachments upon that freedom by individuals or groups seeking to impose their own standards or tastes upon the community at large; and by the government whenever it seeks to reduce or deny public access to public information.
  - It is inevitable in the give and take of the democratic process that the political, the moral, or the aesthetic concepts of an individual or group will occasionally collide with those of another individual or group. In a free society individuals are free to determine for themselves what they wish to read, and each group is free to determine what it will recommend to its freely associated members. But no group has the right to take the law into its own hands, and to impose its own concept of politics or morality upon other members of a democratic society. Freedom is no freedom if it is accorded only to the accepted and the inoffensive. Further, democratic societies are more safe, free, and creative when the free flow of public information is not restricted by governmental prerogative or self-censorship.
- It is the responsibility of publishers and librarians to give full meaning to the freedom to read by providing books that enrich the quality and diversity of thought and expression. By the exercise of this affirmative responsibility, they can demonstrate that the answer to a "bad" book is a good one, the answer to a "bad" idea is a good one.
  - The freedom to read is of little consequence when the reader cannot obtain matter fit for that reader's purpose. What is needed is not only the absence of restraint, but the positive provision of opportunity for the people to read the best that has been thought and said. Books are the major channel by which the intellectual inheritance is handed down, and the principal means of its testing and growth. The defence of the freedom to read requires of all publishers and librarians the utmost of their faculties, and deserves of all Americans the fullest of their support.

We state these propositions neither lightly nor as easy generalizations. We here stake out a lofty claim for the value of the written word. We do so because we believe that it is possessed of enormous variety and usefulness, worthy of cherishing and keeping free. We realise that the application of these propositions may mean the dissemination of ideas and manners of expression that are repugnant to many persons. We do not state these propositions in the comfortable belief that what people read is unimportant. We believe rather that what people read is deeply important; that ideas can be dangerous; but that the suppression of ideas is fatal to a democratic society. Freedom itself is a dangerous way of life, but it is ours.

STATEMENT ON LABELLING

An Interpretation of the Library Bill of Rights

Labeling is the practice of describing or designating materials by affixing a prejudicial label and/or segregating them by a prejudicial system.

The American Library Association opposes these means of predisposing people's attitudes towards library materials for the following reasons:

- Labeling is an attempt to prejudice attitudes and as such, it is a censor's tool.
- Some find it easy and even proper, according to their ethics, to establish criteria for judging publications as objectionable. However, injustice and ignorance rather than justice and enlightenment result from such practices, and the American Library Association opposes the establishment of such criteria.
- Libraries do not advocate the ideas found in their collections. The presence of books and other resources in a library does not indicate endorsement of their contents by the library.

A variety of private organizations promulgate rating systems and/or review materials as a means of advising either their members or the general public concerning their opinions of the contents and suitability or appropriate age for use of certain books, films, recordings, or other materials. For the library to adopt or enforce any of these private systems, to attach such ratings to library materials, to include them in bibliographic records, library catalogs, or other finding aids, or otherwise to endorse them would violate the Library Bill of Rights.

While some attempts have been made to adopt these systems into law, the constitutionality of such measures is extremely questionable. If such legislation is passed which applies within a library's jurisdiction, the library should seek competent legal advice concerning its applicability to library operations. Publishers, industry groups, and distributors sometimes add ratings to material or include them as part of their packaging.

Librarians should not endorse such practices. However, removing or obliterating such ratings—if placed there by or with permission of the copyright holder—could constitute expurgation, which is also unacceptable. The American Library Association opposes efforts which aim at closing any path to knowledge. This statement, however, does not exclude the adoption of organizational schemes designed as directional aids or to facilitate access to materials.

8

Succession Planning

AN OVERVIEW

Imagine this: You come to work one day to find out that your library director has accepted another job, decided to retire, or become ill or had an accident. In any event, you have a top position open. What will happen? The procedure in academic libraries is very familiar. A search committee will be appointed, and a position description will be written and advertised. Occasionally it will be decided to limit the search to current staff members, an in-house search. This will speed up the process.

However, if a national search is conducted, the hiring process will take months. Contrast this scenario with one at a major corporation such as McDonald's Corp. Jim Cantalupo, chair and CEO suddenly died. Within days the corporation was announcing a new chair. Before the stockholders reading the financial page had time to respond, McDonald's was back to business as usual. How can they respond so fast? What planning and preparation make this possible? The answer is called succession planning. Organizations such as Dow Chemical, Eli Lilly, Sonoco, and Dell Computer are anticipating changes in leadership, assessing the skills and knowledge of their employees, identifying those that possess the potential to be effective leaders, and providing training, mentoring, and experience so that when the moment happens the plan is in place.

Companies are not just doing this for the top executive; they are pushing this planning down the ladder. Succession planning is becoming workplace planning. William J. Rothwell, author of the major book on succession planning, defined it as anticipating changes in management, creating a strategic plan to identify potential staff members, determining the gaps in their knowledge, and providing training and coaching, special assignments, and experiences so that they are ready to step up when the time comes.

REVIEW OF THE LIBRARY LITERATURE

Are some libraries following the lead of these corporations and adopting succession planning? A review of the literature turned up only one article about succession planning in academic or public libraries in the United States, "Your Library's Future," a 2004 article published in Library Journal. This stage discusses how one library, the Multnomah County Library in Portland, Oregon, developed a programme to prepare and train younger staff members for the anticipated upperlevel positions. This plan included making staff aware of the future needs, encouraging them to make their interest known, and then providing peer reviews, mentors, and a training programme.

A side bar called "Succession Planning Tool Kit" gives an excellent but brief outline of the steps to take to set up a programme. Besides this object, there is one book on succession planning in libraries, Staff Planning in a Time of Demographic Change, which is based on a series of conferences held in Ontario, Canada, in 2002 and 2003. Libraries in the United Kingdom, Canada, and Australia have more seriously discussed succession planning, and this book provides a thorough discussion of the issues, many which apply to U.S. library situations. With the exception of the Library Journal object and a small set of objects centering on special libraries, there is almost nothing in journal literature about libraries in the United States using succession planning. The lack of objects about U.S. libraries is a red flag. Should libraries use succession planning? Why are U.S. libraries not using such plans? Are libraries just behind the times and missing a technique that could be useful? The primary reason that the business world uses succession planning is the shortage of capable people in the management ranks to fill the senior executive positions. In other words, major corporations cannot hire the leaders they need, so they are growing their own. Are libraries facing the same problem? Is there a shortage of leaders in the library field?

IS SUCCESSION PLANNING SOMETHING LIBRARIANS SHOULD CONSIDER?

A Look at the Leadership Supply in the Library Profession as a Whole

Within the next few years, many librarians, especially those holding the top-level positions, such as directors, deans, associate directors, and heads of libraries, will be retiring. The Bureau of Labour Statistics said that more than three in five librarians are age 45 years or older and will become eligible for retirement in the next 10 years. Mary Jo Lynch, director of American Library Association's Office for Research and Statistics, confirmed that in the near future a surge of retirements will take place peaking between 2015 and 2019. "In total, the decade beginning in 2010 will see 45% of today's librarians reach age 65, representing the early wave of baby-boom librarians reaching the traditional retirement age". Earlier statistics similarly outlined the coming librarian shortage and predicted that 83,366 librarians will be age 65 years by the year 2010. The general conclusion of many objects on the future of the profession is that the cause of the projected shortage is the expected retirements. Not satisfied with this general conclusion Larry Hardesty took a more analytical look at the recruitment and hiring statistics in his object in portal: Libraries and the Academy. He identified and investigated the possible causes: closing library schools, more attractive positions for MLS graduates in information science fields, or low salaries. He concluded, "The most plausible explanation for the current situation is the increased number of retirements". The problem is even more pronounced in Canada, which may explain why the Canadian libraries have been paying more attention to this phenomenon than U.S. libraries.

The Canadian Library Association conducted a questionnaire survey sent to 386 members that focused on retirement trends from 2002–2010 and looked for strategies and the level of preparedness to deal with the future shortage of librarians. The survey found that between 30%–50% of the Canadian librarians will retire by 2010 and most libraries (74%) feel that they are not prepared or only somewhat prepared. Further data indicates that there is a decrease in the number of librarians in the 25–34 age range; the figure is 12% in Canadian Association of Research Libraries (ARL) libraries. These numbers are far from the ideal figures of 20% at the senior level and 20% at the newcomer level. The full report on the Canadian situation has just been released in a publication by the 8Rs Research Team.

Despite statistics that indicate a shortage of librarians and lack of middle-level librarians trained in the competencies of leadership, only 9% of the libraries surveyed have a succession plan in place. ARL libraries in the United States are probably even less prepared. In the past the profession has solved similar shortages by promoting mid-career librarians and filling their positions with new graduates. However, there is now a shortage of mid-career librarians and new MLS graduates. The situation is complicated by the fact that the 1990s were lean times in libraries, and the number of new hires during this time was limited.

Many of the jobs went to boomers who changed careers and became librarians later in life. The result is that many librarians in middle management positions are the same age as the directors and associate directors, and they will be retiring along a similar time table. To further complicate the labour situation, over the past 15 to 20 years, there has also been a shortage of new MLS graduates to fill the ranks vacated by promotions of middle-level librarians. This shortage is predicted to extend into the peak baby boomer retirement years, 2015– 2019. "Estimated retirements outpace graduations in the United States, even accounting for reduced growth in professional-level library staffing in public and academic libraries". The library professional associations have made valiant efforts to address this problem by recruiting more people into the profession, but the prediction is that there is still a shortage of new MLS graduates. The retirement of the boomers coupled with the shortage of new librarians will complicate the already tight recruiting market, but there is yet another phenomenon occurring that is blackening the outlook even more. That is poor retention of new librarians, or "the five year itch." Many new librarians are leaving the profession dissatisfied and restless within their first five years as librarians. In survey research reported by Markgren and her research colleagues, one half of the 464 new librarians who answered their survey said they are thinking of leaving the profession and list some of the top reasons as "limited or no opportunities," and "position or role is not challenging enough."

They feel there are no growth opportunities, that they cannot move up the ladder, and that to advance they need to change jobs. Many are leaving librarianship as a career. So while library managers are despairing because they cannot find qualified staff especially for middle and upper-level positions, the new recruits feel there is no job advancement possible. There seems to be a serious communication gap between the generations. My own personal experience with gen Xers parallels what is written about them. They are described as self focused and impatient but also very motivated and success oriented; they want to learn and take on responsibility including management and supervision. The time is ripe for formal succession planning programmes that open up the discussion of opportunities for leadership and set up educational and training programmes to prepare new librarians to step up.

IS THE SHORTAGE OF LIBRARIANS TRUE FOR BUSINESS LIBRARIANS AND BUSINESS LIBRARY MANAGERS?

Statistics on Business Librarians and the Job Market for Business Librarians

The focus of this journal is business librarianship, and there is data on this niche of the library world. Two objects published since 2000 shed some light.Researchers did a thorough statistical study of business librarians and found that in the United States the average business library manager was a 51-year-old white and as likely to be female as male. As a group business librarians were well educated with 68% of the 25 managers in the survey holding multiple post-undergraduate degrees and about one third of them having a MBA.

They averaged 22 years of experience as a librarian and nearly 17 years as business librarians. Amajor finding of this research was that 50% of the managers indicated that they did not anticipate being an academic business librarian longer than five years. So research indicates that we should be in the midst of a major shift in the managers/directors/heads in business libraries right now. However, a quick review of the Academic Business Library Directors (ABLD), the same group Pagell and Lusk surveyed, indicates little change in the demographics of this group in the last seven years. The average age now is 55 years; their education level is approximately the same with 67% holding multiple higher education degrees; 37% hold a second master's degree other than an MBA, and 30% hold an MBA; and 55% are female So in seven years the group has aged respectively, but the education level has not altered. New directors were more likely female as the ratio of male to female has altered. However, many business library directors are not retiring yet, as Pagell and Lusk's survey expected. To ascertain when the retirement exodus will begin, I asked when each ABLD member plans to retire. Sixteen of the 27 in the group (or 60%) plan to retire by 2014; but only three of these 16 plan to retire within the next two years.

As just as the Census Bureau predicts, the retirement blitz will occur between 2010 and 2015. Are the upcoming business librarians being prepared for these positions? The major way (36%) was by personal contact, followed by internal postings (28%). It is the internal posting statistic that is of interest to this object. If in the 2000 survey over one fourth of the business library directors came to their jobs by internal promotions, then some rudimentary "succession planning" techniques were happening in their library, even if it was not called that.

I found this so surprising that I asked a few related follow-up questions of the ABLD group in August 2007. Sixty per cent stated that they were internal candidates. Twenty-two per cent were internal promotions without any search, in-house or external. Another 11% were promotions after an in-house search, and 26% were internal candidates in an external search. These statistics clearly show that libraries are "growing their own" business library directors. Business librarians in the ranks are being prepared to manage the library and being promoted from within the same library.

Do mid-career, non-managing business librarians feel they are ready and willing to be promoted to leadership positions when the business managers retire? Again some of Pagell and Lusk's survey results give us some clues as they asked skill related questions. Interestingly, non-managing business librarians' self ratings for information skills did not deviate from managers' skills; however, there was a significant gap in management skills in two areas: human resource responsibilities and conflict resolution. There was a wide variation especially in conflict resolution; about 60% of the managers rated themselves high in this area, whereas only 30% of the non-managers felt they were able to handle this. So business librarians in the ranks know their subject but feel they lack management skills, and they feel they particularly lack human resources skills such as conflict resolution skills. The Pagell and Lusk object did not attempt to determine if there will be enough business librarians to fill the upcoming management positions.

However, another object by did address this question. Their research, based on a survey to libraries that had advertised for a business librarian between March 1, 2000 and March 31, 2001, emphasized that at that time there was a lack of available business librarians. The major conclusion was that 70% of the employers were not satisfied with the applicant pool, with the quantity of candidates being the major problem. "Low supply of business information professionals" and "too much competition" for librarians were the major reasons listed by libraries that experienced difficulties in hiring. A huge 40% of the searches were reopened at least once. Researchers concluded that "a good business librarian is hard to find" and "recruiting internally and providing extensive professional development and training may also be a cost-effective alternative" to searching for an outside business librarian.

Their recommendations have the sound of succession planning. Like major corporations, perhaps libraries need to grow their own. All the statistics indicate that there will be a major shortage of librarians, starting in 2010 and peaking at 2015, caused by retirements and shortages of young people choosing librarianship as a career. This shortage will affect business libraries. Succession planning seems like a logical approach. So why are U.S. libraries not readily using it?

One reason is that in most libraries "the bench is too narrow." In other words, libraries do not have enough staff members to mentor and train new leaders. Major corporations have thousands of employees and hundreds of top-level managers. Identifying a handful of them that have the potential and interest to lead is possible. In a library with a few dozen librarians, this may not work. Another reason is that higher education institutions are actively working on increasing diversity; every opening is an opportunity. And the institutions have stated goals to increase the diversity of the faculty and staff; internal promotions do not met this goal.

The whole diversity problem is a topic for another object, but American Library Association's Office for Research and Statistics is following these statistics closely. They concluded that the "persistent lag in diversity in our LIS schools, the number of librarians and library assistants leaving the profession prematurely, the aging of racial and ethnic minority library workers, and the continued under representation of workers with disabilities, suggest a proportionally less diverse library workforce on the horizon". Furthermore, they suggested strategically planning around human resource development and succession planning. A third reason is the "grass is greener" perception. Libraries always want to hire the best candidate, and somehow librarians are not inclined to believe the best is on the staff right now.

The last reason is the "new broom theory"; libraries have a strong desire for a change in management. Unlike the business world that is dependent on stockholders' desire for consistency, libraries use upper-level staff openings as an opportunity to bring in new ideas and people that can implement creative strategic changes. Verbalizing and then discussing these reasons can help a library assess whether succession planning or some strategies of succession planning might be useful. Even if a fully developed succession planning programme is not the choice, there is much to be learned and borrowed from succession planning.

HOW TO START A SUCCESSION PLANNING PROGRAMME

The business literature on the topic is clear on two essentials: succession planning only works if the top-level administrators are 100% behind it; and the programme needs to be an open process.

It cannot be done by the human resource department alone or by middle managers mentoring and grooming staff members reporting to them. The administration has to be deeply involved; likewise staff members need to be involved, with feedback going to the employees that have been identified as possessing the potential for leadership.

The basic steps of succession planning are:

- Analyse the demographics of your key positions
- Identify potential employees for lead positions
- Assess candidates strengths and weaknesses
- Develop a training programme to build competencies.

Analyse Your Demographics

In a large academic or public library this would mean figuring out the age of your current directors, assistant or associate directors, department heads, and any other key positions, such as the main computer technician or business manager. In a smaller library system or a business library within a larger library system this might be a short list including only the managing librarian and possibly the assistant or associate managers. This step is easy to do; the main obstacle, because birth dates may not be readily available, is ascertaining ages.

However a fairly close estimate can be obtained by assuming each librarian was age 22 years when the undergraduate degree was earned. This analysis does give some insights. Using the Purdue Faculty Directory I did this exercise for Purdue libraries just to see what our demographics are. The average age of librarians in management positions has dropped over the past five years as younger people have been hired. One surprise was the number of internal promotions and in-house hires; over one half of the changes were internal promotions. We are not officially using succession planning, but these internal promotions indicate that we are preparing our mid-career librarians for upper-level positions.

Identify Potential Employees

This step is much more involved. Following the philosophy that top level administrators need to be involved in the process does not mean that other people in the library system are not included. Even in business setting, identifying potential employees involves many people; in some instances it is done by committee. For each position the qualifications and competencies need to be agreed upon. These might include such additional skills as ability to speak influentially to a large group, or ability to handle multiple projects at the same time, or ability to influence staff. These skills and competencies need to grow from the libraries' strategic plan and emphasize future needs. One way of developing this list of skills is to interview the staff currently in these positions.

This is also a good opportunity to ask for their nominations for a successor, recommendations for a training programme, and their willingness to mentor candidates for succession. This step is similar to writing job descriptions. Next potential employees are nominated and staff are asked to self identify listing their personal goals. The openness of the process is critical. Doing this step behind closed doors is generally not successful as it leads to staff distrust and accusations of unfair opportunities.

Assess Candidates' Strengths and Weaknesses

Once a list of potential candidates is developed, interview each of these employees to identify his or her interest, experience, and potential skills in librarianship and management. For example, does the candidate have extensive reference skills but lacks supervisory skills? Pay particular attention to management and leadership skills and gaps, and then prioritize the gaps. This needs to be a frank discussion, and help from mentors and supervisors will be critical for the success.

At this point it is important to have an agreement with the incumbents about their skill gaps and willingness to address these gaps and build the competencies needed. Is he or she willing to be mentored and willing to outline a self-development programme? Is the candidate willing to travel to attend association pre-conferences and workshops, to take courses at the university that provide needed skills such as financial management or personnel management skills? Likewise the library administration needs to make a commitment to the incumbents.

This would include funds for training and travel, release time from current responsibilities, and such things as supporting mentors. One of the major challenges of succession planning in libraries is "bench strength." In a small library there might not be anyone in the ranks who has the potential or interest in managing or leading the library. If this is the conclusion then the library needs to look closely at new hires in the future and to search for beginning librarians with career objectives of leadership and management.

Develop a Training Programme to Build Competencies

There are many choices for meeting skill gaps. Many libraries already have extensive training programmes in place, and libraries connected with universities have university employee training programmes as well as formal courses available. The major library associations offer many opportunities to learn leadership and management skills. In addition there are leadership institutes available at the University of California–Los Angeles, Harvard and Emory. The Association of Research Libraries also has programmes on leadership. Besides these formal training programmes, other options are job rotation, job shadowing, or interim positions. Managing a library while the head is on an extended vacation or sabbatical can help fill the management experience gap. Budget planning; staff selection, training, and evaluation; crisis management; and donor relations are all areas that mid-career librarians need training to be ready to step up to director-level positions.

The major one is William J. Rothwell's Effective Succession Planning. A second useful title is Growing Your Company's Leaders. The third recent book is the Whitmell's Staff Planning in a Time of Demographic Change. It is the only book available specifically on succession planning in libraries. It is a collection papers from a conferences held in Ontario, Canada, and covers mentoring, training, and demographic statistics and information from the business literature. Like many of the objects on succession planning, this book focuses on Canadian, Australian, and U.K. libraries. Whitmell is executive director of the Legislative Library for the Legislative Assembly of Ontario.

CONCLUSION

Although the literature indicates that few U.S. libraries are utilizing succession planning techniques, statistics on the demographics of librarians, and business librarians in particular, indicate that there is and will continue to be shortage of qualified middle-level librarians available for the projected management positions. This shortage will peak between 2010 and 2015. The business world has successfully used succession planning to identify, train, and prepare employees to be ready to step up the executive positions. This idea of "grow your own" leaders could help to accomplish the following goals for libraries: increasing career advancement opportunities for interested staff that will lead to the retention of young librarians looking for a more challenges and career development, encouragement of targeted diversity candidates who have leadership potential, as well as being ensured of leadership at a critical moment when the boomers retire.

9

Rules and Regulations

DEFINITIONS

- *Board of Governors:* The Board of Governors of the National Academy of Higher Education/ University Grants Commission.
- *Competent Authorty:* Any authority of the University Grants Commission/National Academy of Higher Education having full financial and administrative powers or part thereof.
- *Director General:* The Director General of National Academy of Higher Education.
- *Employees:* The employees of the National Academy of Higher Education, University Grants Commission and University Grants Commission's Regional Offices.
- *Inter-Library Loan:* Giving or taking of books and other reading material on loan to and from other libraries or agencies.
- *Librarian:* The Librarian of the National Academy of Higher Education's library.
- *Library:* The Library of the National Academy of Higher Education.
- *Members:* Registered members of the National Academy of Higher Education Library as laid down in rules 3and4.
- *Officers:* The employees declared by the Government as officer *i.e.* all employees of BP&-16 and above of the National Academy of Higher Education and the University Grants Commission.
- *Officials:* All employees BP&-l to BP&-15 of the University Grants Commission and the National Academy of Higher Education.
- *Pre-Service/In-Service Training Participatnts:* Participants attending training Programmes in the National Academy of Higher Education.
- *University:* Any University in Pakistan recognized by the Government.
- *University Librarian:* Librarian/ Incharge Librarian/ Acting Librarian/ Chief Librarian of any of the Pakistani Universities.
- *University Departmenta Librarian:* Librarian of a departmental library of any of the Pakistani Universities.

LIBRARY RULES

Working Hours

1 The library shall remain open for service during the working hours observed by the National Academy of Higher Education/University Grants Commission.

2 The" library hours may be changed from time to time according to the service of the National Academy of Higher Education/University Grants Commission.

Loan Privileges

3. The following categories of persons will be allowed to make use of the library resources:
   3.1. Employees of the University Grants Commission/National Academy of Higher Education.
   3.2. In-service and Pre-Service training participants.
   3.3. Teachers/resources persons etc. deputed by UGC/NAHE for teaching.
   3.4. Members of the Board of Governors of UGC/NAHE.
   3.5. Other persons allowed in writing by Director General/Librarian.
   3.6. University/University Department Librarians.
4. Persons desirous of using the library must apply for membership on a form obtainable from t he library.
   4.1. A borrower's card will be issued to each member on presentation of which reading material will be issued (except rule 3.6 for which the Librarian will maintain a proper record). The same procedure will be followed when the books are returned. This card will not be transferable and should be surrendered at the time of obtaining a clearance certificate.
   4.2. A borrowers card will be valid up- to the date mentioned on it. A borrower should get the card renewed before it expires, if he so desires.
   4.3. Members should not mark or write on their borrower cards in any way Defaulters may be dealt with as per rule 30.
5. A Member, who loses his card shall at once inform the Librarian. A duplicate card will be. issued. Any member sub- lending reading material from the library on his card to any other person shall do so at his own responsibility.

Loan Period

6. The following categories of members shall observe the loan schedule mentioned against each. Relaxation of loan schedule will be at the discretion of the Librarian.

7. Books borrowed once may be issued provided these are not required by other members. Books will not be reissued more than twice. Books will have to be presented for re-issue. However, in case of need the Librarian may relax the condition.
8. Reading material of the following nature shall not be issued but can be consulted in.the library (except in special cases *e.g.* classroom use of a teacher for a short period/photocopying purposes)
   8.1 Reference material (*i.e.* Encyclopedias, dictionaries, atlases and the material marked 'R')
   8.2 Theses, reports, pamphlets, syllabi, acts etc.
   8.3 Microfilms, slides, cassettes, tape recorders and other allied material.
   8.5 All unprocessed material.
   8.6 Current periodicals.
   8.7 Other material assigned by the Librarian.

Damage and Loss of Books

9. Book(s) lost, dam ed, or mutilated in any way by a member shall have to be replaced or paid for. The cost of such book(s) shall be double the prevailing cost plus an additional 25% departmental charges. The price of rare book(s) shall be decided by the Librarian.
10. If books and other materials borrowed from the library are not returned notices will be issued. In case the books are not returned even after the second notice, Rule 9 will be applied.
11. The amount realised from a member as cost of lost or damaged book(s) or material(s) or for not returning the books after due notices shall be credited to NAHE Library's head 'Books and Journals'.
12. Book.,(s) or other material lost or found to be lost on stock-taking shall be reported to the competent authority for write-off.
13. If a member leaves his organization without returning books borrowed from this library, the price of the book(s) will be adjusted against his dues with the organization. (In case there is no outstanding balance in his name, the price will be paid by his guarantor).

Weeding

14. On receipt of a written request from the Librarian, the Director General shall depute one or two members other than the library staff for weeding out outdated worn-out and/ or seriously damaged or mutilated books and other materials. He/ She/ they shall submit their recommendations in writing to the competent authority for approval.

Write-off Losses

15. The Librarian shall report all books/ non- print material damaged, and/or worn-out through fair wear and tear to the competent authority for write off action.
16. Losses to the extent of 3% per annum of the available stock in an open access library shall be written off by the competent authority.
17. Losses to the extent of 2% per annum of the available collection of a close access or partially open access library shall be written off by the competent authority.
18. Losses written off by the competent authority shall be struck off from the stock and the records of the library, including public catalogues, and transferred to the with-drawl register indicating the authority under which the losses were written off.
19. The permanent irrecoverable loans of mutilated, damaged and worn-out books found to be beyond repairs during the physical verification of the library shall also be reported to the competent authority for write-off.

Mail Loan

20. The library shall offer postal loan service to the Librarian(s) of the out station Universities provided Rule 4.2 is followed. University Librarian/Department Librarian will be responsible for Safe return.
21. In view of the insecurity of mail, inconveniences of the postal-loan service and other discrepancies of non-receipt of materials expected to arise by this/these facility (ies) loss of book(s) and other materials shall be safeguarded by adopting the Registered Parcel procedure of dispatch to avoid loss in transit.
22. In case there is a loss in transit, it shall be recorded by the Librarian and reported to the competent authority for write-off action.

Inter-Library Loans

23. With a view to extending and/or utilizing book and non-book resources of other institutions of higher education in the country, the Librarian shall enter into, and maintain any mutually agreed upon interlibrary loan system with Academic, Research, Special, Public and Government Departmental Libraries.

General Rules

24. Members shall not mutilate, or damage by writing or marking on pages, any book or publication, nor shall they trace or perform mechanical reproduction of any material belonging to the library

without formal permission of the Librarian. Violation of this rule shall require replacement of the damaged volume or payment of its price as specified under rule 9.

25. If one volume of a set/series is damaged and it is not available separately, the whole set shall have to be replaced or paid for by the member as specified under rule 9.
26. Following Rules 24 and 25 paying the cost the member may, if he/she so desires, retain the damaged book(s) or volumes for which the price has been recovered from him/her.
27. Members are advised to inspect books or other material at the time of issue. They must direct the attention of the staff at the Charging Desk to defects, if any.
28. The Library Reading Room shall remain open during stock-taking but the borrowing privileges will remain suspended for the same period. All books on loan 'with the members must irrespective of the date-due, be returned to. the library before the date of stock-taking. Two week advance notice will be given.
29. All members must without fail intimate, the librarian of any change of address.
30. The Librarian is authorized to withdraw library facilities from any member who is found misusing the library material or facilities.
31. Members of the library shall deposit their personal belongings at the counter near the entrance.
32. In case any personal reading material has to be taken in-side the library, permission must be sought from the Librarian. All reading material issued to them shall be shown to the attendant at the exit before leaving.
33. Eating, sleeping, smoking and audible conversation within the library premises is prohibited.
34. Members shall make their own arrangement for carrying book(s) etc. from and to the library.

10

Professional Organizations in Library

INDIAN LIBRARY ASSOCIATION (ILA)

Indian Library Association (ILA) was established on September 13, 1933, on the occasion of the First All India Library Conference held at Calcutta (now Kolkata). The ILA is the largest and renowned professional body in the field of Library and Information Science in India with a membership of more than 7000.

The main objectives of the Association are:

- Promoting library movement in the country,
- Developing Library and Information Science education,
- Training and research, betterment of library personnel,
- Cooperation at the national and international levels,
- Promotion of standards, norms, services and guide-lines, and
- Providing a forum for professionals and publication of materials.

INDIAN ASSOCIATION OF SPECIAL LIBRARIES AND INFORMATION CENTRES (IASLIC)

The IASLIC, acronym for the Indian Association of Special Libraries and Information Centres, was established on 3 September 1955 as a non-profit making national, professional body to:

- Promote the quality of Library and Information Services
- Coordinate the activities, and
- Foster mutual cooperation and assistance among the special libraries, scientific, technological and research institutions, learned societies, commercial organizations, industrial research establishments as well as centres of studies in social sciences and humanities
- Improve the technical efficiency of the professionals
- Act as a centre of research and studies in special librarianship and documentation techniques
- Act as a centre of information in scientific, technical and other related fields of LIS in pursuance of the aforesaid objects.

INDIAN ASSOCIATION OF TEACHERS OF LIBRARY AND INFORMATION SCIENCE (IATLIS)

The idea of founding an association of library science teachers was floated at the Unesco Regional Seminar held at the University of Delhi in October 1960 and later on discussed at the following three seminars:

- All India Seminar on Education for Librarianship held at Banaras Hindu University (1963),
- All India Seminar on Education for Librarianship held at SNDT Women's University (1965), and
- All India Seminar on Teaching of Library Science held at Delhi University (1966). To elicit the opinion from teachers in library schools, a circular was issued by Prof Bashiruddin in collaboration with the late Prof. Das Gupta and P.N.Kaula from the Rajasthan School. At the Delhi Seminar in 1966, the same issue was reviewed but without yielding any result.

Mr Derek Langridge, principal lecturer, North Western Polytechnic School (England) delivered Sarada Ranganathan Endowment Lectures at DRTC, Bangalore on 'Teaching of Library Classification' from 15-19 December 1969. This provided a fortuitous opportunity to discuss the issue of having an organization for teachers of Library Science.

FORMATION OF THE ORGANIZATION

On 19th December 1969, a meeting of the teachers of library science attending the Sarada Ranganathan Endowment Lectures was convened by Mr. P. N. Kaula at DRTC with Mr. C. K. Langridge in the chair. This was attended by teachers from several Library schools. Dr. D. B. Krishna Rao asked Mr. P.N. Kaula to give his opening Address stating the purpose of the meeting. Mr. P. N. Kaula described the structure of Library education in the country and the need for having an association of teachers of Library science.He also stated the efforts made in the past and the interest shown by the teachers at the seminar.

Dr. D. B. Krishna Rao declared that the Indian Association of Teachers of library science be formed with an ad-hoc committee constituted for this purpose. Mr. Ganesh Bhattacharya proposed a vote of thanks. In the end a Committee was formed with Dr. D. B. Krishna Rao as its Chairman and Mr. P. N. Kaula as the Secretary.

Thus was born the Indian Association of the Teachers of Library and Information Science (IATLIS) a national professional organization to further the cause of library education in India. The General Body meeting of IATLIS was held on 21st December 1970 to adopt the draft constitution circulated to members earlier with Mr. P. B. Roy in the chair. The constitution was discussed and adopted unanimously.

THE REVIVAL

After the foundation meeting in 1969, the first 'National Seminar' was held in 1970 at DRTC, Bangalore with the blessings of Dr Ranganathan and dynamic leadership of Prof P.N.Kaula. Dr D.B.Krishna Rao, Padmasri Bashiruddin, Prof A.Neela-meghan, Prof M.R.Kumbar played a key role in the formative years of the Association.

However, the Association was remained dormant from 1973-80. In March 1980, Prof Kaula conducted an All India Seminar on Relevance of LIS Education to the changing needs of the country at BHU. At this Seminar IATLIS was revived with Prof Kaula as President and Prof Kumar as General Secretary. Since 1981 it was active once again and IATLIS Communication and several other activities were initiated by Prof Kumar. National Seminars are being conducted regularly since 1986.

AIMS AND OBJECTIVES

To promote exchange of ideas on education in library and information science, To promote research in education in library and information science, To promote the publication of books and periodicals on education in library and information science. To hold conferences, seminars, and colloquia for the development and propagation of ideas on education in library and information science, to give consultation service on education in library and information science, to promote training of the teachers of library and information science in India, and to promote welfare of teachers of library and information science in India.

AMERICAN LIBRARY ASSOCIATION (ALA)

The American Library Association (ALA) is a non-profit organization based in the United States that promotes libraries and library education internationally. It is the oldest and largest library association in the world, with more than 62,000 members. Founded by Justin Winsor, Charles Ammi Cutter, Samuel S. Green, James L. Whitney, Melvil Dewey (Melvil Dui), Fred B. Perkins and Thomas W. Bicknell in 1876 in Philadelphia and chartered in 1879 in Massachusetts, its head office is now in Chicago.

During the Centennial Exposition in Philadelphia in 1876, 103 librarians, 90 men and 13 women, responded to a call for a "Convention of Librarians" to be held October 4–6 at the Historical Society of Pennsylvania. At the end of the meeting, "the register was passed around for all to sign who wished to become charter members," making October 6, 1876 to be ALA's birthday.

In attendance were 90 men and 13 women, among them Justin Winsor (Boston Public, Harvard), William Frederick Poole (Chicago Public, Newberry), Charles Ammi Cutter (Boston Athenaeum), Melvil Dewey, and Richard Rogers Bowker. Attendees came from as far west as Chicago and from England.

The aim of the Association, in that resolution, was "to enable librarians to do their present work more easily and at less expense." The Association has worked throughout its history to define, extend, protect and advocate for equity of access to information. Library activists in the 1930s pressured the American Library Association to be more responsive to issues put forth by young members involved with issues such as peace, segregation, library unions and intellectual freedom. In 1931, the Junior Members Round Table (JMRT) was formed to provide a voice for the younger members of the ALA, but much of what they had to say resurfaced in the social responsibility movement to come years later.

During this period, the first Library Bill of Rights (LBR) was drafted by Forrest Spaulding to set a standard against censorship and was adopted by the ALA in 1939. This has been recognized as the moment defining modern librarianship as a profession committed to intellectual freedom and the right to read over government dictates. The ALA formed the Staff Organization's Round Table in 1936 and the Library Unions Round Table in 1940. The ALA appointed a committee to study censorship and recommend policy after the banning of *The Grapes of Wrath* and the implementation of the LBR. The committee reported in 1940 that intellectual freedom and professionalism were linked and recommended a permanent committee–Committee on Intellectual Freedom.

The ALA made revisions to strengthen the LBR in June 1948, approved the Statement on Labeling in 1951 to discourage labeling material as subversive, and adopted the Freedom to Read Statement and the Overseas Library Statement in 1953. In 1961, the ALA took a stand regarding service to African Americans and others, advocating for equal library service for all. An amendment was passed to the LBR in 1961 that made clear that an individual's library use should not be denied or abridged because of race, religion, national origin, or political views. Some communities decided to close their doors rather than desegregate. In 1963, the ALA commissioned a study, *Access to Public Libraries*, which found direct and indirect discrimination in American libraries.

In 1967 some librarians protested against a pro-Vietnam War speech given by General Maxwell D. Taylor at the annual ALA conference in San Francisco; the former president of Sarah Lawrence College, Harold Taylor, spoke to the Middle-Atlantic Regional Library Conference about socially responsible professionalism; and less than one year later a group of librarians proposed that the ALA schedule a new round table programme discussion on the social responsibilities of librarians at its next annual conference in Kansas City. This group called themselves the Organizing Committee for the ALA Round Table on Social Responsibilities of Libraries. This group drew in many other under-represented groups in the ALA who lacked power, including the Congress for Change in 1969. This formation of the committee was approved in 1969 and would change its name to the Social Responsibilities Round Table (SRRT) in 1971). After its inception, the Round Table of Social Responsi-bilities began to press ALA leadership to address issues such as library unions, working conditions, wages, and intellectual freedom. The Freedom to Read Foundation was created by ALA's Executive Board in 1969. The Black Caucus of the ALA and the Office for Literacy and Outreach were set up in 1970.

In June 1990, the ALA approved "Policy on Library Services to the Poor" and in 1996 the Task Force on Hunger Homelessness, and Poverty was formed to resurrect and promote the ALA guidelines on library services to the poor. The ALA archival materials, non-current records, are currently held in the University of Illinois archives. These materials can only be used at the University of Illinois.

MEMBERSHIP

ALA membership is open to any person or organization, though most of its members are libraries or librarians. Most members live and work in the United States, with international members comprising 3.5% of total membership.

GOVERNING STRUCTURE

The ALA is governed by an elected council and an executive board. Since 2002,Keith Michael Fiels has been the ALA executive director (CEO). Policies and programmes are administered by various committees and round tables. One of the organization's most visible tasks is overseen by the Office for Accreditation, which formally reviews and authorizes American and Canadian academic institutions that offer degree programmes in library and information science. The ALA's current President is Molly Raphael (2011-2012). Notable past presidents of the ALA include Theresa Elmendorf, its first female president (1911–1912), Clara Stanton Jones, its first African-American president (1976-1977), Loriene Roy, its first Native American president (2007-2008), Michael Gorman (2005-6), and Roberta Stevens..

Activities

The official purpose of the association is "to promote library service and librarianship." Members may join one or more of eleven membership divisions that deal with specialized topics such as academic, school, or public libraries, technical or reference services, and library administration. Members may also join any of seventeen round tables that are grouped around more specific interests and issues than the broader set of ALA divisions.

Notable Divisions

- ALA Editions (book publishing)

- American Association of School Librarians (AASL)
- Association for Library Collections and Technical Services (ALCTS)
- Association for Library Service to Children (ALSC)
- Association of College and Research Libraries (ACRL)
- Library Information Technology Association (LITA)
- Public Library Association (PLA)
- Reference and User Services Association (RUSA)
- Young Adult Library Services Association (YALSA)

Notable Offices

- Office of Intellectual Freedom (OIF)
- Office for Accreditation (OA)
- Office for Literacy and Outreach Services (OLOS)
- Office for Information Technology Policy (OITP)

Notable Sub-organizations

In 1970, the ALA founded the first lesbian, gay, bisexual and transgender professional organization, called the "Task Force on Gay Liberation", now known as the GLBT Round Table. On July 23rd, 1976, the Committee on the Status of Women in Librarian-ship was established as a Council Committee of the ALA on recommendation of the Ad Hoc Committee with the same name (which had been appointed by the President of the ALA in December of 1975) and of the Committee on Organization.

The Committee on the Status of Women in Librarianship works to "officially represent the diversity of women's interest within ALA and to ensure that the Association considers the rights of the majority (women) in the library field; to promote and initiate the collection, analysis, dissemination, and coordination of information on the status of women in librarianship; to coordinate the activities of ALA units which consider questions of special relevance for women; to identify lags, gaps, and possible discrimination in resources and programmes relating to women; in cooperation with other ALA units, to help develop and evaluate tools, guidelines, and programmes designed to enhance the opportunities and the image of women in the library profession, thus raising the level of consciousness concerning women; to establish contacts with committees on women within other professional groups and to officially represent ALA concerns at interdisciplinary meetings on women's equality; and to provide Council and Membership with reports needed for establishment of policies and actions related to the status of women in librarianship; and to monitor ALA units to ensure consideration of the rights of women." In 1979 the Committee on the Status of Women in Librarian-ship received the Bailey K. Howard-World Book Encyclopedia-ALA Goal Award to develop a profile of ALA personal members, known as the COSWL Study. In 1980 the Committee on the Status of Women in Librarianship was awarded the J. Morris Jones-World Book Encyclopedia-ALA Goals Award with the OLPR Advisory Committee to undertake a special project on equal pay for work of equal value.

National Outreach

The ALA is affiliated with regional, state, and student chapters across the country. It organizes conferences, participates in library standards development, and publishes a number of books and periodicals. The ALA publishes the magazines *American Libraries* and *Booklist*. Along with other organizations, it sponsors the annual Banned Books Week the last week of September. Young Adult Library Services Association (YALSA) also sponsors Teen Read Week, the third week of each October, and Teen Tech Week, the second week of each March.

Awards and Honours

The ALA annually confers numerous book and media awards, primarily through its children's and young adult divisions (others are the Dartmouth Medal, Coretta Scott King Awards, Schneider Book Awards, and Stonewall Book Award). The children's division ALSC administers the Caldecott Medal, Newbery Medal, Batchelder Award, Belpré Awards, Geisel Award, and Sibert Medal, all annual book awards; the Odyssey Award for best audiobook (joint with YALSA), and the (U.S.) Carnegie Medal and for best video. There are also two ALSC lifetime recognitions, the Wilder Medal and the Arbuthnot Lecture.

The young-adult division YALSA administers the Margaret Edwards Award for significant and lasting contribution to YA literature, a lifetime recognition of one author annually, and some annual awards that recognize particular works: the Michael L. Printz Award for a YA book judged on literary merit alone, the William C. Morris Award for an author's first YA book, the new "YALSA Award for Excellence in Nonfiction for Young Adults", and the "Alex Award" list of ten adult books having special appeal for teens. Jointly with the children's division ALSC there is the Odyssey Award for excellence in audiobook production. The award for YA nonfiction was inaugurated in 2012, defined by ages 12 to 18 and publication year November 2010 to October 2011. The first winner was '*The Notorious Benedict Arnold: A True Story of Adventure, Heroism and Treachery* by Steve Sheinkin (Roaring Brook Press, November 2010) and four other finalists were named.

Beside the Alex Awards, ALA disseminates some annual lists of "Notable" and "Best" books. The annual awards roster includes the John Cotton Dana Award for excellence in library public relations. From 2006 the ALA annually selects a class of Emerging Leaders, typically comprising about 100 librarians and library school students. This minor distinction is a form of organizational outreach to new librarians. The Emerging Leaders are allocated to project groups tasked with developing solutions to specified problems within ALA divisions. The class meets at the ALA Midwinter and Annual Meetings, commonly January and June. Project teams may present posters of their completed projects at the Annual.

Conferences

The ALA and its divisions hold numerous conferences throughout the year. The two largest conferences are the annual conference and the midwinter meeting. The latter is typically held in January and focused on internal business, while the annual conference is typically held in June and focused on exhibits and presentations. The ALA annual conference is notable for being one of the largest professional conferences in existence, typically drawing over 25,000 attendees.

POLITICAL POSITIONS

The ALA advocates positions on United States political issues that it believes are related to libraries and librarianship. For court cases that touch on issues about which the organization holds positions, the ALA often files amici curiae briefs, voluntarily offering information on some aspect of the case to assist the court in deciding a matter before it. The ALA has an office in Washington, D.C., that lobbies Congress on issues relating to libraries, information and communication. It also provides materials to libraries that may include information on how to apply for grants, how to comply with the law, and how to oppose a law.

Intellectual Freedom

The primary documented expressions of the ALA's intellectual freedom principles are the Freedom to Read Statement and the Library Bill of Rights; the Library Bill of Rights urges libraries to "challenge censorship in the fulfillment of their responsibility to provide information and enlightenment." The ALA Code of Ethics also calls on librarians to "uphold the principles of intellectual freedom and resist all efforts to censor library resources." The ALA maintains an Office for Intellectual Freedom (OIF) headed by Barbara M. Jones, former University Librarian for Wesleyan University and internationally known intellectual freedom advocate and author. She is the second director of the Office for Intellectual Freedom, succeeding Judith Krug, who headed the office for four decades.

OIF is charged with "implementing ALA policies concer-ning the concept of intellectual freedom," that the ALA defines as "the right of every individual to both seek and receive information from all points of view without restriction. It provides for free access to all expressions of ideas through which any and all sides of a question, cause or movement may be explored." Its goal is "to educate librarians and the general public about the nature and importance of intellectual freedom in libraries."

The OIF compiles lists of challenged books as reported in the media and submitted to them by librarians across the country. Its actions are not without controversy; for example, Nat Hentoff noted "An issue facing all members of the ALA is their leaders' shameful exception of the Cuban people's freedom to read." Hentoff's characterization contradicts the ALA's official position on Cuba, which urges the Cuban Government "to eliminate obstacles to access to information" and expresses "deep concern" for political dissidents in Cuba. In 1999, radio personality Laura Schlessinger campaigned publicly against the ALA's intellectual freedom policy, specifically in regard to the ALA's refusal to remove a link on its web site to a specific sex-education site for teens. Sharon Presley said, however, that Schlessinger "distorted and misrepresented the ALA stand to make it sound like the ALA was saying porno for 'children' is O.K."

In 2002, the ALA filed suit with library users and the ACLU against the United States Children's Internet Protection Act (CIPA), which required libraries receiving federal E-rate discounts for Internet access to install a "technology protection measure" to prevent children from accessing "visual depictions that are obscene, child pornography, or harmful to minors." At trial, the federal district court struck down the law as unconstitutional. The government appealed this decision, and on June 23, 2003, the Supreme Court of the United States upheld the law as constitutional as a condition imposed on institutions in exchange for government funding. In upholding the law, the Supreme Court, adopting the interpretation urged by the U.S. Solicitor General at oral argument, made it clear that the constitutionality of CIPA would be upheld only "if, as the Government represents, a librarian will unblock filtered material or disable the Internet software filter without significant delay on an adult user's request."

Privacy

In 2003, the ALA passed a resolution opposing the USA PATRIOT Act, which called sections of the law "a present danger to the constitutional rights and privacy rights of library users". Since then, the ALA and its members have sought to change the law by working with members of Congress and educating their communities and the press about the law's potential to violate the privacy rights of library users.

ALA has also participated as an *amicus curiae* in lawsuits filed by individuals challenging the constitutionality of the USA PATRIOT Act, including a lawsuit filed by four Connecticut librarians after the library consortium they managed was served with a National Security Letter seeking information about library users. After several months of litigation, the lawsuit was dismissed when the FBI decided to withdraw the National Security Letter. In 2007 the "Connecticut Four" were honoured by the ALA with the Paul Howard Award for Courage for their challenge to the National Security Letter and gag order provision of the USA PATRIOT Act.

In 2006, the ALA sold humourous "radical militant librarian" buttons for librarians to wear in support of the ALA's stances on intellectual freedom, privacy, and civil liberties. Inspiration for the button's design came from documents obtained from the FBI by the Electronic Privacy Information Center (EPIC) through a Freedom of Information Act (FOIA) request. The request revealed a series of e-mails in which FBI agents complained about the "radical, militant librarians" while criticizing the reluctance of FBI management to use the secret warrants authorized under Section 215 of the USA PATRIOT Act.

Copyright

The ALA "supports efforts to amend the Digital Millennium Copyright Act (DMCA) and urges the courts to restore the balance in copyright law, ensure fair use and protect and extend the public domain". It supports changing copyright law to eliminate damages when using orphan works without permission; is wary of digital rights management; and, in ALA v. FCC, successfully sued the Federal Communications Commission to prevent regulation that would enforce next-generation digital televisions to contain rights-management hardware. It has joined the Information Access Alliance to promote open access to research. The Copyright Advisory Network of the Association's Office for Information Technology Policy provides copyright resources to libraries and the communities they serve.

SPECIAL LIBRARIES ASSOCIATION

Special Libraries Association (SLA) is an international professional association for library and information professionals working in business, government, law, finance, non-profit, and academic organizations and institutions.

While Special libraries include law libraries, news libraries, corporate libraries, museum libraries, and medical libraries, many information professionals today do not actually work in a library setting. They actively apply their specialized skills to support the information needs of their organizations.

SLA was founded in 1909 in the United States. It is now an international organization with over 9,000 members in over 75 countries. SLA is organized by Chapters (geographic) and Divisions (topical) and special interest groups. The association has a CEO (employee of the association) and an elected President (mandate of one year). Members of SLA typically possess a master's degree in library or information science. Given the rapid adoption of information technologies for selecting, analysing, managing, storing, and delivering information and knowledge, the average SLA member might be performing a range of services and employing a diverse mix of skills related to, but not exclusive of, library science. Association activities include conferences, professional education, networking and advocacy.

CHARTERED INSTITUTE OF LIBRARY AND INFORMATION PROFESSIONALS

The Chartered Institute of Library and Information Professionals (CILIP) is a professional body representing librarians and other information professionals in the United Kingdom. It was formed in 2002 by the merger of the Library Association (abbreviated to LA or sometimes LAUK)–founded in 1877 as a result of the first International Conference of Librarians and awarded a Royal Charter in 1898–and the Institute of Information Scientists, founded in 1958. Membership is not compulsory for practice, but members can work towards *Chartered Membership* which entitles them to the postnominal letters MCLIP, and subsequently towards *Fellowship* (FCLIP). Affiliated members can also obtain ACLIP upon completing certification. Honourary Fellowship (HonFCLIP or FCLIP(hc)), a qualification akin to an honourary degree, is granted to a small number of people who have rendered distinguished service to the profession.

FUNCTIONS

CILIP accredits degree programmes in library and information science at universities in the UK, including City University, London, Loughborough University, the Manchester Metropolitan University, the Robert Gordon University, the University of Sheffield and University College London. CILIP is perhaps best known to the general public for awarding the Carnegie and Kate Greenaway Medals for children's books. CILIP publishes a monthly magazine, *CILIP Update with Gazette,* including listings of job vacancies. It also runs a publishing imprint, Facet Publishing.

There are several local branches across the United Kingdom, 28 special interest groups and over 20 organisations in liaison including such bodies as the African Caribbean Library Association, the Librarians' Christian Fellowship and the Society of Indexers. CILIP hosts a conference every two years called "Umbrella" (containing 'LA' the acronym of the Library Association). Umbrella 2009 was held in Hertfordshire and so was Umbrella 2011 (July 12-13 at Hatfield). The title is abbreviated from "Under One UmbrelLA" a Library Association event held every two years.

ROLE IN LIS EDUCATION

CILIP's policy is to improve all aspects of professional practice through its work in education, maintaining a framework of universally recognised qualifications and providing a wide range of opportunities for CPD. In 2002 CILIP undertook a review of its qualifications framework. The new *Framework of Qualifications* was launched in April 2005. It is designed to be flexible and adaptable, as the areas will evolve and develop over time to accommodate changing needs. It is appropriate to library and information professionals across the sector as a whole. As such it has a degree of overlap with the knowledge base of other professions.

The framework consists of four levels–certification, chartership, revalidation and fellowship. Certification provides recognition from the association for library and information work by para-professionals. Those who gain admittance to the Register of Certified Members are entitled to work towards Chartered Membership.

There are two categories of applicant for Chartership:

- Firstly para-professionals with over five years experience;
- Secondly those who have some evidence of training and have been working for two years.

Chartership is CILIP's standard for information professionals. Chartered members are entitled to use post nominal letters and describe themselves as qualified library and information professionals. All candidates for Chartership must work with a Mentor and demonstrate through their portfolio that they meet the required criteria. Chartership is not an academic qualification but a recognition of the highest standards of professional practice. The individual makes a commitment to continued professional development. Normally applicants will have completed a degree in LIS and have been working for at least one year.

INTERNATIONAL FEDERATION OF LIBRARY ASSOCIATIONS AND INSTITUTIONS

The International Federation of Library Associations and Institutions (IFLA) is the leading international association of library organisations. It is the global voice of the library and information profession, and its annual conference provides a venue for librarians to learn from one another. The IFLA forum promotes international cooperation, research and development in all fields related to library activities. A very important and close partner of the IFLA is UNESCO. Several of the manifestos prepared by committees of the IFLA have been recognized as UNESCO manifestos.

IFLA is part of the International Committee of the Blue Shield (ICBS), which works to protect the world's cultural heritage threatened by wars and natural disasters, and whose Director General is currently Mr Julien Anfruns from the International Council of Museums (ICOM). IFLA was founded in Edinburgh, Scotland, in 1927 when library associations from 14 European countries and the United States signed a resolution at the celebration of the 50th anniversary of the Library Association of the United Kingdom. Isak

Collijn, head of the National Library of Sweden, was elected the first president. The first constitution was approved in Rome in 1929 during the World Congress of Librarianship and Bibliography. During the 1930s the first library associations from outside Europe and the US joined, these being China, India, Japan, Mexico and the Philippines. By 1958 membership had grown to 64 associations from 42 countries.

A permanent secretariat was established in 1962. By 1970 there were 250 members from 52 countries. The secretariat was moved to The Hague in 1971. By 1974 IFLA membership had become virtually global with 600 members in 100 countries. Membership criteria were expanded beyond library associations in 1976 to include institutions, *i.e.* libraries, library schools and bibliographic institutes. At this time, the word *Institutions* was added to the organisation's name. Since then further new categories of membership have been created, including personal affiliates. IFLA has now grown to over 1,700 members in 155 countries. It is headquartered in the Koninklijke Bibliotheek, the National Library of the Netherlands, in The Hague.

MISSION

IFLA's objectives are:

- To represent librarianship in matters of international interest
- To promote the continuing education of library personnel
- To develop, maintain and promote guidelines for library services

Core Values

The objectives are informed by the following core values:

- The endorsement of the principles of freedom of expression embodied in Article 19 of the Universal Declaration of Human Rights
- The belief that people, communities and organizations need universal and equitable access to information, ideas and works of imagination for their social, educational, cultural, democratic and economic well-being
- The conviction that delivery of high quality library and information services helps guarantee that access
- The commitment to enable all Members of the Federation to engage in, and benefit from, its activities without regard to citizenship, disability, ethnic origin, gender, geographical location, language, political philosophy, race or religion.

Committee on Free Access to Information and Freedom of Expression (FAIFE)

One of the core activities of IFLA is the Committee on Free Access to Information and Freedom of Expression, which monitors the state of intellectual freedom within the library community worldwide, supports IFLA policy development and co-operation with other international human rights organisations, and responds to violations of free access to information and freedom of expression. IFLA/FAIFE is a member of the International Freedom of Expression Exchange, a global network of non-governmental organisations that monitors freedom of expression worldwide.

It is also a member of the Tunisia Monitoring Group, a coalition of 16 free expression organisations that lobbies the Tunisian government to improve its human rights record.

CONSERVATION BOOK REPAIR

Most of a public library's resources are spent on collecting, cataloguing and circulating material. While much effort goes into acquiring books and paper materials, little follow-up occurs in caring for that same material. Book and paper materials receive a great deal of use: they are pulled off the shelf roughly, stuffed into backpacks, forced onto photocopiers and dumped into book drops. In addition to ongoing patron and staff use, the books in a library collection are constantly aging; many are expensive and difficult to replace.

Caring for a library collection is a large task. Each library, regardless of size, must choose how to care for its collections. Successful book repair is an important component of a collection development and maintenance programme. In the past, maintaining a library collection was usually accomplished with plastic tape and household glue. Unfortunately, these products do not lead to successful repairs. Books return for repairs again and again or are discarded when they are damaged beyond repair.

In many cases, the fault lies with the repair choices, not the book. The basic concepts used in conservation book repair, such as using materials that are stable and reversible, were originally introduced to care for rare book collections. These same practices and materials can be successfully adapted to repairing non-rare books, and it is the intent of this manual to teach these techniques for use in circulating and reference collections.

USING THIS MANUAL

While it can be difficult to learn practical, hands-on skills from a book and tempting to jump right into a repair technique without reading the introduction, Please resist the urge. The introduction to each technique explains how to choose a particular technique and why that technique works while others do not. With a solid understanding of these principles and techniques, it is possible to quickly evaluate damaged books and choose the treatment that will lead to a successful repair.

CHOOSING BOOKS TO REPAIR

Choosing which books to repair is the first step in any successful book repair programme. Because each library is unique, one library's guidelines for retaining or repairing books may be very different from another's, Taking the time to create guidelines that are realistic and consistent with the needs of a collection can insure the well being of library materials and the effective use of staff time.

Before choosing to repair a book, ask questions such as:

- Is this book a candidate for weeding? Is the information misleading or has it been superseded by a new edition or a better book on the subject? Is the information trivial, of no discernible literary or scientific merit or irrelevant to the needs and interests of the library's patrons?
- Has the book previously been repaired using improper or damaging techniques? Is the book worn beyond mending or rebinding? Should this book be replaced or sent to the bindery? Is it easier and cheaper to purchase a replacement copy rather than repair the old volume?

It can be a difficult decision to not repair a book. However, the urge to save every book is unrealistic because some books cannot be effectively repaired and should be replaced. Learn to choose the books that can be repaired and those that cannot so the library collection will be in better condition and staff time will be better utilized. Choosing the proper repair for a book and carrying out that repair takes knowledge and skill. In a small library, the person who makes the repair decision will probably be the person who repairs the book.

In a larger library, that process might be shared by two staff members, in which case, both people need to understand the principles of book construction and repair. After deciding to repair a book, choose the best kind of treatment.

If a volume is to be replaced or withdrawn after one more circulation or when a replacement is purchased, mending it quickly using non-conservation repair methods such as clear plastic tape, might be an option. If the book is needed for a longer period of time or is part of a permanent collection, always repair it using conservation repair techniques such as those outlined in this book.

DETERMINING WHY A BOOK NEEDS REPAIR

It is important to determine why a book needs repair:

- Has it been damaged through carelessness or simply through use?
- Was it manufactured in a way that caused the damage?
- Has an old repair failed or caused more damage?
- How have previous repairs hindered the mechanics of the book?

Look at the kind of paper used in the book and how the book is constructed:

- Is the book constructed in signatures?

- Is the book constructed in single sheets glued or over sewn together?
- Is the paper coated and shiny?

All these factors should be considered when choosing to repair a book and deciding what techniques to use.

PLANNING REPAIRS AND THE WORKSPACE

- Read the directions for any repair thoroughly before attempting the repair.
- Make sure the workspace is large enough to work comfortably. Clear away excess objects and have the tools and materials needed close at hand.
- Think about where the repaired books will dry. Materials that are glued or pasted must dry under weight or the paper will buckle.
- If the book has several problems, start with the simplest and work towards the most complex. In general the text block is repaired first then the cover. The last part of the book to be repaired is the attachment of the text block to the cover.
- Try to group similar types of repairs together. In addition to saving time and materials, repeating the same repair several times is a good way to improve repair techniques.

PRACTICING REPAIRS

- Initially, it's a good idea to practice each repair either on a book that has been withdrawn from the collection or on plain paper. Different types of paper and different book structures will react differently to the paste or glue. For instance, shiny, coated paper will not absorb as much moisture as uncoated paper so less paste is used on the latter kind of paper.
- Read the explanation and instructions before beginning a repair. Take time to assemble all the tools and materials called for in the instructions.
- Reread the instructions after practicing a repair two or three times. They will probably be more understandable and some questions that came up during the repair may be answered. Once it is clear why and how a repair works, it is easier to choose a technique to match a particular repair need and not rely on the written instructions.

The materials and techniques used in conservation book repair should not damage books and, if a repair is not successful, it can usually be reversed and repeated. Be aware of your skill level and limitations. If a repair is too advanced, wait until you have more experience. Practice these techniques to improve your skills. Above all, keep working.

THE BASIC INFORMATION

Understanding book construction, the materials used to repair books and the proper way to handle tools are important components of a successful repair programme. Books are constructed in several ways. Many repair materials work best on certain kinds of paper or in specific parts of a book. "The right tool for the right job' is an axiom that applies to book binding as well as other fields. Having a few specialized tools and understanding how to use them will save time and energy.

BOOK STRUCTURE AND CONSTRUCTION

The pages of a book, whether they are sewn or glued together, are called the text block. The covers of a book are called the case. The case is made of the front cover, the spine and the back cover.

Text Blocks in Signatures

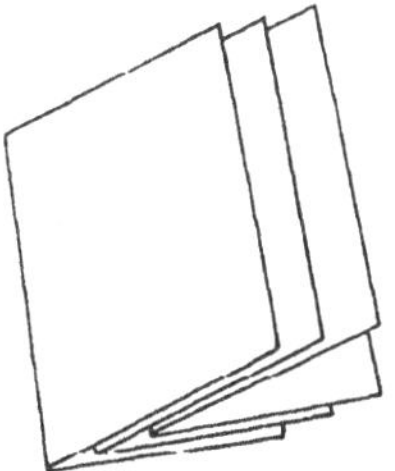

When the text block is sewn, the pages are gathered together in groups; then each group is folded in half.

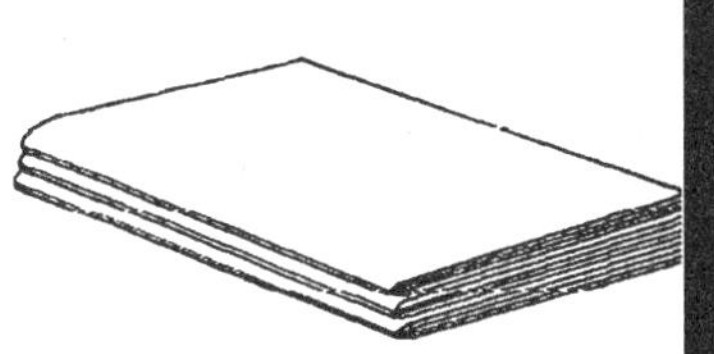

A group of folded pages is called a part or signature and is usually four to eight pieces of paper. Books that are constructed of sewn signatures tend to function best because the pages are securely attached to one another and they open flat.

Modern manufacturing techniques enable book manufacturers to create a text block with signatures, cut small notches in the folded edge and insert glue to hold the pages together instead of sewing thread. These books look like they are sewn, but they are not. Open the text block to the centre of a signature and look for the thread, if it's not there, the book is glued.

Text Blocks in Loose Sheets

Text blocks can also be single sheets glued together in a process called adhesive, perfect, or fan binding. In this process, fast drying glue is applied to the spine of the text block. Adhesives that dry very quickly are often brittle and that is why the spine of a book cracks when the book is opened. Once the spine glue is cracked, the pages will begin to fall out. In addition to the problem of brittle glue, there is often very little glue attaching each page to the adjoining pages. When the glue is only in contact with the very thin edge of each sheet of paper, pages can easily separate over time.

Single and Double Fan Binding

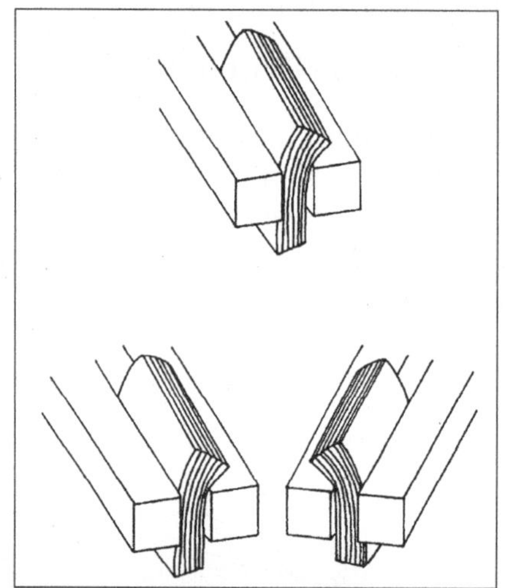

In single-fan binding, the pages of the text block are fanned in one direction and glued along that fanned edge. In this style of binding, a thin line of glue penetrates the inner margin of each page, not just the spine edge. Double-fan adhesive binding goes another step beyond single-fan binding. After the pages are fanned in one direction and glued, they are also fanned in the opposite direction and glued along the second fanned edge. Double-fan binding applies glue on the inner margin of each side of the page, not just on the spine edge or the inner margin of one side of the paper.

It is much stronger than single-fan binding. When library binders bind a book using double fan binding, they use adhesives that dry slowly and flexible. In addition, they usually reinforce the spine edge of the adhesive bound text block with cloth and paper so it is stronger and the text block opens flat. A library binder can be a good source of information to understand the binding processes.

Keep in mind the bindery is selling a product and as the customer, you can question the binder until all the techniques are fully explained. The services offered must meet the specifications that a library has defined for its collections. In order to set minimum levels of excellence in library binding, the Library Binding Institute has published the Standard for Library Binding. This booklet explains the different types of bindings and what standards should be met in library bound books. The Guide to the Library Binding Institute Standard For Library Binding written by Jan Merril-Oldham is a plain English explanation of the Standard.

Oversewn Text Blocks

Before library binderies began to fan bind books, the most common form of library binding was oversewing. In the over-sewing process, the folds of the signatures are trimmed off and the pages of the text block are oversewn to one another with a diagonal whip stitch. Since the sewing threads tend to pierce deep into the inner margin, the pages are restricted from turning easily.

Oversewing is a strong form of binding, but it is often so strong that over time the pages can break out of the binding as they are forced to turn against the sewing threads. Oversewn books may not be candidates for rebinding since much of the inner margin was trimmed off or damaged by the oversewing threads. Books should not be oversewn unless they are very heavy and have wide gutter margins to accommodate the sewing threads. Many libraries stipulate their binders must have permission to oversew a volume.

Sewn Text Blocks: Flat Back and Rounded and Backed Text Blocks

The pages of a book attached together by sewing or gluing is called a text block. Before a text block is attached to a paper or book board case, it can be treated in several ways.

Flat Back Text Blocks

Flat back books are a type of binding which has a flat text block spine. The case spine of flat back books is usually a piece of book board covered with book cloth. The spines of flat back text blocks have a tendency to become concave over time. To prevent this, the spine of the text block can be rounded and backed.

Rounded and Backed Text Blocks

Text blocks are rounded and backed to shape the flat spine of a text block into a curved spine with shoulders. Rounding a text block is the process of molding the spine of a text block into an arc of approximately onethird of a circle. Rounding takes place after the pages of the text block are attached to one another by sewing or gluing. A light coat of adhesive is applied to the spine which is then worked into shape with light pressure, applied with your fingers or a special hammer called a backing hammer. Backing is the process of shaping a ridge or shoulder on each side of the spine of a text block prior to attaching the spine lining material.

Using a backing hammer, the folds of each signature or glued pages are bent over from the centre to the left and right until shoulders are formed against which the boards will fit. The width of the shoulders is determined by the thickness of the cover boards. In addition to providing space for the cover boards, backing also distributes the swell caused by the sewing threads or adhesive and helps maintain the round of the text block over time.

Book Case Construction

Regardless of how the text block is assembled, modern books are usually manufactured in two stages.

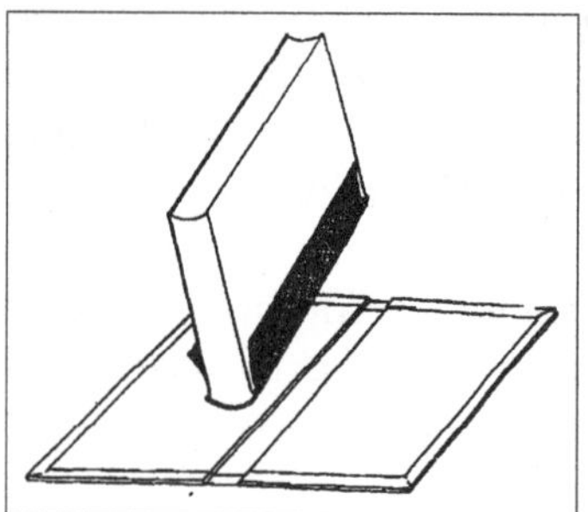

The text block is constructed in one operation where the pages are attached to one another, the spine covered with a cloth liner, called crash, and a paper spine liner is added over that. The book case, consisting of a front cover, a spine and a back cover, is constructed separately in a second operation and the two parts of the book are attached by gluing the crash and end papers to the case covers. The crash holds the text block into the case while the end papers cover up the crash.

PAPER AND BOOK CLOTH

Many types of paper or book cloth can be used in manu-facturing, binding and repairing a book.

Paper

Although many different types of papers are used to print and manufacture books, three important types of paper to be familiar with in book repair are uncoated paper, coated paper and acid-free paper.

Uncoated Paper

Uncoated paper is the most common type of paper and is made from plant or tree fibres that are processed into sheets. Originally, most uncoated paper was handmade from linen or cotton rags. These older papers age very well because they contain few damaging chemicals. In the 1860s, a process was developed to turn cellulose fibre from trees into paper. This type of paper can be made in large quantities but contains some very damaging chemicals that cause paper to become brittle more quickly than paper made from cotton or linen.

Coated Paper

A sheet of paper can be impregnated with very fine clay to produce a very fine printing surface. Introduced at the end of the 19th century, coated papers is ideal for printing halftone illustrations. Unfortunately it is not very strong and is highly susceptible to water damage. Often the text pages of a book are printed on uncoated paper while the pages that contain illustrations are printed on coated paper. The coated paper may be part of the signature or tipped onto a page uncoated page.

Acid-free Paper

Acid-free is a designation given to paper that has a pH value of 7.0 or greater on a scale of 1 to 14. Fibres from any source can be made into paper that is acid-free. Both coated and uncoated papers can be acid-free. Acid-free paper used in conservation book repair includes photocopy paper and Japanese repair tissue.

Book Cloth

Book cloth is a specially woven cloth backed with thin paper. The paper backing gives the cloth support, minimizes stretching and allows the material to maintain a crease.

There are three main categories of book cloth:

- Starch-filled book cloth in which the weave of the cloth is filled with starch. This type of cloth is sometimes called sized book cloth;
- Acrylic-, pryoxylin-, or vinyl-impregnated book cloth;
- Plastic coated book cloth.

Heavier book cloth is sometimes called buckram.

Paper and Book Cloth Grain

Paper and book cloth have a grain just as fabric does and it is important to understand how that grain affects repairs.

Reprinted from Library Materials Preservation Manual

When the grain of the paper and book cloth runs parallel to the spine of the book, the cover and pages open freely and stay open without much effort. This is called 'with the grain'. Paper that is bound into a book with the grain running perpendicular to the spine of the book is called 'against the grain'.

Modern publishers often print the pages of a book against the grain to get more pages on a large sheet of paper. When the grain runs perpendicular to the spine of a book, the book can be difficult to open and it will not remain open without a great deal of pressure. Books printed against the grain are easily damaged since patrons must force the book open to read or photocopy it. When pages or the case of a book are repaired, the grain of the repair materials should always run parallel to the spine of the book.

Determining the Grain of Paper or Book Cloth

All paper and book cloth has a dominate grain. Paper can be tested for grain using the bend test, the tear test or the water test. The grain of book cloth usually runs parallel to the selvage or bound edge of the fabric. If the selvage of the book cloth has been cut off or if there is any doubt about the grain of book cloth, the bend test or the tear test can be used to determine the grain.

Bend Test

The quickest way to test the grain is to bend the paper or cloth slightly in each direction.

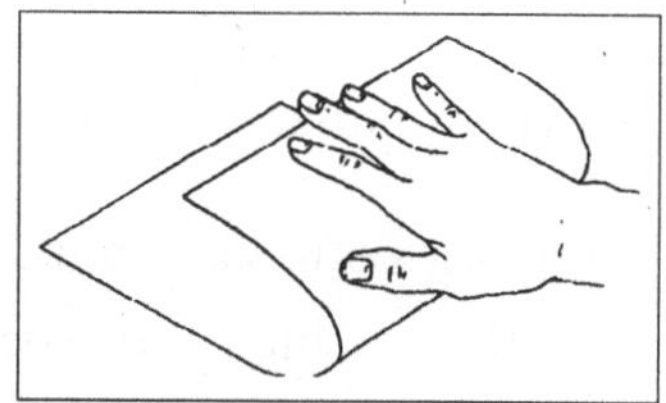

Bring two opposite edges of a piece of paper or cloth together but do not crease. Instead, gently press down on the bend with minimal pressure. Feel any resistance Now bring the other two opposite sides of the paper or cloth together and repeat the process. In one direction there is more resistance than the other. The greater resistance means the paper or cloth does not want to bend in that direction because it is bending against the grain. When the paper or cloth is bent in the opposite direction, there is much less resistance. The bend that offers the least resistance is the bend that goes with the grain of the paper or book cloth. Mark the direction of grain on the paper for future reference.

Tear Test

Another way to test for the grain is to tear the paper or cloth. Paper or cloth will tear easily and straight along the direction of the grain. When forced to tear against the grain, the paper or cloth will be difficult to tear and the tear will tend to curve until it meets the grain. Tear the cloth or paper close to a comer and then pencil a small straight line in that comer indicating the direction of the grain so it won't need to be determined every time it is used.

Water Test

When grain is particularly difficult to find, a water test can be used. Use this test only to test paper being used to repair a volume, not on pages bound in a book. Draw a 4" straight line along one comer of a large sheet of paper. This line will not necessarily be the grain line, it is simply an orientation line. Cut a square out of the comer, including l/2 of the line. Moisten the small square of paper and lay it on a work surface. As the water is absorbed into the paper fibres, the square will begin to curl. The two edges that curl towards one another are parallel with the grain. Mark the correct grain on the square.

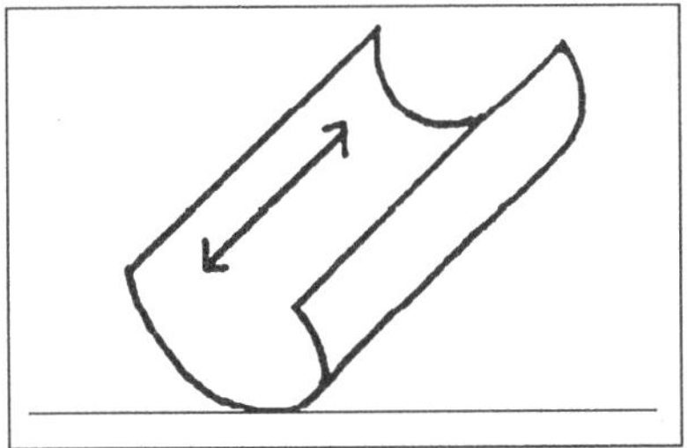

Replace the curled square in position on the large sheet of paper and mark the correct grain on the large sheet. Remember, the first pencil line is not necessarily the grain line.

PAPER REPAIR MATERIALS

Conservation book repair generally usesJ apaneser epair tissue, wheat paste, and heat-set tissue or archival repair tape to repair paper tears.

Japanese Repair Tissue

Japanese repair tissue is sometimes called 'rice' paper, but this thin paper is made from the fibres of the mulberry tree, not from rice as the nickname implies. The strength of Japanese repair tissue comes from its long fibres which make the paper very strong, even though it is very thin. Hand made Japanese repair tissues are made on a mold and have mold or 'chain' lines which can be seen in the paper. These lines generally run the same direction as the paper grain. The lines are visible when the paper held up to a light or held down to let the light shine from above.

The grain can also be determined by using the tear, bend or water test discussed previously. In general, Japanese repair tissue is torn rather than cut. A piece of torn Japanese tissue has a delicate feather that blends into the repaired paper, so there is no sharp edge for the repaired page to turn against. Different methods of tearing Japanese tissue are discussed later in the Book Repair Tools and Techniques part. Japanese repair tissue can be purchased in different weights and colors. Generally, three weights will cover most repair needs. Since most paper is not truly white, buy the 'natural' or 'toned' colours:

- TENGUJO light weight for working over type or illustrations

- KIZUKISHI medium weight for most repairs
- S~KISHU heavy weight for heavier paper

Although Japanese repair tissue may seem very expensive, only a small amount is used on any one tear. One sheet of Japanese repair tissue will last a long time.

Heat-set Tissue

Heat-set tissue is a thin tissue that has been coated with a heat activated, acrylic adhesive. The tissue is tom or cut to fit the tear or paper loss, laid in position and covered with silicone release paper. The tissue is adhered to the paper with a heated iron. A standard household iron or tacking iron from a book repair supply house or hobby store can be used to adhere heat-set tissue. Heat-set tissue is sold with the silicone release paper. Heat-set tissue tends to be more brittle than Japanese repair tissue as it does not have the long, strong fibres of the Japanese tissue. It is not recommended for use on the folds in paper or areas that need to flex and bend. Since heat-set tissue is not applied with moisture, it works quite well on shiny, coated paper that can buckle when wet.

Document Repair Tape

Document repair tapes differ from common clear plastic in several ways. The carrier is thin, acid-free paper, not plastic. It is not as stiff as plastic tape so a page can turn and bend more easily. The adhesive used is a neutral acrylic adhesive that should not dry up, yellow over time or seep out the edges of the document repair tape. Because this adhesive is neutral, it should not react chemically with the paper. The manufacturers of these tapes have tested the materials using artificial aging tests and they believe these tapes will remain stable over time and can be removed easily. Actual experience is not always so positive. Some libraries are finding that these tapes dry hard and crack or that the adhesive dries up and the paper carrier falls off leaving the paper discoloured.

In addition, some tapes are not reversible over time. Because of these problems, document repair tapes should not be used on valuable books or books that are a part of a long-term permanent collection. Document repair tape has become accepted for use in some circulating collections and is definitely better than clear plastic tape. Some libraries choose to use document repair tape on materials that will not remain in the collection for a long time, such as reference books or children's books. Document repair tape can be a quick way to repair paper tears, and staff can use it easily after very little training. Document tape is sold under several brand names. Some of these are Fihnoplast P, Filmoplast P-90, and Document Repair Tape.

Clear Plastic Tape

Many library books are repaired with clear plastic tape. What appears to be a quick solution can become a long term headache in a library repair programme. Before using plastic tape, it is important to understand how it works and how it affects books. Plastic tape is dangerous to use in books because it is unstable and causes a great deal of damage. Often two or three layers of tape will cover a single repair. The first repair did not work and additional layers of tape were added to correct the problem. Unfortunately, adding more layers of tape only creates a thick pile of tape; it does not repair the book..

Plastic tape has two main parts: a clear plastic carrier and an adhesive that sticks to the paper. As the tape ages on a piece of paper, the adhesive penetrates the paper fibres of the page and causes a chemical reaction that stains the paper and makes it brittle. Once the adhesive has dried, the plastic carrier falls away and the stain remains. The adhesive on the tape seeps out the edge of the plastic carrier, attracting dirt or adhering one page to another. Once tape is in a book it is very difficult, if not impossible to remove. Simply lifting the tape off the page will damage the paper because the top layer of paper is removed with the tape. If the tape covers the text, it cannot be removed without damaging the print. Removing plastic tape is difficult even for trained conser-vators who work with chemicals and special tools. Using tape to reattach a loose page restricts the page from turning freely. The tape has a sharp edge and makes the original paper heavier than before so the paper tends to turn against the edge of the tape and not at the hinge. Soon the paper breaks against the edge of the tape and falls out of the book. Now a second repair is needed and if the page is repaired a second time with plastic tape, the same problem occurs. Wide, clear plastic tape is also used to repair the cover spine or corners of a book and special 'repair wings' are sold to repair comers as well. While tape covers up the problem but it does not repair it.

Often the tape slides out of position or detaches entirely while the adhesive remains on the book cover attracting dirt or sticking books to one another on the shelf. Some libraries that practice conservation book repair may use plastic tape in very specific instances. Plastic tape might be used when a book will not remain in the collection for a long tune, such as children's books, reference books that are updated regularly, or books that need 'one more circulation' before they are discarded. Decisions regarding when and how to use clear plastic tape should be made ahead of time. Be certain a book is not important in a long term collection policy before repairing it with plastic tape. Keep in mind that once the tape is in the book, it cannot usually be removed without damaging the book.

REPAIR ADHESIVES

There are two main kinds of adhesives used in conservation book repair: paste and glue. Each has special properties and should be used in specific instances.

Paste

Paste is generally a cooked mixture of water and vegetable starch, such as wheat or rice. Repairing paper with paste will give a stronger bond than repairing it with glue because the paste soaks into the paper fibres and bonds them together. Since paste contains water, it can stretch and cockle paper. It dries slowly and can usually be reversed with water.

Wheat Paste

Wheat paste is used to mend tom paper, attach Japanese tissue or soften old paste and glue. It is not usually used on book cloth or the case of a book. Wheat paste can be purchased uncooked, instant or pie-made. Wheat paste prepared from scratch will last for 3-4 days before it begins to mold. Prepare a small amount of paste and keep it refrigerated. Instant commercial or prepared pastes can be convenient in some situations.

Thick Wheat Paste:

- 6 TBS wheat starch
- 2 Cups cold water
- Place the wheat starch in the top of a double boiler.
- Mix the water into the starch stirring constantly.
- Bring the mixture to a boil.
- Lower the heat and stir constantly as the mixture simmers.
- Cook until mixture thickens.
- Remove from heat and cool.
- Put through a sieve and store refrigerated for 3-4 days.

Thin Wheat Paste:

- 3 1/2 TBS wheat starch
- 2 Cups cold water
- Follow the instructions for Thick Wheat Paste above.

Microwave Wheat Paste:

- One tablespoon wheat starch
- Five tablespoons distilled water
- Place the wheat starch in a deep container, add distilled water and place in microwave. Microwave on high setting 20-30 seconds, remove paste and stir. Return to microwave and cook another 20-30 seconds. Remove and stir again. Continue this process for 3-4 minutes depending on the power of your microwave. Paste should stand a few minutes before using.

Glue

Several types of glue have been used in bookbinding over the years, the most common being animal hide glue. In recent years, animal-based glues have been replaced with synthetic vinyl resin glues, the most common of which is polyvinyl acetate emulsion.

Polyvinyl Acetate (PVA)

PVA is a good all-around adhesive. It has a low moisture content and dries quickly. It dries flexible, so it can be used to tighten hinges, repair book cover comers and reattach loose book cloth to book board. PVA is not affected by mold or fungi. However, it is damaged by freezing, so most book repair supply houses will not sell PVA by mail from October to March. If PVA freezes, it separates and loses its adhesive properties.

PVA can be thinned with water or thin wheat paste for different consistencies and effects. Thinning PVA with water adds moisture and does not add any additional adhesive properties while thinning with wheat paste adds the adhesive qualities of the paste to the glue. Many book binders or repair technicians use a 50/50 mixture of PVA and wheat paste strained through a sieve.

Other books may describe different adhesives or mixtures of adhesives. PVA glues cover a wide range of brand names and not all are used to repair books. For instance Elmer's glue is technically a PVA but is not flexible when dry so it has limited use for repairing books. Two common brand names for PVA glues used in book repair are AT-l 100 from Colophon Book Arts Supply and Jade 403 available from Talas. These companies are listed in the Supply Sources.

Working with Adhesives

Most people learning to repair books use too much adhesive. The belief seems to be that if a little is good, a lot is better. In book repair, that just isn't true. A thin, even coat of adhesive makes the best bond. Too much adhesive will ooze out of the edges of a repair and bond to the pages. Also, too much adhesive causes the paper to wrinkle and takes longer to dry. Watch each repair carefully. If there is excess glue or paste, wipe it away. Next time, try to use less paste or glue. When applying adhesive, choose a brush that matches the size of the surface. When pasting or gluing a small area, use a small brush. When the area is larger, use a bigger brush.

LINEN THREAD

Books are traditionally sewn with linen thread which is very strong and can be purchased in several sizes. Choosing the right thread is important for a successful repair. Using thread that is too thick can damage a book because the text block may not fit back in the original case. Thread that is too thin can tear through the folded signature paper. In general, it's best to use as thin a thread as possible, but choosing the right thread depends on the kind of paper and how many signatures are being resewn.

Thread Sizes

Common sizes of linen thread are 12/4,18/3,25/3,35/3 and 60/3. The first number is the thickness of the strand or ply and the second number is the number of strands or ply per thread. So 12/4 is composed of 4 strands that are 12 thick. The 12 refers to an industry designation that relates to the weight of the wholesale quantities of thread.

In this sizing system, the smaller the number, the thicker the thread so 12 thread is thicker than 60 thread. 35/3,30/5, and 18/3 are a good assortment of thread to have on hand. It can be hard to recognize a particular thread size so it's a good idea to mark the size of thread on the inner cardboard spool before discarding the paper wrapper.

Waxing and Threading Linen Thread

Like all thread, linen thread has a tendency to tangle. Waxing sewing thread with beeswax keeps the thread from tangling and helps the thread 'grip' the paper. Run the thread through a cake of beeswax two or three times to coat it with wax, then run the thread through your fingers. The heat generated from the friction will melt the wax into the thread.

Measuring Thread Length

The length of thread needed depends on the height of the book and how many signatures need to be resewn. Save time by measuring the thread directly on the book. For instance, a book with one unattached signature will need a piece of thread that is at least three text block heights long plus one text block height for tying knots.

Adding Additional Lengths of Thread

It's not a good idea to try to work with more than 4-5 book heights of thread at one time. There are two ways to add additional lengths of thread discussed in Tying Knots In Thread, which follows.

Tying Knots in Thread

There are two basic knots used in book repair, the weaver's knot and the square knot.

The Weaver's Knot

Since sewing with a very long piece of linen thread can be difficult, the weaver's knot is used to tie on additional lengths of thread so shorter lengths can be used. Tie on additional thread when there is about 6" of thread left on the needle. Tie the knot inside the signature, as close to the last sewing station as possible.

A knot cannot easily pass through a sewing station hole so it should lie between the sewing station holes on the inside of the signature.

- Make a loop of the remaining thread and hold it in your left hand, with the short end of the loop on the bottom.
- With a new thread, make a loop with the short end on the bottom and hold it in your right hand.
- Insert the left-hand loop underneath and into the right-hand loop and hold both in place with your left thumb.
- Take the short end of the right-hand loop under and through the left-hand loop as illustrated.
- Pull the short end of the left-hand loop and both ends of the right-hand loop away from each other until the knot is secure. Trim both ends.

The Square Knot

Square knots are used to tie off sewing thread when resewing a text block or attaching materials into pamphlet binders:

- Take one end of thread in each hand.
- Pass the right-hand thread over the lefthand thread and through the loop. Pull tight.
- The original right-hand thread is now on the left side. Place it over the right-hand thread and bring it through the loop. Pulltight. Trim the end of the original thread. Do not cut the added thread..

SEWING NEEDLES

Using the right needle will make sewing easy and more successful. Needles should be as small in diametre as possible, have a blunt point, and have an eye no larger than the shaft of the needle. If the sewing needle is much bigger than the thread used, it will make a hole that the sewing thread cannot fill up. Many book suppliers advertise needles that are very large, sometimes much larger than the sewing thread. Leather harness called Egg Eye needles work very well with most thread and are available in leather shops. Sources are listed in the Supply Sources list.

Index